Celebrating Christmas

Pamela Westland

Hundreds of ideas, recipes and flower, food, gift and decorating projects

Celebrating
Christmas

Pamela Westland

Hundreds of ideas, recipes and flower,
food, gift and decorating
projects

Photography by
Nelson Hargreaves

SMITHMARK

This edition published in 1993 by
SMITHMARK Publishers Inc.
16 East 32nd Street
New York
NY 10016

SMITHMARK books are available for bulk purchase for sales
promotion and premium use. For details write or call
the manager of special sales, SMITHMARK Publishers Inc.,
16 East 32nd Street, New York, NY, 10016; (212) 532–0600

Produced by Anness Publishing Ltd
Boundary Row Studios
1 Boundary Row
London SE1 8HP

ISBN 0 8317 1260 0

Editorial Director: Joanna Lorenz
Project Editor: Lindsay Porter
Designer: Tony Paine
Photographer: Nelson Hargreaves

Printed in Hong Kong

CONTENTS

INTRODUCTION

The celebration of Christmas is deeply woven into the fabric of family life, and often comprises the most precious childhood memories. Many of these memories are centred on the kitchen which, as the culinary preparations get under way in the helter-skelter run-up to Christmas, more than ever becomes the heart of the home. We may cherish memories of stirring the Christmas pudding and making a secret wish; of scraping out the mixing bowl and delighting in the warm spiciness of the blend; of rolling out left-over pastry into personal pies and, later, of making gingerbread men to hang on the tree and give to our friends.

Other memories might be of hand-made Christmas cards for friends and family, of making presents with paper and paint, needle and thread, or clay and beads; and of thinking up ingenious ways of wrapping those gifts.

The text and the photographs throughout this book should help to rekindle your own memories of family Christmas celebrations, and fire you with renewed enthusiasm to create new and cherished ones.

There are sections devoted to decking the home with holly and ivy, mistletoe, fruit, flowers and candles in traditional and original ways. There are ideas to make the most of Christmas presents, and the wrappings and gift tags to decorate them.

The book moves on to the fun and games of Christmas and proves that entertaining even on a large scale can be as enjoyable for the host and hostess as for the guests.

At one of these parties someone will suggest playing party games. Memories have been made for generations of the family-favourite pencil and memory games, guessing and word teasers, card tricks and team games in a just-for-the-fun-of-it section of the book, complete with lists of suggested prizes and forfeits (penalties).

The games, which are largely (but by no means wholly) for children, are followed by a section of projects and ideas especially for them, brilliant paper-flower designs; step-by-step photographs of making gingerbread house biscuits; candy decorations to hang on the tree and adorn the table, and stunning papercraft designs for window panels and candleholders.

It comes as no surprise that over 30 pages are devoted to the preparation and presentation of the Christmas dinner, with photographs showing you exactly how to prepare every course.

Eat, drink and be merry is the theme of the following section, itself a celebration of Christmas imbibing, from Champagne cocktails to spicy mulls, sparkling fruit cups to foamy egg flips. There are also recipes and ideas for appetizers and snacks to serve with drinks of all kinds to help you plan a galaxy of trouble-free gatherings.

The smooth running of the Christmas catering programme calls for a fair amount of advance planning and, nearer the day, meticulous timing. The final sections of the book take you through the tasks of making your Christmas puddings, mincemeat and cakes and all the extra cakes and cookies, candies and sweets you will need to entertain in style.

The wealth of practical projects and stunning colour photographs throughout the book will inspire you to share the kind of Christmas that memories are made of.

Pamela Westland

As we warm to the annual ritual of filling our kitchens with the homely smell of rich, spicy baking; as we welcome carol singers to the door with a glass of steaming hot mull, and gather the branches of evergreens to decorate our homes; as we write Christmas card messages to friends and relatives, and wrap presents for family and those we love; as we light candles, hang glittering ornaments on the tree and assemble for midnight mass; as we gather round the table for Christmas dinner, and later join in party games, we are carrying on traditions that have been perpetuated through over two thousand years and have evolved, with remarkable similarities still, in many parts of the Christian world.

The festival of Christmas as it is celebrated today has its origins in pagan times, when ancient peoples throughout the northern hemisphere gathered together to feast and frolic at the winter solstice. On December 21 the Vikings held the festival of *Juul* (from which the word Yule derives), in honour of their god, Odin, while the Druids, a tree-worshipping sect, celebrated the festival of *Nolagh* at which they dragged a huge log into their homes and celebrated for as long as it could be kept alight. They held mistletoe in particularly high regard, believing it possessed sacred powers as a protection against witchcraft and evil spirits, and as a symbol of fertility. It was also associated with sacrificial rites, a connection that makes the plant unacceptable as a decorative element in many churches today.

The ancient Romans celebrated the feast of Saturnalia, when they worshipped the god of agriculture and heralded, after the shortest day of the year, the return of the sun. This was a time of benevolence. Wealthy Romans gave presents of money and clothing to their servants, who reciprocated with gifts of garlands and evergreen boughs. Presents were exchanged between family and friends at the Roman New Year or *Kalends* celebration, when villas were decked with holly as a symbol of the renewal of life.

Then, as now, the celebrations extended through December and well into the New Year, with many an excuse for a convivial drink. The custom of wassailing, drinking from a communal bowl of hot spiced ale or cider, had many variations. It began with the Anglo-Saxons, for whom the seasonal toast of *Wes-hal* (be whole!) invited the response *Drink-hal* (good health!). Wassailing was celebrated as a fertility rite in English apple orchards to ensure a bountiful crop in the coming year, and inspired groups of youths to roam villages banging drums and clashing cymbals to ward off evil spirits. They then claimed a reviving drink as a reward. With more restraint, wassail time was also marked by processions of young girls carrying wassail bowls decorated with ribbons and greenery, and asking householders to drink from the bowl and then replenish it. Centuries later,

LEFT: A St Lucia crown, composed of small evergreen leaves and seven white candles, is worn by young

Scandinavian girls in a procession on the saint's feast day, December 13th.

LEFT: Trimmings from a Christmas tree, a Norwegian spruce, and small red check gingham bows comprise an unusual evergreen wreath to decorate a fireplace.

carol singers who walked from house to house were offered a few coins and a sup from the steaming punch bowl as a gesture of seasonal goodwill.

The transition from a string of pagan festivals to the festival of Christmas was gradual. In the early days of Christianity the birth of Christ was not only not celebrated; it was not even marked by a specific date. It was only in the fourth century that the church fixed the date of Christ's birth as December 25. Then, when St Augustine arrived in Britain, he instructed the faithful to adopt many of the existing customs, applying new meanings and Christian standards to the ancient rituals. In that way, followers were not asked to forego traditional pleasures.

In Medieval Britain the emphasis fell heavily on the merrymaking aspect of the festival. Groups of masked mummers, usually men, performed plays in local villages and towns throughout England, receiving money, fruit and other seasonal foods in return for their entertainment. The plays usually centred on a fight between a hero and a villain, with a quack doctor arriving in the nick of time to revive the fallen hero with a magic potion.

In some regions the lord of the manor appointed the aptly named Lord of Misrule to preside over the celebrations and lead the community in often disorderly fun and games throughout the festival. This role reversal, of a servant becoming the master of ceremonies, had its beginnings in the Roman Saturnalian festival.

With the rise of Puritanism in the seventeenth century the merrymaking and, indeed, the celebration of Christmas had to stop. The Puritans denounced the festival and passed an Act of Parliament prohibiting any celebrations, announcing that the only fitting way to commemorate the birth of Christ was to fast. They even employed troops to patrol the streets and ensure that no-one broke the law and cooked lunch. In New England the Pilgrims and Puritans, in protest against what they saw as the laxity of the Church of England, refused to recognize Christmas Day as a holiday and eschewed all those customs with pagan origins.

With the Restoration of the Monarchy in Great Britain in 1660, Christmas feasting became increasingly lavish, and a journal of the time records that a London merchant's table was set with '. . . turkies, geese, capons, puddings of a dozen sorts . . . besides brawn, roast beef and many things . . . minc'd pies and a thing called plumb pottage'.

Although the turkey, after having been discovered in South America, had been brought to England in the sixteenth century, it did not become widely popular until the nineteenth century when Mrs Beeton, the Victorian writer on household management, pronounced it as 'one of the most glorious presents made by the New World to the Old'.

THE VICTORIAN CHRISTMAS

It was in Victorian Britain that many existing Christmas customs were practised with renewed enthusiasm, and many innovations were introduced, customs which are now deeply woven into the fabric of Christmas as it is celebrated today.

With marked lack of restraint, the Victorians covered their homes with evergreens, draping boughs across mirrors and picture frames, over mantels and furniture and weaving them in and out of the banisters. Those who could not gather greenery for themselves bought it from streetsellers whose barrows were piled high with holly and mistletoe.

Then, in 1841, came the Christmas tree, which had played a prominent role in German festivities since the fifteenth century. When Queen Charlotte, wife of King George III, erected a tree at Windsor Castle in the late eighteenth century, its introduction had passed largely unnoticed. But when Prince Albert, Consort of Queen Victoria, reintroduced the custom, decorating the tree with glittering trinkets and baubles from his native Germany, it was as if everyone had been waiting for the moment. A photograph of the Royal Family gathered around their tree appeared in a

ABOVE RIGHT: Christmas decorations from the north-eastern states of America.

London journal and from then on a decorated and illuminated tree became the focal point of the festivities in Britain and, shortly afterwards, in the United States.

Although many tree decorations were made at home, manufacturers became more and more inventive, creating delicate and exquisite glass bells, balls, stars and other fancy, festive shapes, as well as twisted candles that fitted into 'safety' holders.

The idea of decorating a tree with lighted candles is thought to have originated with Martin Luther, professor of theology at the Saxon University of Wittenburg in the early sixteenth century, as a way of reminding children that the birth of the infant Jesus brought light into the world. The first electric tree lights appeared in New York in 1882 when an associate of Thomas Edison used strings of coloured lights to illuminate his tree. A decade later, when they were manufactured commercially by The General Electric Company, this form of safety lighting became generally available.

The 1840s heralded the introduction to Victorian Britain not only of the Christmas tree, but of Christmas cards and Christmas crackers as well. Christmas greetings cards evolved over several decades from an eighteenth-century

BELOW: Christmas cards began to be mass-produced in the Victorian Era.

snowballs. The romantic idea of a 'white Christmas' emanates from this time, a period of particularly harsh winters and deep snow and persists long after the weather pattern has changed. Other cards were designed around seasonal rhymes of a religious or secular nature and one, revealing links with the winter solstice celebrations, was written in praise of holly, which 'helps to drive stern Winter away'.

SANTA CLAUS, FATHER CHRISTMAS, SAINT NICHOLAS OR WHOEVER!

'Christmas won't be Christmas without presents', begins Louisa M. Alcott's, Victorian novel, *Little Women*, expressing a sentiment that would be echoed throughout the Christian world if Father Christmas, Santa Claus, St Nicholas, St Basil, Christkindl, La Befana, Grandfather Frost, Julenisse or any of the other benefactors were to fail in their customary distribution of gifts in December or January.

The familiar figure of Santa Claus or Father Christmas, red-robed, white-haired and jolly, has a somewhat confused ancestry. The distribution of gifts at that time of the year was part of many pagan rituals – Norsemen, for example,

school practice in Britain of writing 'Christmas pieces', an end-of-year report presented by children to their parents to indicate what progress they had made at school. It was this custom, and the fact that the 'pieces' had become ever more elaborate, that prompted Henry (later Sir Henry) Cole, the first director of the Victoria & Albert Museum in London, to commission in 1843 the first known Christmas card. The hand-coloured and printed card, designed by his friend Sir John Callcot Horsley, R.A., showed a close family group seated at a table drinking red wine, and is flanked on either side by allegorical sketches depicting charitable acts. Surrounded by a rustic vine entwined with ivy, a panel carries the seasonal message, 'A Merry Christmas and a Happy New Year to you'.

Three years later, a thousand copies of the card were sold – at considerable expense. This and the heavy price to be paid by the recipient of mail would have put greetings cards beyond the reach of the masses. However the introduction of the 'penny post' and the invention of cheaper colour reproduction made Christmas cards at first an affordable and soon an essential part of the celebrations.

Later designs depicted scenes of the typical Victorian Christmas: children dancing round a tree, gathering foliage, and playing games; families expressing delight at the entry of the Christmas pudding; skating on ponds, and playing with

ABOVE LEFT: Scandinavian children hope to find the lucky almond in their Christmas Eve bowl of rice porridge.

BELOW: Collecting evergreens, nuts and cones can be a pleasant family pastime during the weeks before the holiday.

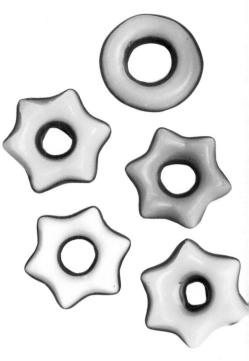

OPPOSITE: *A vine-wreath form entwined with dried hops and displayed with a group of gourds may decorate the home from Thanksgiving through to Christmas.*

RIGHT: *In homes and in churches, one candle of the Advent ring is lighted on each of the four Sundays before Christmas.*

believed that their god Woden brought them gifts in honour of the winter solstice. And then, in the Christian church, a number of legends built up around St Nicholas, a fourth-century bishop of a Turkish See. He is said to have distributed baskets of grain, fruit and honey cakes to poor children, thrown bags of gold into a house where there were three young girls, and even brought back to life three boys who had been murdered. With so much good work to his credit, early churchmen conferred on St Nicholas the honour of being the distributor of Christmas gifts.

The legend of the bags of gold had far-reaching consequences. It is said that the gold landed in the girls' stockings which were hung up by the fire to dry, and this gave rise to the custom that is dear to children's hearts today. One of the traditional tokens placed in children's stockings, gold-wrapped chocolate coins, commemorates the wealthy prelate's gift. And the fact that the stockings were originally hung by the fire prompted St Nicholas – Father Christmas or Santa – to enter the house by the most direct route – down the chimney.

Originally the stockings hung up in eager anticipation would have been workaday ones, perhaps outgrown by the youngest child, but gradually they became an art form in themselves, ranging from those made of homespun check gingham cotton in the Shaker community of Pennsylvania – where sugar plums and molasses toffee were customary fillers – to the elaborate petit-point designs of the Victorians, where clove-studded oranges and nuts were obligatory gifts.

Children in some northern-European countries still look to St Nicholas, the patron saint of boys and girls, to bring them presents. Lucky children in Germany have two bene-factors: St Nicholas who distributes the gifts from house to house on his feast day, December 6, and the Christkindl, a fair-haired girl with a crown of candles, a messenger of the Christ child, who brings a basket of presents to each house on Christmas Eve.

In the Netherlands, where St Nicholas is called Sinte Klaas, he arrives on December 6 on a white horse, wearing his bishop's mitre and robes and accompanied by his servant, Black Peter, whose function is to note which are the good children. Only those with an unblemished record will find gifts in their shoes on Christmas morning.

In Britain, the Protestant Reformation in the sixteenth century, which led to a lessening of emphasis on saints, stopped St Nicholas in his tracks. When he eventually re-emerged it was in the avuncular form of Santa Claus or Father Christmas. He was summed up in a poem written in 1822 by Clement Clark Moore, who established in his *A Visit from St Nicholas* that 'He was dressed all in fur from his head to his foot' and, further, 'He was chubby and plump – a right jolly old elf –'. This description still influences the image we have today.

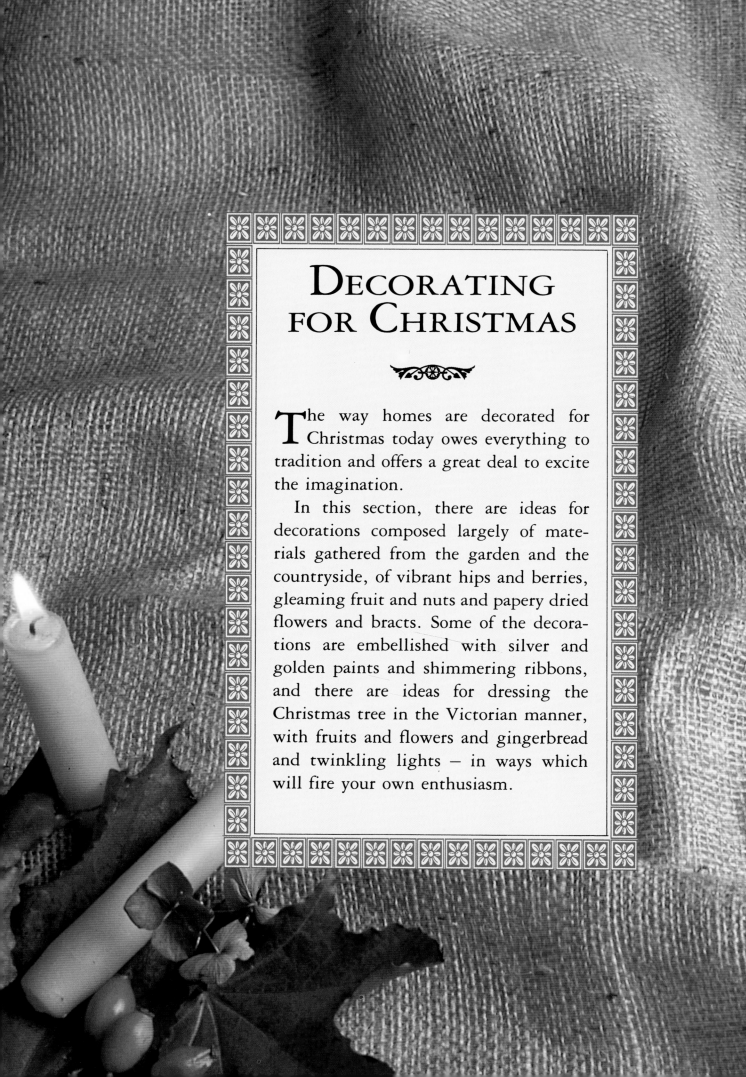

DECORATING FOR CHRISTMAS

The way homes are decorated for Christmas today owes everything to tradition and offers a great deal to excite the imagination.

In this section, there are ideas for decorations composed largely of materials gathered from the garden and the countryside, of vibrant hips and berries, gleaming fruit and nuts and papery dried flowers and bracts. Some of the decorations are embellished with silver and golden paints and shimmering ribbons, and there are ideas for dressing the Christmas tree in the Victorian manner, with fruits and flowers and gingerbread and twinkling lights — in ways which will fire your own enthusiasm.

WELCOME WREATHS

THE TRADITION of hanging evergreens and decorative wreaths on the door, and of suspending 'kissing rings' in a hall or living room, has its origins in pagan times. Ancient peoples believed that evergreens had magical powers because they retained their leaves in winter when other branches were bare. They came to symbolize eternal life, as did wreaths, rings and circles garlanded with plants. Holly, ivy and mistletoe were also seen as powerful life symbols because they bore fruit in the winter. They were hung in people's homes and exchanged as gifts in the hope of warding off evil spirits and bringing eternal good fortune.

The decorative use of these plants outlived the ancient beliefs in their supposed powers, and they were adopted by the early Christians, too; though not without some misgivings. The early Fathers of the Christian Church were fearful that 'bringing in the holly' at Christmastime would keep alive memories of pagan rituals, and for several centuries the use of 'green boughs' as a winter decoration was banned by the Church. A similar attitude was adopted by the Puritan Fathers in New England, who took a firm line on the association between Christmas and evergreens until as late as the early nineteenth century.

All that is history, and for many families throughout the world, both Christians and non-Christians, the festival would not be complete without a holly wreath hung on the door as a sign of welcome and good fortune, and a sprig of mistletoe in the hall. From its ancient beginnings as a fertility charm, a supposed cure-all for countless illnesses and a force against evil, mistletoe now has purely romantic associations. At the beginning of this century every young man who

stole a kiss under the mistletoe bough or kissing ring had to pluck a berry from its depths. When there were no more berries left, the kissing had to stop.

Over the centuries, evergreens came to be decorated with ribbon bows and other embellishments and in Victorian times red and green tartan ribbons, which matched the vibrant colours of the holly itself, became fashionable. In those days too it was the custom to add candies and bon-bons, tiny toys for the children and other purely decorative and fanciful items to the basic evergreen wreaths. This delightful practice continues today.

COUNTRY WREATHS

Today, creative expression is given free rein, and Christmas decorations, whilst still deeply rooted in tradition, make imaginative use of all types of plant material.

Preserving the fruits of the countryside or the garden in readiness for Christmas is one of the most pleasant of preparatory tasks. Rosehips – if they survive the onslaught of winter-hungry birds – can be preserved in a solution of glycerin and water to rival the brilliance of holly berries. Preserved rosehips and other fruits and seeds such as rowan (mountain ash), hawthorn and pyracantha (firethorn) berries can be incorporated into an evergreen wreath to supplement or replace holly berries, or used alone in all their glory. Rosehips inserted into a twisted willow wreath form make a bold statement that, where Christmas decorations are concerned, bright is beautiful. This is also true of cranberries, a vibrant, and popular component of Christmas decorations.

RIGHT: Since time immemorial people have hung wreaths composed of holly, ivy and other evergreens as a symbol of good fortune, and of welcome. The addition of tartan ribbon was especially popular in Victorian times.

OPPOSITE: Vibrant rosehips rival holly berries as the brightest plant materials around. Cut short the stems and push them between the intertwined stems of a willow (as here) or vine wreath form. A few stray rose leaves add a natural look.

COUNTRY WREATH

In the time-honoured tradition of natural wreaths, this design blends the contrasting colours and textures of horse chestnut and sweet chestnut cases, dried red chillies and bunches of cinnamon quills.

EQUIPMENT

* raffia
* fine silver wire
* medium stub wires
* wire cutters
* scissors
* 25cm/10in vine wreath form
* hot glue gun

DECORATIVE MATERIALS

* cinnamon sticks
* dried red chillies
* horse chestnuts
* sweet chestnut cases
* 7.5cm/3in-wide shiny ribbon

1 Tie short cinnamon sticks into bundles with raffia and thread small chillies in clusters onto fine silver wire.

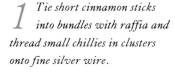

2 Cut the stub wires in half, bend into U-shapes to make staples and push through the raffia ties. Fix the cinnamon bunches to the wreath form by pushing the wires between the vine twigs. Glue the horse chestnuts and sweet chestnut cases at random around the ring, adding the long red chillies last, as colour accents.

3 Tie the ribbon in a bow, and attach to the wreath with a stub wire (floral pin). Because it is composed of weatherproof materials, the wreath could be hung on an exterior wall.

ALL AGLOW

The contrasting characteristics of matt and spiky juniper bunches and golden, glowing quinces combine to compose a striking wall decoration.

1 Cut the evergreen stems to about 20cm/8in long and gather them into bunches of three, four or five, depending on thickness. Tie the twine to the ring frame and bind on the bunches so that the tips of one cover the stems of the next. Continue until the frame is covered.

2 Measure the heavy-gauge wire around the inside of the completed evergreen ring and, allowing for a short overlap, cut it to size. Thread the quinces onto the wire and, when it is complete, push the two ends into the first and last of the fruits to be threaded. If the wire will not hold its position, wire the two fruits together at the back with a stub wire.

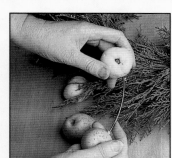

3 Bind the evergreen and the fruit rings together with silver wire, making a loop for hanging. The decoration may be hung on a door, or a wall, either inside or outside. It is especially effective in a kitchen or living room, where the aroma of the fruit may be appreciated.

EQUIPMENT

* florists' scissors
* binding twine
* 25cm/10in wire ring frame (from florists)
* heavy-gauge flexible wire
* wire cutters
* medium stub wires
* fine silver wire

DECORATIVE MATERIALS

* evergreens such as juniper (cypress or yew would give a similar effect)
* small quinces

GLISTENING WREATHS

Just as holly and ivy leaves were once valued for their sheen and the consequential brilliance they brought to the house in the dark days of winter, so artificial glitter sprays, paints and powders have come to play a significant role in Christmas decorations. Although all that glisters may not indeed be gold, a spatter of gold or silver paint here and there, as a highlight on evergreen or fallen leaves, on nuts, dried seedheads and flowers (and even on gift wrapping paper) transforms and uplifts decorations of all kinds.

It is a matter of personal preference whether this decorative Midas touch is employed to give the merest hint of gold – as if, for example, a bunch of holly had been spattered by golden raindrops – or is used for a complete cover-up for a look of gilded luxury. Both approaches lay claim to decorative merit.

The wreath of mixed evergreens, wheat and linseed (flaxseed) combines the best of both worlds in decorative terms. The bunches of seedheads are totally gilded, the ivy, eucalyptus and false flowers only splattered with gold, and the cypress left in its natural state.

A similar all-and-nothing combination of gilded and not gilded materials has been used on the nut ring, where gold-sprayed walnuts and almonds contrast vividly with the natural colours and textures of unsprayed pecans, hazelnuts (filberts) and nutmegs formed into clusters and wired into the natural willow ring.

Ribbon bows and trails can do much to add a sparkle or a colour highlight to evergreen and other decorative wreaths. Choose them as carefully as you would fashion accessories. Your choice of ribbons determines whether a wreath has an informal and countrified look (check gingham typifies this style); has a more elegant and classic feel, which the use of tartan ribbon does so much to promote; or has the frankly festive air of the Christmas party season. Sparkly gold and silver woven thread ribbons, ribbons with a shot-silk effect, and printed metallic ribbons are all delightfully luxurious and festive options.

LEFT: A natural willow ring, gold spray-paint, a hot glue gun and a handful of nuts are all you need to create this striking table design. Add a glittering bow as an eye-catching finishing touch. You can glue it to the ring frame or fix it in position with a bent stub wire.

MISTLETOE RING

A symbol of romance and Christmas frivolities, mistletoe is combined with other evergreens and gilded seedheads in a wayward wreath that is at once elegant and casual.

EQUIPMENT

* binding twine
* gold spray-paint
* 30cm/12in stem wreath form
* medium stub wires
* wire cutters
* scissors

DECORATIVE MATERIALS

* wheat stalks
* linseed (flaxseed)
* evergreens such as cypress, ivy, mistletoe and eucalyptus
* artificial Christmas roses
* 7.5cm/3in-wide shiny ribbon

1 Gather the wheat stalks into bunches of three or four and bind the stems. Form the linseed (flaxseed) into bunches of uneven lengths, to give the design its wispy outline, and bind the stems. Lightly spray the wheat, linseed (flaxseed), artificial Christmas roses and a few of the evergreens with gold paint.

2 Using mixed bunches of the plant materials, secure them to the ring with half a stub wire bent to make a U-shaped staple. Continue all around the ring, so that the heads of each bunch cover the stems and staples of the one before.

3 Push the stems of the Christmas roses into the ring at irregular intervals. Shape 2 ribbon bows, trim the ends by cutting them slantwise and fix them to the wreath with stub wire staples.

CANDLE WREATHS

The combination of candles and evergreens in a wreath formation is most powerfully expressed in the symbolic Advent wreath. By tradition in the Christian church – and it is a tradition that is carried out both in churches and at home – one of the four candles is lighted on each of the four Sundays prior to Christmas. Not only does this practice have a deep religious significance, but it results in an asymmetrical design brought about by the unevenness of the candles.

The interpretation of an Advent candle wreath illustrated on these pages breaks with the visual though not the religious tradition, and uses a partnership of delicate flowers and pastel candles. The blend of fresh flowers is a herald of spring, and the slender tapers are in a myriad of colours from traditional holly green and berry red to palest apricot and pink. A design like this would make an eye-catching table centre-piece, a stunning focal point on a sideboard or side table or an inspiring, outward-looking decoration on a wide windowsill.

LEFT: Adopt the Victorian tradition and embellish an Advent ring with tiny gift parcels to be opened on Christmas Eve. The decoration is made on a pre-formed absorbent foam ring covered first with small sprays of evergreen – it could be variegated holly, ivy or box (boxwood) – and the snippings of sea lavender dyed pink, pink rosebuds and dried everlasting flowers. One candle is lit on each of the Sundays during Advent.

A Ring for all Seasons

A fresh flower decoration with four pale-coloured tapers is inspired by the tradition of an Advent ring. This one combines winter-flowering laurustinus (viburnum) and summery blooms with sprays of minute white flowers, like pretty snowflakes.

Equipment

* 25cm/10in diameter absorbent foam ring, soaked in water
* 25cm/10in in diameter
* florists' scissors

Decorative Materials

* selection of flowers such as spray carnations, Peruvian lilies, freesias, gypsophila (baby's breath)
* flowering shrub such as laurustinus (viburnum)
* 4 slender tapers

3 Fill in the ring until it has a pleasing balance of colour, and add short sprays of gypsophila (baby's breath) all around, like delicate snowflakes. Insert the tapers firmly into the foam at the chosen focal point.

1 Cut short sprays of the flowering shrub and arrange them around the foam so that they largely cover the inside and outside rims. Position the Peruvian lilies around the ring so that they are evenly spaced.

2 Arrange a special feature at one end of the ring, where it will surround the tapers and become the focal point. In this design, deep pink freesias were used for this purpose.

ALTERNATIVE CHRISTMAS TREES

EVER SINCE people began bringing boughs of evergreens into their homes an unrecorded number of years ago, the tree has held a place of honour – first at the winter solstice festival and then at Christmas. Boughs of greenery were hung over doors to represent both welcome and hoped-for good fortune. On walls they were sometimes arranged to resemble the shape of the living tree.

However, the custom of transplanting an entire evergreen tree and installing it as the focal point of the Christmas festivities is a comparatively recent innovation. Prince Albert, Queen Victoria's husband, introduced the idea to Britain in 1841, and brought with it a number of other Christmas customs from his native Germany.

If you decide this year to have a natural tree, you may still have room for another one – a designer tree that clings to the spirit of Christmas past and yet explores the creative possibilities of the concept. The projects illustrated are certain to tempt the most confirmed traditionalist!

LEFT: This tree is composed on a pre-formed foam ball shape and the clumps of lichen are fixed with stub-wire staples (floral pins). The harvest includes gilded peanuts, clusters of cinnamon sticks tied with raffia and kumquats pushed onto toothpicks.

BRIGHT AS A BERRY

Evoke the artistry of clipped hedges and shaped trees with a spherical tree design of glossy evergreens and shiny fruits.

DECORATIVE MATERIALS

* clippings of glossy evergreen such as box
* rosehips
* false berries (optional)

EQUIPMENT

* damp sphagnum moss
* 2.5cm/1in wire mesh netting
* wire cutters
* 18cm/7in-diameter flowerpot
* florists' adhesive tape
* scissors
* florists' scissors

1 Place the moss on the wire mesh netting, turn the corners into the centre to enclose the moss and crush the wire into a ball shape. Tuck in or cut off any stray ends with wire cutters. Place the wire ball on the flower-pot and secure it with two or three short lengths of adhesive tape. Cut the evergreens to more or less equal lengths and push the stems into the wire ball.

2 Continue filling in the ball with evergreens, then push in the rosehips and, if you use them, the stems of false berries.

3 The evergreen 'tree' is a welcoming sight in a porch, and looks good in a fireplace or a room corner where there is enough light to enhance the colour of the leaves.

TOPIARY TREES

Some of these designs are based on the pre-formed dry and absorbent stem-holding foam shapes available from florists' shops, department stores and through flower clubs. These are reassuringly simple to use as the hidden bases for spherical and conical tree shapes. The foam spheres, which can be bought in a wide range of sizes, encourage design notions of neatly clipped bay trees, the classical topiary decorations that grace the entrance halls of the grandest of establishments. But inspiration need not stop there. Designs may include fresh and dried flowers and seedheads, and nuts, berries and spices.

If you cannot obtain a foam shape in the size you need, it is quite simple to make one. All you need is a length of wire mesh netting and some dry or damp sphagnum moss. Once you have mastered the technique of covering the netting with moss, folding the sides to the middle, and then crushing it between both hands, you can design a tree in any shape and size you wish.

OPPOSITE: This fanciful floor-standing tree, with its trunk firmly secured in a large flower-pot, is made on a foam sphere. It flourishes with colourful dried flowers, honesty, Chinese lanterns (Winter cherry) and other seed heads, and has attracted a dove of peace.

SPICE TREE

A colourful and aromatic table decoration combines two distinctive kitchen ingredients – dried red peppercorns and star anise seedpods.

EQUIPMENT

* gold spray-paint
* 7.5cm/3in-diameter dry foam sphere
* quick-setting glue
* stout twig
* 7.5cm/3in-diameter flowerpot
* modelling clay
* dry moss or hay

DECORATIVE MATERIALS

* star anise seedpods
* dried red peppercorns
* 1.5cm/½in-wide ribbons

1 Spray some of the star anise seedpods with gold paint. Working on small areas at a time, cover the foam ball with glue and press on the red peppercorns. Apply spots of glue and more pepper to fill in any gaps. Glue on the gilded star anise all around the ball, and then glue others on top to make a double layer of natural stars.

2 Fix the twig into the pot with modelling clay, and press the ball onto it. Fill the pot with moss or hay and scatter over a few peppercorns. Decorate the stem with trailing ribbons.

PARCEL GILT

Nut-tree branches planted in an earthenware pot play host to a variety of foliage species: maple, oak, hydrangea, holly, poplar and cherry among others. The fallen leaves are dried, threaded onto stub wires and then sprayed gold.

1 Use medium wire to thread the leaves. Take short 'tacking' ('basting') stitches from the leaf base and along the vein, and spray the leaf and wire with gold paint to create an invisible false stem.

2 Hang tiny golden parcels and a few of your favourite Christmas cards from the tree branches, but not so many that they hide the glittering leaves.

Spherical trees fixed to pedestal stands are effective decorations, and simple enough for beginners. You can use any one of a variety of materials to anchor the stem in place. The support for a small, lightweight design can be held in place with a ball of modelling clay pressed firmly around the 'trunk' and onto the base of the container. Larger, more top-heavy designs can be secured with florists' quick-hardening clay; by pushing the stick into a heavy metal pinholder and securing it to the container with a criss-cross of wires, or with plaster of Paris.

GLITTERING TREES

Designer trees take well to the additional glitter and glitz of baubles and other shiny decorations. This is especially true of those composed of matt foliage. The design composed of lavender cotton is highlighted by a handful of chocolate candies wrapped in purple foil and transparent papers. In another example, an evergreen blend of mainly Jerusalem sage and cypress foliage, in colours ranging from grey-green to yellowy-green, has the added sparkle of gold baubles and a lamé ribbon bow.

Taking the notion a stage further, you can plant a collection of twigs in a pot and hang them with baubles and other shiny decorations for a design that catches every flattering flicker of candlelight. Designs could range from a tree bearing a fanciful crop of silver and white apples and a flutter of silvery butterflies, to one composed of bare nut tree branches wired with gold-sprayed fallen leaves of several species. To further enhance the glamorous effect, you could first spray the branches gold or silver; though to spray branches covered in lichen may be gilding the lily.

CANDY CENTRE-PIECE

Silver-leaved lavender is arranged to form a tree shape, and decorated with wrapped candies in a single colour.

EQUIPMENT

* florists' adhesive clay
* plastic spike (from florists)
* pedestal cake stand
* florists' scissors (knife)
* 23cm/9in-high foam cone
* medium stub wires (floral pins)
* wire cutters
* scissors

DECORATIVE MATERIALS

* lavender cotton (you could also use senecio, lavender or curry plant)
* shiny-wrapped candies
* 1.5cm/½in-wide ribbon

1 Press a piece of florists' clay onto the base of the spike and press it onto the cake stand, making sure the surface is absolutely dry.

2 Cut the lavender cotton stems to graduated lengths, the longest extending beyond the rim of the stand and the others successively shorter, to achieve a conical shape. Position the stems around the foam cone. Cut the wires in half, push them through the candy paper wrapping (not through the candy itself) and twist the ends. Insert the candies at intervals all around the cone.

3 Twist a wire around the centre of 2 lengths of ribbon and press the ends into the top of the cone. The design makes a delightful if somewhat irresistible table centre-piece and looks good under a spotlight.

GOLDEN HIGHLIGHTS

From yellowy-green cypress to grey-green Jerusalem sage foliage, with shiny box for highlights, this conical tree makes the most of clippings from a winter garden.

1 *Place the moss on the wire mesh netting and shape it into a cone. Trim off excess netting at the top of the cone. Tuck in any stray ends of wire. Press a large piece of adhesive clay onto the base of the pinholder and press the pinholder onto the base of the basket. Push the twig onto the pinholder. Secure it by taking two wires from side to side of the basket, wrapping the wires around the twig. Place the cone on the twig and secure it by taking wires from side to side and around the twig. These will also hold the moss in place.*

EQUIPMENT

* damp sphagnum moss
* 2.5cm/1in wire mesh netting
* wire cutters
* florists' adhesive clay
* pinholder
* 18cm/7in diameter cylindrical basket
* stout twig
* medium stub wires (floral pins)
* florists' scissors
* scissors

DECORATIVE MATERIALS

* selection of evergreens such as cypress, Jerusalem sage and box (boxwood)
* dried hydrangeas
* gold baubles
* 7.5cm/3in-wide ribbon

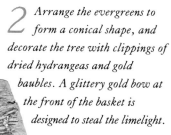

2 *Arrange the evergreens to form a conical shape, and decorate the tree with clippings of dried hydrangeas and gold baubles. A glittery gold bow at the front of the basket is designed to steal the limelight.*

WINDOW LIGHTS

Candles lighted in a window serve a double purpose, giving pleasure to those inside the room and others who pass by outside.

1 *Plastic foam-holders, which you can buy from florists' shops or through flower clubs, are ideal for a design of this kind. If you do not have them, wrap the soaked foam tightly in foil. To position the holders, cut strips of adhesive clay and press them to the undersides. If you are using foil-wrapped blocks, press the clay to the foil. Press the holders in place and insert blocks of soaked foam, or position the wrapped blocks. Press the candles into the foam.*

2 *Cut the stub wires in half, and bend them to make U-shaped staples to fix clumps of lichen to the foam. This will help to conceal the fixings, and give the design a wintry look. Position the planted tree if you use one.*

3 *Arrange the mixed evergreens in a dense mass of varying greens to create a 'forest floor' look. Add more greenery until all the holding materials are covered.*

EQUIPMENT

* plastic foam-holders or foil
* absorbent stem-holding foam, soaked in water
* florists' adhesive clay
* medium stub wires (floral pins)
* wire cutters

DECORATIVE MATERIALS

* green and white candles
* lichen (available from florists' shops)
* selection of mixed evergreens
* pine-cones
* fallen leaves, sprayed gold
* miniature evergreen tree, in pot (optional)

4 *Twist stub wires around a few cones and push the wires at intervals throughout the design. Lastly, arrange the gilded leaves to catch every glint of candlelight.*

CANDLE TIME

CHRISTMAS IS the time to gather your most attractive candlesticks, get in a supply of candles to tone with your seasonal colour theme, and turn the lights down low. It is also a time for improvisation, whether it is to supplement the number of candlesticks you have, or to set the scene for a special party.

You may like to incorporate candles into a large, deep swag filling a wide windowsill or mantelpiece, using thick, stubby candles raised on flowerpots concealed among the greenery. Or position tall candles to taper elegantly from a forest of twigs and pine-cones. (This decorating theme is developed in one of the preceding projects, in which both white and holly-green candles are used to seasonal effect.)

Flowerpots make practical if somewhat rustic holders for candles of all kinds – from the highly-textured beeswax ones to those in traditional colours. Select the most earthy and weatherbeaten flowerpots you have, though for the sake of the table surface they should be scrupulously clean. Plant the candles in heavy holding material such as gravel chippings concealed under (for safety reasons) damp moss or hay. A garland of ivy trailing around the top of the flowerpot, held in place with unobtrusive blobs of clay, will add to the pastoral look while a large green and white gingham bow will add a touch more elegance.

A variety of household items can do festive duty in this way. Pottery mugs and tumblers, casseroles and baking dishes can hold a candle galaxy. A group of beakers supporting beeswax candles and surrounded by pomanders, pine-cones, polished fruits, pearly seashells or glitzy baubles would make a brilliant centre-piece for the dining table or a focal point on a side table.

Plain white altar candles, beautiful in their simplicity, can be trimmed with evergreens, berries and bows to stand as a sign of welcome in a window or, again, as a table centre-piece. Snippings from larger decorations co-ordinate with the candles and at no extra expense.

VERY NEARLY VERDIGRIS

Transform bargain-shop candlesticks with this verdigris look-alike technique. Real verdigris is the green deposit that forms on copper or brass that has been exposed to the elements and oxidized. This interpretation will weather any storm!

EQUIPMENT
* candlestick
* small paintbrushes
* acrylic paints in green, gold and bronze
* turpentine (optional)
* varnish (optional)

1 Paint the candlestick with a base coat of bronze, using criss-crossing brush strokes for an uneven, textured finish. Allow paint to dry.

TARTAN TRIM

Plain white candles enter into the Christmas spirit with a festive trim of ribbon bows and evergreens.

1 *Cut short lengths of the evergreens and seedheads and bind them into mixed bunches. Place a few stems against one of the candles and bind them on with silver wire. Add more bunches, binding them on all around the candle and secure the wire. Hook on false berries, if desired. Tie around the stems with ribbon to conceal the wire. Trim the other candles in a similar way.*

2 *Place the candles in appropriate holders and arrange them in the centre of the dining table or on a windowsill among cuttings of mixed evergreens.*

EQUIPMENT

* 30cm/12 in-long plain white candles
* florists' scissors
* fine silver wire

DECORATIVE MATERIALS

* snippings of evergreen
* linseed (flaxseed), sprayed gold
* artificial holly berries (optional)
* 4cm/1½in-wide and 2.5cm/1in-wide ribbons

2 *Daub the bronze-coloured surface with green paint. If you prefer a more transparent finish, thin the paint with turpentine. Allow to dry for about 10 minutes, then daub on gold paint, again applying in uneven patches.*

ABOVE: *A selection of brass, enamel and earthenware candlesticks, beeswax candles and slender tapers provide informal, country-style decoration.*

3 *A verdigris-style candlestick makes an elegant flower stand when it is fitted with a small foam-holder and a piece of soaked stem-holding foam. Fix the holder to the top of the candlestick with florists' adhesive tape and arrange flowers and foliage. For a festive look, fit the candlestick with a rolled beeswax candle, a ring of glossy evergreens and a handful of cream and gold flowers.*

CANDLE-BRIGHT

Pumpkin-shaped gourds make the brightest candleholders ever. Arrange them in a cluster on a dining table, a sideboard or in the kitchen, or use as decorations for an informal party. But be warned – they will steal the show.

EQUIPMENT

* pumpkin-shaped gourds
* apple corer, sharp knife, or florists' adhesive clay (see below)
* candles

1 If you have more gourds than you will need for candleholders, select those with the most attractive curved stalks and set them aside. Break off the stalks from the others and, if the gourd is soft enough, gouge out a shallow hole wide enough to hold a candle. If the gourd is too hard – and dried ones may well be – fix the candles securely in the indentation with florists' adhesive clay. If candles are fixed in this way, take extra care when they are lighted. Do not leave them unattended with boisterous youngsters or animals.

2 A colourful collection of bright orange gourds is vibrant with yellow and orange candles. Trailing stems of Chinese lanterns (winter cherry) wind through the group, an element which could be repeated in neighbouring flower arrangements, wreaths and decorative swags.

OPPOSITE: Two old weatherbeaten flower pots adopt a decorative role as candleholders. Filled with gravel chippings and with a light covering of damp hay, they hold a galaxy of forest-green candles.

GARLANDS AND SWAGS

FROM A luxuriant garland of blue pine and glimmering ribbon to a ring of ivy leaves wound around a hat brim; from a garland of gold-sprayed hydrangea heads to an unruly composition of twigs and baubles over a fireplace; from a neat and orderly swag of nuts, resembling an intricate wood-carving to a casual and colourful pairing of orange Chinese lanterns (winter cherry) and shimmering honesty – swags and garlands enhance our homes at Christmas in myriad ways.

Gathering the materials for the decorations can be very much a family affair – involving forays into the countryside or the garden weeks in advance of the festival to cut the evergreens and twigs and hunt for fallen cones, beech nuts, chestnut cases and all the other natural materials.

MIXED BLESSINGS

An evergreen garland bringing together a host of natural materials comes close to the beauty of the forest or wayside in winter. All you need is a touch of frost for total realism.

EQUIPMENT

* wire mesh netting (see below)
* wire cutters
* absorbent stem-holding foam, soaked in water
* knife
* florists' scissors
* secateurs (pruning shears)
* stub wires (floral pins)

DECORATIVE MATERIALS

* selection of evergreens such as pine, holly, ivy, cypress, juniper and spruce
* bare twigs such as apple and teasels
* dried ferns, sprayed gold (optional)
* large cones
* ribbon or baubles, for the centre (optional)

LEFT: Trails of ivy outlining the dresser; an arrangement of evergreens and golden lilies; and candles trimmed with ribbons and dried flowers.

1 Measure the length of the fireplace, doorway or arch to be decorated with the garland, allowing for any curve or drape you wish it to have. Cut the appropriate length of wire mesh netting, and trim it to a width of about 25cm/10in. Cut blocks of absorbent foam into 6 and place them end to end along the centre of the netting. Fold the netting over from both sides to enclose the foam and secure it by bending and twisting together the cut edges of the wires. Measure and mark the centre of the garland length.

2 Decorate the garland with the evergreens and natural materials, pushing the stems under the wire mesh and into the foam. This design is planned to have an unruly and somewhat shaggy appearance, but you could make it neater and more orderly. Continue adding more materials until you reach the end of the wire cone and the fixings are concealed. Return to the centre of the garland and decorate it outwards in the opposite direction. There is no need to match the two sides stem for stem, but the garland should have a pleasing balance.

3 Twist stub wires (floral pins) around a few cones and push the wires into the foam at intervals along the garland.

4 Twist stub wires around the garland in the centre and at the high points to hang it securely. Decorate the centre with a ribbon bow, a cluster of baubles, or a few large cones, as you wish.

CORE MATERIALS

Garlands composed of heavy materials or a variety of components will need a core material, to provide a base to attach the decorations. This core rarely has decorative appeal, and is usually hidden. Depending on the size and weight of the embellishments, the core material can vary through every gauge and type of wire, from fine silver wire to the thickest one that remains pliable and flexible. Rope of various thicknesses, from parcel twine and thin string through heavy-grade tufty string and cord, can also be used.

For the lightest of garlands you can use a tightly rolled paper core that, when opened out, reveals itself as attractive paper ribbon, and is decorative so that it need not be completely concealed.

At the other end of the size and weight scale, for a garland composed of woody evergreen sprays and wired fruits, a substantial core can be made of thin strips of wire mesh netting rolled around damp sphagnum moss. The core is best shaped and draped to its finished pattern before being decorated. It is much more difficult to coax a wire roll into gentle arcs once it is generously laden with wired-on fruits.

When using thick cord or rope to bear the weight of heavy evergreens, concealing the core can be a problem. One way to overcome this is to cover it first with dry sphagnum moss or hay. Handfuls of the covering material bound on with well-camouflaged green twine will thicken the core and give it more 'body'.

Moss- or hay-covered rope, and cores constructed of wire mesh netting and moss can be used as a base for vertically hanging swags. Other core materials, which you can buy in florists' shops or make yourself, include thick plaits (braids) of raffia or straw. A more substantial and woody-looking braid may be made of vine twigs.

VERTICAL
TAKE-OFF

Three metallic birds perch
on a colourful dried-flower
swag. It is composed on a
raffia plait (braid) and made
in moments.

EQUIPMENT

* fine silver wire
* raffia plait (from florists'
  shops)
* hot glue gun or stub wires
  (floral pins) and wire cutters

DECORATIVE
MATERIALS

* dried seedheads such as
  Chinese lanterns (winter
  cherry), honesty, Jerusalem
  sage and poppy
* decorative birds (optional)

*OPPOSITE: This simple swag of
ivy leaves and dried
hydrangeas draped over a
small bedroom fireplace has
golden highlights in keeping
with the festive season. Any
dried flowers that have lost
their natural colour over time
can be sprayed silver or gold
for a pretty cover-up.*

1 Cut the dried materials to
stems of equal lengths and
bind them with the silver wire
into mixed bunches. Attach the
bunches to the plait, some facing
to either side, with hot glue, or
with U-shaped staples made from
stub wires (floral pins).

2 With the song-birds in
place, the swag is ready to
hang on an interior door. The
dried materials are too fragile to
brave some winter climates.

EVERGREEN GARLAND

A garland of evergreens is the perfect seasonal decoration to transform the corner of a room, highlight a special piece of furniture or enhance a fire-place, doorway or arch.

EQUIPMENT

* thick cord or rope
* scissors
* green binding twine
* dry hay or sphagnum moss
* secateurs (pruning shears)
* hot glue gun
* stub wire (floral pins)

DECORATIVE MATERIALS

* wheat stalks, sprayed gold
* blue pine (spruce) or similar foliage
* selection of pine- and fir-cones
* 7.5cm/3in-wide glittery ribbon

1 Measure the length required for the garland, allowing for generous drapes. Cut the rope to length, tie the twine to one end and bind on handfuls of hay all along. Fasten the twine at the other end. Mark the centre of the garland.

3 Bind the bunches of wheat - at intervals along the garland. Work in this way until you reach the centre, then start at the other end, binding on one stem of the blue pine with the tip covering the end of the rope. Continue binding on more evergreens and wheat until you reach the centre of the rope.

4 Using the hot glue gun, stick the cones at intervals along the garland. You can use them to conceal or fill in any gaps in the decoration.

2 Cut the evergreen into short lengths and sprays, and bind the first one, tip facing outwards, onto the hay-covered rope. Bind on others so that the tip of each spray covers the stem end of the previous one.

5 *Tie the ribbon into a bow.
Fix to the garland with a
stub wire (floral pin).*

TWISTED
CORD

A vertical swag of mixed
nuts, a bunch of seedheads
and two curtain tie-backs
comprise a decoration that is
reminiscent of eighteenth-
century bell-pulls.

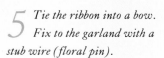

EQUIPMENT

* 60cm/24in-long willow or
  raffia plait (braid) from
  florists
* hot glue gun or clear, quick-
  setting glue
* stub wires (floral pins)
* wire cutters
* florists' scissors

DECORATIVE
MATERIALS

* selection of nuts
* dried seedheads and cones

1 *Glue the nuts to the plait,
   mixing the colours, shapes
and textures for a varied look.
Cones and any seedheads
which do not have
stems will have
to be wired.*

2 *To wire a cone,
   wrap a stub wire around
the lowest 'petals', bring the two
ends of the wire together
beneath the cone and
twist them tightly.*

3 *To wire a lotus
   seedhead, push a
stub wire through the
seedhead close to the base,
bring the two ends of
the wire together at
the base and twist.*

4 *Form the
   seedheads
and cones into a
bunch with the heads
at varying levels and
wire them to the top of the plait
(braid). Loop two ends of the cord
tie-backs together to make one
continuous cord. Wrap it around
the top of the plait where it will
conceal the wire fixings, and twist
it around the plait. Secure the
cord with half stub wires pressed
into the back of the plait.*

DRESSING THE CHRISTMAS TREE

TRIMMING THE Christmas tree is one of the most enchanting of all Christmas preparations. Weeks before the festivities begin, various members of the family can set to work making new decorations, each one maximizing his or her culinary or artistic skills. Some decorations will be so pretty that they will be brought out year after year; others so tasty that it will be touch and go whether they will survive the twelve days of Christmas.

Many families have adopted the charming custom of giving a take-home gift from the tree to anyone who calls at their home during the holiday – to visiting carol singers; friends and neighbours who drop by to deliver a Christmas card, gift or invitation; houseguests and those invited to a party. In Northern Europe, and in Holland, Germany and Scandinavia particularly, specially decorated biscuits and shaped chocolates are offered as a sign of welcome and friendship to anyone who calls during Advent, the four weeks leading up to Christmas.

A tall order? Not if you start building up a stock of home-made and specially wrapped candies, gingerbread and other spiced biscuits and cookies, kumquat or tangerine pomanders and tiny inexpensive baskets filled with bought candies, dried flowers and trinkets for the children.

The decorations on these pages, and others throughout this book, will provide you with ideas for decorations to keep for the tree, and others that would make ideal gifts. Some are just asking to be eaten (when they should be suitably wrapped) and others, such as the walnut clusters and the dried mushrooms sprayed with gold paint, have moved out of the food category and into the realms of fantasy.

RIGHT: Collect pine- and fir-cones on woodland walks or buy them by the bagful in florists' shops. Wrap a wire around the top layer of 'petals', bring the wire up at the back and twist it into a loop. Finish with a gingham bow.

RIGHT: Use clear, quick-setting glue or a hot glue gun to stick nuts together in clusters. You can spray all or some of them with gold or silver paint, keep them in clusters of a single kind, or mix walnuts, pecans, hazel nuts and others. Pecans, especially, look best if some are left unsprayed; the rich pinky-red is too attractive to hide. When the glue has set, push a stub wire (floral pin) through a gap between the nuts, twist it to make a loop and tie on a decorative ribbon bow.

LEFT: Collect miniature baskets from charity shops and fill them with the most colourful candies around. A perky bow in a contrasting colour increases the eye appeal. And so do the candy sticks, hooked over the branches!

LEFT: Wedge a small piece of dry stem-holding foam into the bases of small baskets – off-cuts saved from large arrangements are suitable – and fill them to over-flowing with dried flowers and seedheads. Those shown here are Chinese lanterns (winter cherry), honesty and hops. Strawflowers, gypsophila (baby's breath) and statice would also be suitable.

RIGHT: Entering the realms of fantasy, dried and gold-sprayed mushrooms and toadstools make unusual tree decorations in weird and wonderful shapes. Dry the fungi in an airing cupboard or an oven at the lowest setting with the door slightly open. After spraying, tie them singly, in pairs or in groups with bright and shiny ribbons.

ABOVE: A posy from small everlasting flowers is attached to the tree with golden ribbon.

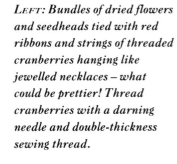

LEFT: Bundles of dried flowers and seedheads tied with red ribbons and strings of threaded cranberries hanging like jewelled necklaces – what could be prettier! Thread cranberries with a darning needle and double-thickness sewing thread.

RIGHT: Select gourds in all shapes and sizes and spatter-spray them with gold or silver paint. Fix a hook to the stalk and tie on a bow that will catch every flicker of light from the Christmas tree candles.

RIGHT: *White wooden curtain rings take on a new role as dried flower holders. Cut 4 slits in a Chinese lantern (winter cherry) or Cape gooseberry (physalis) case and open it out like a flower. Stick it to the base of a ring and stick a pink everlasting flower inside it, with another at the top. Tie a ribbon bow through the small metal ring.*

BELOW: *Make decorative 'candleholders' by sticking a small white cake candle, the wick burnt for a look of realism, to the base of a white curtain ring. Cut a piece of gold sequin trim to fit and stick it on the back of the ring. Add a gold-sprayed star anise seedpod at the front for a decoration certain to become a family heirloom.*

ABOVE: *Thick, shiny orange rings look good enough to eat, even when they have been dried. Cut 6mm/¼in slices from a large orange, place on a rack and dry in an oven at the lowest temperature for about 1 hour. Push a knife through just below the peel and thread with a ribbon.*

LEFT: *Tie decorative bundles of cinnamon sticks together with ribbon for a sweetly scented tree trim. Fix cranberries to the ribbon with a strong, clear adhesive, to complement the jewel-bright garlands of cranberries threaded onto sewing cotton.*

IN FOCUS
A Guide to Better Photos

NEWSLETTER 1993   YORK® PHOTO LABS   ISSUE III

Photo Contest Winners

We have a winner!

Ms. Jeanne Griffin of Sangerville, Maine sent in this magnificent picture of her daughter, Shelly Mae. Ms. Griffin writes, "This picture of my 6 year old, Shelly Mae, was taken after she rescued a dragonfly from a spider's web. Both she and the dragonfly look pleased with each other."

The Griffin family will be going to WALT DISNEY WORLD® Resort as Grand Prize winners of our first photo contest, introduced in our April issue of IN FOCUS. We have twenty-five second place winners as well, who will receive Fuji QuickSnap cameras. You'll see many of these photos in our upcoming catalogs and flyers. Our second place winners are:

Rebecca Allen, Challis, ID; *Richard Betts*, Lemont, PA; *Christa Chilson*, Seneca, SC; *Noel Cruz*, Olathe, KS; *Sandra Daley*,

Killeen, TX; *Linda Erlandson*, Sleepy Eye, MN; *Wayne Farnum*, N. Scituate, RI; *Susan Filter*, East Grand Forks, MN 56721 (three pictures); *Lynette Goodale*, New Hudson, MI; *Carol Hookham*, Bellingham, WA; *Sarah Jepsen*, Delta Junction, AK; *Nancy Ishimoto*, Honolulu, HI; *Shelley Logan*, Manhattan, KS; *Sheila Manning*, Fairdale, WV, *Michelle McDonough*, S. Walpole, MA; *Julie McKeen*, Fredericksburg, VA; *Sue Murphy*, Yalesville, CT; *Saida Nassirruddin*, Birmingham, AL; *Lois Rice*, Winchendon, MA; *Diane Sackett*, Ft. Meade, MD; *Chris Venema*, Marysville, WA; *Barbara Wagner*, Smithsburg, MD; *Gail Wurmstein*, Enid, OK.

Thank you to everyone who participated! To enter our next Photo Contest, read on . . .

Flash Pictures
Without Fear!

When the sun goes down, or when you step indoors, do you pack your camera away because you're afraid to use your flash? Don't be! You CAN take great flash photos. Just follow these tips and those annoying flash problems will be a thing of the past.

REFLECTIONS—Be aware of reflective surfaces when you're composing your flash pictures. If you can't avoid them (say, if your subject is wearing glasses) shoot from an angle so the flash won't reflect back into the camera.

RED EYE—Avoid this flash "gremlin" by increasing the overall room lighting, and reminding your subject not to look

(continued on other side)

Photo Contest!
Win A Royal ⚓ Caribbean Cruise

FAMILY & FRIENDS

Ports of Call: Aruba, Curacao, St. Maarten, St. Thomas and St. John

With the holiday season fast approaching, it's time to think about fun-filled get-togethers with family and good friends. Be sure you take pictures whenever you're with people you care about, because this year one could win you a fabulous Royal Caribbean cruise for two! That's right! It's another great photo contest from York.

First Prize is a Royal Caribbean Cruise for Two.

- 5 Second Place winners will receive automatic Fuji Discovery 190 point-and-shoot 35mm cameras.

Picture This! Magazine

Learn to improve your photography skills with easy to understand, step-by-step instructions. Get information on cameras and equipment, and enter your new and improved pictures in the photo contests! Charter subscriptions are now available to York Photo Labs customers, and you can even receive a **FREE ISSUE.**

Complete the order form at right; make checks payable and mail to:
Picture This! Magazine, Subscription Dept., Suite 804, 1102 Pleasant St., Worcester, MA 01602.

directly at the camera. Some automatic cameras offer "red-eye reduction"—a "pre-flash" that goes off ahead of the main one to make your subject's pupils contract. Helpful, but it won't eliminate "red-eye" entirely.

OVEREXPOSURE—

"Washed out" faces usually mean you were too close to your subject to use your flash. Check your camera's manual for recommended flash distances.

UNDEREXPOSURE—A grey,

foggy look belongs at the seashore—NOT in a brightly lit room! You were probably too far away for an effective flash.

Ordering Reprints & Enlargements

1. Reprints and enlargements can be made from your negatives, photos or 35mm slides. For best results, send us your negatives.

2. Send negatives in whole strips - *don't cut them apart!* Specify which negative number you want prints from by finding the frame number beneath it and writing that number on the negative bag before inserting negative strips.

3. Be careful with your negatives. Send them in a negative bag whenever possible to keep them free of dust, dirt or fingerprints. Never cut, tape, staple or put labels on negative strips.

4. If you're sending us a print to copy, we'll have to make a negative of it first. Please add $1.00 extra for

this service for each print you send. Attach personal address labels to the BACK of prints, not the front.

5. Pick the size and quantity of reprints and enlargements you want on the handy chart below, and fill in the rest of the order form.

6. Send your negative strip(s), print(s) or 35mm slide(s) along with the order form and a check or money order in a York envelope. If you don't have a York envelope handy, mail in a plain envelope to:

York Photo Labs
National Headquarters
400 Rayon Drive
Parkersburg, WV 26101

Frame It – It's Fun!

When you have pictures so important you've just GOT to share them, why not show them off in a big way: Order 11" x 14", 16"x 20" or even 20" x 30" enlargements, mount and frame them, and give them as gifts.

Yes, frame them! You can do it like a pro, right at home. It's easy, inexpensive and fun! Just follow these simple steps:

Here's what you'll need:
✓ A towel
✓ A pre-cut frame, matte and glass
✓ Brown cardboard (same size as the matte)
✓ A clean brown paper bag
✓ A spray bottle with warm water
✓ White glue
✓ A blow dryer
✓ Hanging hook, u-nails (or glazier's points)
✓ A small hammer

1. Put a towel on a clean, flat surface and lay the frame on it so it won't get scratched.

2. Clean the glass on both sides and lay it in the frame—keep a sharp eye out for fingerprints and lint.

3. Lay the matte in the frame, followed by your print

(face down and centered, you may want to tape your print in place), and finally the piece of cardboard.

4. Gently hammer u-nails or push glazier's points (about 1 every 4 inches) into the frame to secure your matte, print and cardboard "sandwich."

5. Cut the brown paper bag about 1/8" smaller than the back of the frame. Apply a *thin* line of glue directly to the frame, then press the brown paper in place, wiping off any excess glue immediately.

6. Spray the paper with warm water—wet thoroughly, but don't soak. Use the blow dryer to dry the paper. The heat will shrink and tighten the paper. Dry the paper *completely*—it should be smooth, tight, and wrinkle-free when you're done.

7. Very carefully hammer a hanging clip into the back of the frame.

Turn your handiwork over and admire it. You've framed a print just like the pros!

RIGHT: Pretzel sticks are tied into bundles with festive ribbon, and decorated with a gold-dusted leaf.

ABOVE: Deck the tree with the prettiest of citrus fruits, tiny egg-shaped kumquats, by threading them onto medium stub wires. Loop the circlets over the tree branches, or tie them with toning or contrasting ribbons.

LEFT AND BELOW: These traditional tree decorations are as popular and tasty as ever. Use a gingerbread cutter to cut out the basic shapes and create a variety of characters – some bald, bearded, young or old – with the icing.

BELOW: Save a few salty pretzels from the snack tray and shape them into bright tree ornaments. Or, stick circular biscuits together with fondant icing to make a hoop.

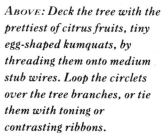

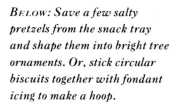

PRECIOUS METALS

THE GLINT of metal containers takes on an extra-special quality at Christmastime, when every curved or faceted surface of silver, pewter, copper or brass reflects the flickering flames of the candles and the pin-points of lights on the tree. Make the most of this seasonal bonus and gather together several well-polished metal items to play their part in the decorative scene. Arrange them with evergreens and berries, fresh flowers in fire-glow hues and dried flowers and seedheads in every colour of the rainbow.

You may have a silvered teapot no longer in use that would make a charming container for a precious bunch of pink and coral roses to create a delightful centre-piece at teatime; or a decorative tray you could press into service to flatter a candle and flower arrangement. You may have a pewter plate – not the shiniest of metals but one with depth and a certain amount of warmth – that prompts a medieval-style arrangement of gilded leaves, nuts and seedcases; a pewter cake-stand that elevates a selection of fresh and sugared fruits and flowers to new heights; or a pewter tankard that would look magnificent with nothing more than a few simple sprays of holly stripped of the leaves to highlight the berries.

An old copper kettle would help to transform a kitchen corner with a flourish of ruby and white lilies and, for good measure, a tray of utilitarian nightlights; or a small copper jug could hold a still-life of pyracantha (firethorn) berries, rosehips, clematis seedheads and blackberry leaves, all arranged to frame the last rose of winter. Where the brass section is concerned, fill to the brim a gleaming preserving pan with a selection of pine- and fir-cones. At Christmastime every glimmer of reflective light counts.

ABOVE: A collection of copper brings a warm glow to a kitchen corner. The kettle is arranged with a display of ruby and white lilies.

TOP BRASS

An old brass watering can spills over with a dazzlingly colourful collection of leaves and seedheads, from the natural brilliance of the Chinese lanterns (winter cherry) to the deep, rich purple of the dyed poppy heads.

1 Crumple the wire netting, push it into the neck of the container and secure it with 2 or 3 short lengths of adhesive tape wrapped around a strand of wire and stuck onto the rim. Arrange the foliage to make a fan shape with the tallest stems in the centre and shorter ones positioned to the side.

EQUIPMENT

* wire mesh netting
* brass or copper container; a kettle or jug would be suitable
* florists' adhesive tape
* fine silver wire
* florists' scissors

DECORATIVE MATERIALS

* dried leaf sprays
* selection of dried natural and dyed seedheads such as Chinese lanterns (winter cherry), globe thistle (echinops), poppy and thistle

2 Fill in the design with tall stems of poppy seedheads and short-stemmed clusters of spiky dyed thistles, positioned so that they will conceal the wire netting and fixings.

3 Repeat the fan shape of the leaves, poppy and thistle on the other side of the design. Position the vibrant Chinese lanterns (winter cherry) at varying heights, with some trailing over the rim to create glowing reflections.

EASTERN FLAVOUR

Break with the tradition of decorating the home with greenery and explore the dramatic and long-lasting effect that can be created with dried flowers and seedheads. The arrangement on these pages, whilst still paying lip service to the powerful combination of red and green, is created with a medley of dried materials that may not be as familiar as many others, but is equally striking.

Some of these plant materials may be bought in florists' shops in a bag simply labelled 'exotics'. To prepare such materials the heads can be mounted on false stems made of thin wooden canes bound onto the head with fine silver wire.

LOOK EAST

Capture the spirit of the East with a casual composition of dried flowers, leaves and seedheads in warm, woody browns and vibrant reds.

EQUIPMENT
* wire mesh netting
* deep, round earthenware container; a flowerpot or jug would be suitable
* florists' adhesive tape
* scissors
* florists' scissors
* secateurs (pruning shears)

DECORATIVE MATERIALS
* selection of dried flowers and seedheads such as shumag, caspia, nigella Orient, bottle brush and amaranthus.

1 Crumple the wire mesh netting, push it into the neck of the container and secure it with 2 short strips of adhesive tape criss-crossed from side to side and pressed onto the rim of the container. Commence the outline of the design by placing stems graduated in length to form a fan shape.

ABOVE: Two incense burners heated with nightlights – one of which is burning myrrh crystals – and dried verbascum flowers. These are still used in place of wicks in remote country areas of Greece. The soft, gentle and timeless light of these simple lamps exemplifies the spirit of Christmas.

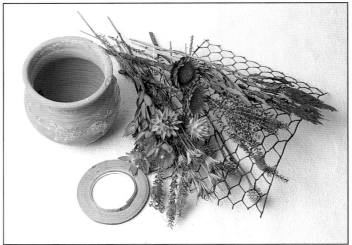

LEFT: Mount dried flower heads and seed heads on false wire stems using thin florists' wire. Thread the wire through the head and secure at the base of the flower or seedhead. Bind the wire with floral tape.

2 *Fill in the design so that the red bottle brush, the most colourful of the materials, is prominently seen. The daisy-shaped seedheads, the most clearly defined of the materials, form the focal point at the heart of the arrangement.*

3 *Complete the design by positioning some of the cone-like seedheads to cover the container rim, where they echo the rough texture of the pot. Arrange complementary accessories – pots, plaques or lamps – to compose a still-life group.*

CHRISTMAS POSIES

NATURAL POSIES probably come closest of all Christmas decorations to the original concept of bringing in bunches of evergreens in celebration of the winter festival. For at their simplest such posies need be no more than a handful of leafy twigs, brilliant berries or papery bracts hanging in a doorway, over a stairwell or in a room corner.

Selecting materials for Christmas posies is influenced not only by tradition but by design considerations. A bunch of deep green ivy and holly endowed with a few berries may be strong on tradition but could appear as a dense, featureless mass if it were not spot-lit with particular sensitivity. The inclusion of a variegated component makes all the difference, and it provides the ray of lightness necessary to bring the bunch into focus. There are a great many examples of variegated holly whose leaves are tinged with cream, white or yellow; some also have well-defined yellow streaks and others – *Ilex aquilfolium bacciflava* is an example – bear sunshine-yellow berries.

Ivy, too, is a plant of many colours and, for the sake of appearances, it is worth seeking out varieties which have especially glossy leaves, are in the green-going-on-yellow colour range, or have intricate and interesting reddish-brown veining.

In a year when holly is richly endowed with berries it is a good decorative idea to strip some stalks of the leaves. This will go some way towards diminishing the all-over greenness of a bunch, maximize the vibrant impact of the berries, and yet stay within the bounds of tradition.

Breaking away from the bounds, Christmas posies can comprise a decorative wealth of other natural materials, as examples on these pages show. Gather a handful of wayward spindle twigs (cotoneaster) thick with their distinctive pinky-crimson fruits opening to show orange-scarlet seeds. With a few contrasting, yellowing leaves clinging to the branches, the posy needs no further adornment. Because of its spindly nature, it is advisable to hang such a bunch where it will be viewed against a plain wall, door or panel. Any degree of pattern on the background would impose unfair visual competition.

LEFT: As simple as can be – a bunch of spindle branches (cottoneaster) vibrant with berries.

A TOUCH OF ROMANCE

A heart-shaped frame covered with evergreen and fragrant rosemary is decorated with a posy of romantic red rosebuds and seasonal holly and ivy.

EQUIPMENT

* strong, flexible wire
* fine silver wire
* hollow wheat straw

DECORATIVE MATERIALS

* rosemary
* dried red and cream rosebuds
* honesty, holly and ivy
* 2.5cm/1in-wide ribbon

1 Bend the wire into a circle, bind the 2 ends securely with silver wire and shape the wire frame to form a heart. Cover the frame with short sprays of rosemary, so that the tips of each bunch cover the stem ends of the one before.

2 Bind the dried flowers and seedheads, holly and ivy on the wheat stalk to give the appearance of a posy.

3 Use the wire to bind the evergreen and dried flower posy to the heart-shaped frame. Decorate the design with a flourish of shining ribbons.

DOOR POSY

Gilded wheat and evergreens, as glittering as the ribbon bow, are formed into a welcoming door posy.

EQUIPMENT
* newspaper or scrap paper
* fine silver wire
* gold spray-paint
* scissors

DECORATIVE MATERIALS
* wheat stalks
* selection of evergreens such as blue pine (spruce), cypress, ivy and yew
* dried grasses
* 4cm/2½in-wide gold ribbon

1 Cover the work surface with newspaper or scrap paper. Gather 10 or 12 wheat stalks to form a bunch and bind them with silver wire. Spray the wheat and ivy with gold paint and leave to dry.

2 Place the largest component on the work surface and arrange the other materials over it. Bind the stems firmly together with wire and tie the ribbon to form a bow. Cut the ends slantwise.

ABOVE: Twisting hop vines with papery bracts compose a delightful posy with understated colour. A single stem of pale orange Chinese lanterns (winter cherry) and a single woody seedhead complete the design. The stems are bound with fine silver wire, concealed beneath the ribbon.

SALT DOUGH DECORATIONS

Attractive but inedible salt dough decorations, thought to have originated in Germany, are popular throughout Northern Europe where they are frequently exchanged as Christmas gifts. Following this basic recipe you can make a posy as shown in the photograph; simple plaited rings as candleholders or tree decorations; or a bell, Christmas tree or other festive shapes cut out with cookie cutters.

INGREDIENTS

200g/7oz/2 cups plain (all-purpose) flour
200g/7oz/2 cups salt
1 tsp glycerin
100ml/4fl oz/½ cup cold water

1   Pre-heat the oven to *100°C/200°F/Gas ¼. Sift the flour and salt into a mixing bowl, add the glycerin and slowly pour on the water, mixing continuously to form a firm but pliable dough. Do not make the dough too wet, or it will be too sticky to handle. Dust a pastry board with flour and roll out the dough to a thickness of about 6mm/¼in.*

2   *Cut the basic shape of the posy, almost that of an hour glass. Cover the shape with non-stick baking paper while you shape the rest of the design. Cut out the leaves and mark the veins with the point of a knife. Cut thin strips of dough and roll them around to form rose shapes. Cut out and shape the flat-faced flowers and the berries. Roll some dough into thin sausage shapes for the stalks. Cut a rectangle for the bow and pinch it into shape between your thumb and forefinger.*

3   *Brush the background shape with water and arrange the decorations. Use a skewer to push a hole at the top of the design.*

4   *Lift the posy onto a well-floured baking sheet and bake in the pre-heated oven at 100°C/200°F/Gas ¼ for 30 minutes. Increase the temperature to 150°C/300°F/Gas 2 and continue baking for about 2 hours, or until the decoration is dry and hard all the way through.*

* sieve (flour sifter)
* mixing bowl
* pastry board
* rolling pin
* non-stick baking paper
* knife
* pastry brush
* metal skewer
* spatula
* baking sheet
* cooling rack
* paintbrush
* clear polyurethane varnish
* 2.5cm/1in-wide ribbon

5   *Transfer the baked decoration onto a wire rack to cool. Brush the posy all over, on the front and back surfaces, with varnish. Leave to dry for 24 hours, then apply another coat. Leave to dry again, then insert the ribbon and tie a bow at the top.*

DECORATING WITH FRUIT

THERE IS nothing new in decorating the home and dining table with fruits at Christmastime. The Romans and ancient Greeks well understood the decorative properties of home-grown fruits and lavished them around their feast-tables, their couches and even their guests with generous abandon. Indeed, those eras evoke images of bunches of grapes spilling lusciously over the side of an exquisite bowl, or a garland of pomegranates embellishing an archway.

They are, it seems, images that we cherish still, for what household would care to be without fruit at Christmas; what decoration scheme would seem complete without it?

The fruits of the forest, fields and hedgerows, in the form of hips and berries, are the very stuff that Christmas decorations are traditionally made of – the glossy red berries that do so much to complement the deep, mysterious greens of the holly and ivy. It can scarcely be coincidence that red and green, two colours which are opposite each other on the artists' colour wheel, are known as complementary or harmonizing colours. These bring out the best in each other when shown together.

If the holly you buy or gather is short on berries, this can be a blessing in disguise, encouraging you to supplement its vibrancy with other fruits of the season. These could include the last of the rosehips; orangey-red pyracantha (firethorn) berries; berberis (barberry) or spindle (cotoneaster). If need be, cut them early and preserve them in most of their natural glory in a solution of glycerin and hot water. A tankard of holly and ivy, cypress and ballota would also show how effective rosehips can look in verdant surroundings.

Edible fruits, too, have a vibrant part to play in Christmas decorations, and may be eaten later if the fruits are attached to the core material – the wreath form, garland core, pre-formed foam ball or whatever – with non-corrosive materials. Fine silver wire, wooden toothpicks and hot glue (which can be snapped off the skin of a tangerine, for example) are acceptable when eating the fruit is the ultimate goal; stub wires, which may be corrosive, are not.

But fruits do not have to form even a semi-permanent attachment to a decoration to become an integral part of the scheme. Tip a basket on its side – the one shown on these

RIGHT: A Greek basket, propped cornucopia-style, cascades with rosy apples and scarlet roses. The rose stems, split at the ends, are pushed into small blocks of soaked foam wrapped in foil.

OPPOSITE BELOW: A tempting bowl of fresh and sugared fruits can be a highlight of the Christmas dinner or an eye-catching table decoration. Dried fruits and frosted or sugared fruits and petals should last throughout the holiday – as long as the guests don't eat them first! The rose stem is held in water in a plastic orchid phial.

BELOW: There are so many traditional styles for kissing rings, and they do not all include mistletoe. This ball of evergreen cypress and holly is composed on a large, scrubbed potato, which acts as a source of moisture. The kumquats are speared onto wooden toothpicks.

pages is, appropriately enough, a Greek fruit-picking basket – insert a piece of soaked stem-holding foam wrapped in foil and you have a cornucopia-style container which would not look out of place at a Roman feast. Fresh crimson roses, evergreens and waxy-white Christmas roses can tumble out in disorderly profusion, with polished rosy apples, nuts and bunches of grapes among them.

A true cornucopia, or horn of plenty, is a variation on this theme. This decoration may be of slightly more pastoral appearance, spilling forth a dried corn-on-the-cob (Indian corn) chosen for its unusually speckled nature, gourds, pomegranates and green-to-orange Chinese lanterns (winter cherry). Find a space where a free-style decoration of this kind can be left undisturbed – as a gesture of welcome in the hall or as the centre of attention on a buffet table – have the components ready to hand, and you can arrange them (perhaps scatter is a more accurate term) in moments.

Fruits of the most familiar and everyday type can be used as accessories to flower arrangements, intensifying the colour factor, providing a visual platform, extending or emphasizing a line, and so on. Apples, for example, may be placed in this way, as an integral part of the design to give visual stability at the base of an arrangement.

FLORAL ARCH

Arranged in a seemingly haphazard way around the base of a container, rosy apples become an important and eye-catching accessory. When space is of the essence, pile the fruit in a small red or green bowl beneath the arch of foliage and flowers.

EQUIPMENT

* scissors
* florists' adhesive clay
* plastic foam-holding saucer
* tall straight-sided container
* cylinder of absorbent stem-holding foam, soaked in water
* florists' adhesive tape
* florists' scissors

DECORATIVE MATERIALS

* selection of flowers such as carnations, spray carnations, *Euphorbia fulgens* and laurustinus (viburnum)
* eucalyptus foliage

1 Cut strips of the adhesive clay, press them to the underside of the plastic saucer and push it firmly onto the top of the container. Insert the foam cylinder and secure the holding material in place with two criss-crossing strips of adhesive tape, taken over the foam and onto the container. Arrange the foliage and long flower sprays to form an arch on either side of the container, then position the carnations at the heart of the design.

2 Fill in the arrangement with spray carnations and short sprays of laurustinus (viburnum) and position some foliage stems to thrust almost vertically downwards where they will partially obscure the container. Arrange the apples around the group.

OPPOSITE PAGE: *Gold-sprayed lychees and leaves are casually arranged with russet-coloured fruits and pecans, creating a simple yet glowing display for the festive season.*

Small is beautiful when it comes to designing with fruits, and small, oval, orange-coloured kumquats are virtually unrivalled in this regard. Pierce them on wooden toothpicks or split wooden skewers and you can use them as the colour focus of a flower arrangement or as highlights in an evergreen ball, and eat them when they are no longer needed as decoration.

Simplicity can be the keynote of Christmas decorations of all kinds, and often need not be any more complex than a plate of fruit and nuts. Make your selection with an eye to colour, scale and texture and position coral-red pears next to russety-brown apples; gilded lychees (no longer suitable for eating) against pinky-red pecans; long and slender cinnamon quills beside partly opened and rounded Cape gooseberry

(physalis) cases; gold-sprayed leaves with bronze ones. The overall effect has medieval overtones.

Develop the theme in other ways – fill a bowl with green apples colour-spiked with stripped stalks of holly berries; a bowl of silver-sprayed apples and pears teamed up with a plate with a casual grouping of fruits and nuts or black figs and black grapes highlighted with a scattering of gold-covered chocolate coins.

While notions such as these strike a note of informality there is usually a place in the scheme of things for a more stylized arrangement; perhaps a pyramid of fruit, flowers and foliage. The example on the following pages, created on a flat pottery plate and with the support of blocks of stem-holding foam would make an effective centre-piece.

PERFECT PYRAMID

Tempting fruits and coral-coloured carnations and roses, clusters of nuts and gilded evergreens combine to form a seasonal pyramid that would steal the limelight on a sideboard or buffet table.

EQUIPMENT

* scissors
* florists' adhesive clay
* 2 plastic prongs
* 30cm/12in-diameter large, flat plate
* 2 blocks of absorbent stem-holding foam, soaked in water
* florists' scissors
* medium stub wires
* clear quick-setting glue or hot glue gun
* gold spray-paint

DECORATIVE MATERIALS

* selection of evergreen foliage such as mahonia, yew, cypress, ivy and eucalyptus
* selection of fruits such as pineapples, satsumas and lychees
* selection of flowers such as carnations, roses and spray chrysanthemums
* nuts and seeds such as pecans and iris seeds

1 Cut 2 strips of adhesive clay and press one onto the underside of each of the plastic prongs. Making sure that the plate is absolutely dry, press the prongs onto it, one just behind the central point and one in front to the right. Push the blocks of foam onto the prongs. Outline the arrangement with mahonia leaves and other evergreens, the tallest ones positioned at the centre back and low on the right.

2 Lean the pineapple against the central foam block. Secure with a stub wire wrapped around the stem and with the ends pushed into the foam. Position the carnations and roses behind the pineapple, creating almost a fan shape.

3 Position short stems of ivy and spray chrysanthemums as 'fillers' between the feature flowers. Arrange the colourful iris berries on stems of graduating height to distribute their contrasting texture throughout the design.

4 Using clear, quick-setting glue or a hot glue gun, stick several lychees into a cluster. Push a stub wire through a gap between the cases, twist the ends and push them into the foam. Form a nut cluster in a similar way and position it on the other side of the design. Thread a stub wire through the back of a satsuma, twist the ends and push them into the foam above the lychees.

5 Complete the design with sprays of ivy spattered with gold paint. Turn the arrangement around and complete the back with sprays of ivy and cypress.

CHRISTMAS CRACKERS

CHRISTMAS CRACKERS have been making Yuletide festivities go with a bang ever since the mid-nineteenth century, when the idea spread from its native France. On special occasions, children were given bags of sugared almonds, which when pulled apart, burst with a bang, revealing the treasures inside.

For many families, Christmas would not be complete without a box of crackers, chosen as much for their outward appearance – which can vary from understated elegance to unrestrained garishness – as for their contents. And yet, relatively few families make crackers to their own colour scheme and design. The photographs on these pages show you how simple, inexpensive and rewarding it can be.

FESTIVE CRACKER

EQUIPMENT

* craft knife
* ruler
* pencil
* double-sided adhesive tape
* fine silver wire

For each cracker

* cardboard roll 4.5cm/1¾in in diameter, 22.5cm/8¾in long (use the inner roll from kitchen or lavatory paper)
* decorative paper 18.5 × 33 cm/7¼ × 13¼ in
* 1 cardboard 'bang' strip, available from joke and novelty shops (see Stockists)
* 1 or more toys or trinkets
* trimmings (see below)

1 Cut the card roll in half and cut one length in half again. Place the largest piece in the centre of one long edge of the decorative paper and the other two pieces 2cm/1½in to either side of it. Secure the rolls to the paper with strips of double-sided adhesive tape. Insert the snap and the 'presents' in the centre.

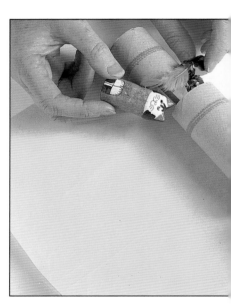

LEFT: A cracker made from pale pink paper is trimmed with star anise seedpods, a nutmeg and a poppy seedhead dusted with gold craft powder, and tied with a ribbon bow.

3 The cracker is now ready
for trimming. You can use
scraps of ribbon; evergreen leaves
such as holly and ivy (spray them
with gold or silver paint if you
wish); dried seedheads and spices
such as star anise and nutmeg;
pine- and larch-cones; gold beads
and miniature baubles; dried
fruit rings; Victorian-style paper
scraps; fresh flowers – the list is
endless. This cracker is trimmed
with a posy of yellow winter
jasmine and a cream Peruvian
lily flower, the stems bound with
fine silver wire and fixed to the
cracker with a pin. Green and
gold satin ribbon wired at the
edges is ruched and wrapped
around the flower stems.

2 Wrap the paper around the
cardboard roll and secure it
with strips of double-sided tape.
Pinch the paper in the gap
between two of the cardboard
rolls. Cut a piece of silver wire,
bind it around this 'waist' and
pull it as tightly as possible. Tie a
knot in the wire and cut off the
ends. Repeat at the other end of
the cracker.

4 A completely co-ordinated
table setting is achieved by
carrying the cracker trimmings
through to the toning napkin.
The green and yellow ruched
ribbon takes the place of a
conventional napkin ring and
holds a few stems of winter
jasmine.

CHRISTMAS GIFTS TO MAKE

What do a scented candle, a zingy flower arrangement in a cone-covered basket, a rosebud pomander, a box of Turkish delight and a jar of pickled vegetables have in common? They are just a few of the many suggestions for gifts you can make throughout the year to delight your family and friends, and to give meaning to the phrase, 'It's the thought that counts'.

Many of the ideas are grouped together in the form of 'theme baskets', so that you can make a collection of co-ordinated items as a composite present, or choose to create a single gift as a smaller token.

SCENTED GIFTS

THINK OF Christmas and you think perhaps of the mingled aromas of spices and seasonal fruits, of flickering candlelight and a general sense of well being. And that is just what the varied elements in this gift basket are meant to convey. Who could ask for anything more!

The basket itself, of humble origin, had been painted, restored and repainted time and time again – the perfect candidate, in short, for another and more important new look. It is covered with cinnamon quills, stuck to the vertical sides with hot glue, which give it a rugged, log-cabin look and a lingering, spicy aroma. Even the handle decoration contributes to the heady scent with its trio of larch-cones and kumquats.

The basket is filled with even more spicy items, some you can make and some to buy. There are tiny orange-coloured kumquats, orange-scented candles and a pot-pourri blend of whole spices and dried orange peel. From a herbalist came orange-scented burning sticks and small bottles of frankincense and myrrh oils.

You could compose a similar gift collection with a variety of different scents, focusing instead on the scents of lemon and lime combined with equally refreshing eucalyptus, or on the woody aroma of sandalwood. Take a cue from the essential oils you can buy in herbalists' shops. You can use them to scent both candles and pot-pourri to create an aroma-coordinated gift.

RIGHT: Any straight-sided basket or box may be decorated with cinnamon quills held in place with clear quick-setting glue or hot glue. If the cinnamon sticks are not long enough to cover the depth of the basket, stick one above the other and conceal the joins with an encircling ribbon or raffia plait (braid).

LEFT: Co-ordinated for both colour and scent, this basket evokes the very essence of Christmas. Once the individual gifts have been used, the basket could be filled with cones, dried flowers or a collection of spice jars.

POMANDERS

Pomanders were made in the Middle Ages to scent rooms and sweeten the air, and to give fragrance to linens and clothes.

EQUIPMENT

* citrus fruits
* whole cloves
* 1.5cm/½in-wide tape, to mask pattern
* nail or darning needle
* orris-root powder
* 1.5cm/½in-wide ribbon

1 You can use any citrus fruits such as oranges, lemons, clementines and satsumas, kumquats and limes. Stud them with whole cloves either all over, in a geometric pattern, or at random.

2 The traditional pattern for a divided orange is made by wrapping tape around the fruit in criss-crossing directions to divide it into four segments. The tape may be outlined with cloves to fill in the segment, or simply to make the pattern of a cross. Use a nail or thick darning needle to pierce the skin.

3 When you have completed the design, put the fruit in a paper bag, sprinkle in 1tbsp of orris-root powder for each large fruit, and close the bag. Leave the fruit in an airing cupboard for two or three weeks so the fruit will dry and spices mellow. Remove the masking tapes and replace them with pretty, decorative ribbons.

4 Clementine and satsuma pomanders tied with ribbons make attractive tree decorations, and spicy kumquats make pretty fillers for a gift basket. Fruits closely studded with cloves, which form a vacuum as the fruit dries and shrinks, will last from year to year; designs with more of the fruit's skin exposed are more short-term decorations.

SCENTED CANDLES

Making your own candles is a satisfying and creative hobby, and also provides you with a wealth of festive gifts. You can buy moulds in a variety of seasonal themes – Christmas pudding and tree shapes, angels and snowmen among them. The group shown here is chosen from a wide selection of fruit shapes and includes oranges, pears, grapes and apples.

EQUIPMENT

* 4 fruit-shaped candle moulds
* vegetable oil for brushing the moulds
* paintbrush
* darning needle
* scissors
* 1 metre/1 yard candle wick
* 4 small bowls or tumblers
* 4 small sticks or pencils
* 450g/1lb paraffin wax
* 150g/5oz stearin, a wax-like hardener
* cooking thermometer
* heatproof jug
* candle dye
* 8 drops orange or lemon essential oil
* soft cloth

1 Brush each mould with oil. Cut the wick into 4, and thread one piece through the needle. Pierce the top of each mould with the needle and thread through a length of wick, leaving a short length outside the mould and about 7.5cm/3in at the base. Wrap the free end of the wick securely round a stick or pencil and suspend it over a bowl.

2 Heat the wax and stearin in a heavy pan to 82°C/180°F. Remove from the heat, pour one-quarter of the wax into a heatproof jug and stir in the dye and scent.

3 Pour into the appropriate mould. Reheat the wax and add the appropriate colour and scent for each mould. When the wax has settled in the moulds, and the level dropped, add a little more wax to level them.

4 Allow to cool, carefully peel off the moulds and cut the wick level at the base. Trim the top to 1cm/½in. Polish each candle with a soft cloth.

DECORATIVE BASKETS

A BASKET OF shiny evergreens spiced up with cinnamon quills and rosy apples, pine-cones and berry-red flowers; a cone-encrusted basket arranged with an equally arresting green and scarlet theme, or one with an imaginative combination of brilliant red peppers and the most colourful blooms around – who could resist baskets like these? They serve as ready-made Christmas decorations and make thoughtful presents for a busy host or hostess, or for a friend who may not have ready access to a selection of seasonal greenery.

Choose the basket with special care. It forms an important part of the gift, since it will remain as a functional memento long after the flowers and foliage have faded. A suitable idea might be a shallow rectangular Shaker basket made from wide, woven slats. It looks beautiful simply piled with cones or apples; lined with checked napkins holding muffins or bread rolls; or laden with cookies and cakes to take to a bring-a-dish party.

BASKET OF EVERGREENS

All things bright and beautiful and appropriate to the Christmas season are here in this cheerful gift basket. Tartan ribbons on the handle bring together the red and green of the contents.

EQUIPMENT

* florists' adhesive clay
* 2 plastic prongs
* shallow rectangular basket
* 2 pieces absorbent stem-holding foam, soaked in water
* foil
* medium stub wires (floral pins)

DECORATIVE MATERIALS

* selection of evergreens such as holly, ivy, yew, cypress and spruce
* red spray carnations
* Christmas roses
* dried poppy seedheads
* pine-cones
* fruits such as pineapples, apples and grapes
* cinnamon quills

LEFT: Cut the top from a red pepper, fill the cavity with soaked absorbent stem-holding foam and you have a brilliant container for vivid flowers.

1 Press a piece of florists' clay to the underside of each plastic prong and press them in position, one on each side towards the back of the basket. Wrap the two pieces of foam in the foil and press each onto a prong.

2 Position sprays of evergreen to fan out over the four corners of the basket, so that neighbouring textures and foliage shapes contrast as much as possible. Arrange the spray carnations, poppy seedheads, and Christmas roses against the background of foliage.

3 Twist stub wires around the lowest row of 'petals' in the pine-cones. Twist the ends together beneath the cones, and push the false stems into the foam.

4 Arrange the fruit to fill the basket; it should have a generous look. Tie ribbon bows around the handle on each side. The arrangement would look good in a hallway or a hearth, on a dining table or a sideboard.

VIVID CONTRAST

For a gift that is out of the ordinary, contrast the rugged look of a basket covered with pine-cones with the delicate beauty of rosebuds and freesias. You can cover any sturdy basket with pine-, larch- or other cones, using a hot glue gun and pressing them firmly onto the surface for a few seconds until they are fixed.

1 Cut two or three short lengths of florists' clay and press them to the underside of the plastic saucer. Insert the foam in the saucer and place the saucer in the basket.

2 Cut short sprays of the evergreen and arrange them to follow the shape of the basket, with the tallest stems just reaching the handle. Position the roses to follow the outline created by the foliage, with tall stems near the handle and short ones around the rim.

3 Fill the arrangement with the freesias, placing some so that they face out to either side and, from the front, are seen in profile. Add a gift tag and, if you wish, a bright glass bauble.

4 Bright scarlet roses and glossy evergreens make the perfect colour combination.

EQUIPMENT
* florists' adhesive clay
* scissors
* plastic foam-holding saucer
* cylinder of absorbent stem-holding foam, soaked in water
* cone-covered basket
* florists' scissors

DECORATIVE MATERIALS
* evergreen leaves such as escallonia or variegated holly
* red rosebuds
* cerise freesias

LAVENDER BASKET

Tʜɪs ɢɪꜰᴛ basket has more than a hint of nostalgia: it has something old – the lace table mat turned into a lavender bag; and something new – lavender soap made into practical bundles, each stick ideal for guests' use. The colour theme is enhanced by the dried-flower posy ringed around with fragrant blue-mauve flowers.

The basket, woven from twisted cane, is painted with lavender blue emulsion (latex) paint highlighted at intervals with streaks of purple poster colour, available from artists' suppliers in appropriately small pots. The basket is lined with dry, sweet-smelling hay blended with a spoonful of lavender flowers so that, even without the goodies, it has a pleasing aroma.

LAVENDER-SCENTED SOAP

Victorian recipes for lavender soap used whole flowers, which gave a rather gritty texture. Grind the flowers in a food processor for a smoother product.

EQUIPMENT

* 100g/4oz unperfumed white soap, grated
* 5tbsp water
* 3tbsp lavender flowers, ground
* 1–2 drops lavender oil
* 1 drop food colouring (optional)
* funnel
* cardboard tubes, such as discarded cigar tubes, to use as moulds
* vegetable oil
* 1.5cm/½in-wide lace edging

1 *Place the soap and water in a large bowl in the microwave and process on high for two to three minutes, or melt in a bowl over a pan of simmering water. Stir the melted soap and water mixture and add the ground lavender flowers, oil and colouring, if used.*

2 *Pour the mixture through a funnel into the mould, sealed at one end, and stand it upright until the soap is set, in two or three hours.*

3 *Remove the mould and cut the soap diagonally into short sticks. Polish with a few drops of oil on a soft cloth and tie into bundles with lace edging.*

LAVENDER DOLLIES

A century or so ago people used lavender bunches, called 'dollies', to scent their clothes cupboards and to sweeten the air. It is an ingenious design, because the lavender seeds, held in a 'cage' of stems and woven ribbon, cannot disperse.

EQUIPMENT

* an uneven number of lavender stalks; 9 or 11 is suitable
* 1 metre/1 yard 1.5cm/½in-wide satin ribbon

1 Tie the stalks together with the ribbon.

2 Bend the stalks down to cover the flowers. Pull the ribbon through to the outside.

3 Weave the ribbon in and out of the stalks, under one and over the next, until the flowerheads are covered.

4 Fasten the ribbon in a knot and cut off the end. Tie the end around the 'dolly' and make a bow.

LAVENDER JELLY

A few blackberries are added to tint the preserve. The more you use the deeper the colour will be.

INGREDIENTS

1kg/2lb cooking apples, washed and quartered
about 1tbsp blackberries (optional)
2tbsp lavender flowers
900ml/1½pt water
about 750g/1½lb sugar

1 Place the apples and blackberries, if used, in a preserving pan. Add the lavender flowers and water, bring to the boil, then simmer until the fruit is soft, about 30 minutes. Press the apples against the sides of the pan to mash them as much as possible.

2 Turn the contents of the pan into a jelly bag suspended over a bowl and allow to drip for about 2 hours. Do not squeeze the bag to hasten the process, or the jelly may become cloudy.

3 Measure the juice and return it to the pan with 450g/1lb sugar to each 600ml/1pt. Bring slowly to the boil, then fast-boil for about 10 minutes, or until setting point is reached. To test that the fruit jelly is ready for bottling, put a small amount on a cold saucer and leave it to cool. Push a finger across the surface. If the jelly has reached setting point, the preserve will form wrinkles.

4 Skim off any foam, pour the preserve into clean, warm jars and cover with waxed discs and transparent or screw-on covers. Add decorative covers of your choice.

THAT'S THE SPIRIT!

MAKING A *Rumtopf* must be the most exotic way of preserving the fruits of the seasons – and so it goes without saying that it makes the most luxurious of gourmet gifts. Layers of gleaming fruit are covered in the spirit of your choice, and left to allow the flavours to blend.

Rum is used for the traditional Christmas and New Year delicacy in Germany and Austria while in France the preserving spirit is brandy. The method is beautifully simple and the result is delicious.

You can follow tradition and begin with the earliest fruits of the season, adding others in layers as they become available. Or make a one-season's preserve with, for example, the colourful currants and berries of early summer. If you freeze some of the soft fruits of summer, the preserve can be made in one delightfully therapeutic operation a month or so before Christmas.

Use slightly under-ripe or only-just-ripe fruits in prime condition – the slightest bruise or blemish could spoil the preserve – and prepare them according to type. Peel, core and slice apples, pears, peaches and nectarines and drop them at once into water acidulated with lemon juice to preserve their colour. Peel, core and slice pineapple, and cut slices in halves or quarters. Peel, segment and skin citrus fruits such as oranges, tangerines and satsumas. Hull strawberries and raspberries, top and tail gooseberries and remove currants from their stalks. If you need to wash soft fruits, sprinkle them with a fine mist of water – do not leave to soak.

As you arrange each layer of fruit in the jar, sprinkle it with caster sugar (superfine sugar). When you have added as much as you intend to at any one time, pour on enough spirit to cover the fruit. If the jar is not full, put a weight inside to keep the fruit below the level of the alcohol. In a wide-necked pot such as a traditional earthenware *Rumtopf* a saucer or plate may be used. In a narrow-necked preserve jar, a small can of beans will provide enough weight.

The proportions of fruit and sugar may be varied according to the sweetness of the fruit. As a general guide, allow about 150g/6oz caster (superfine) sugar to each 450g/1lb of the prepared fruit.

The choice of spirit may be a matter of personal choice too. While dark rum and brandy are traditionally used, you may also use white rum, gin or vodka, or any other spirit. Leave the preserve for at least four weeks for the flavours to blend and store it in a cool, dry, dark place. Tempting as it may be to put a clear glass jar filled to the brim with *Rumtopf* on a sunny windowsill, this would draw out too much colour from the fruits.

PRESENTATION IDEAS

It would be a thoughtful gesture to accompany a gift of *Rumtopf* with a card, giving the recipient a few ideas for serving it. This might include the following ideas:

● Celebrate Christmas morning with a *Rumtopf* cocktail. Mix a little of the liquor with Champagne and add small fruits to decorate.

● Serve *Rumtopf* in wine glasses with cream and a few berries floating on top.

● Serve the *Rumtopf* as a sauce poured over ice-cream or other frozen desserts and mousses.

● Simply enjoy on its own.

*ABOVE: All the ingredients needed for **Rumptopf**: glistening fruits, sugar, and the spirit of your choice.*

*LEFT: Jars and containers awaiting **Rumptopf** preserve. Make an appetizing gift as lovely to look at as it is to eat by choosing the prettiest container around, or adorn a simple glass jar with a ribbon in festive colours.*

MAKING POT-POURRI

POT-POURRI, an aromatic blend of dried flowers and petals, herbs and spices, was an essential part of the home environment in the Middle Ages, when it was made in large households to scent rooms and mask unwelcome odours. It was sewn into linen bags to hang in cupboards, displayed in large open bowls, packed into perforated holders and even scattered on the floor or the hearth. Centuries later, pot-pourri is making a strong comeback, appreciated now as much for the therapeutic joy of making it as for the endless permutations of colours, textures and aromas it offers.

There are two distinct ways of making it, known respectively as the moist and the dry methods. The moist method, the one with the longer pedigree, consists of layering partially dried flowers, petals and leaves in a moisture-proof lidded box (this must not be made of metal) with salt, which acts as a desiccant and draws out the natural moisture in the plant materials. The box is covered and set aside for ten days, after which the mixture will have fermented and formed a solid block. This is broken up, placed in a jar or crock and blended with powdered spices such as cinnamon, allspice, cloves, mace and nutmeg, and with a fixative such as ground orris-root powder or gum benzoin. It is then set aside, except for daily stirring, for six weeks. A few drops of an essential plant oil such as attar of roses may then be added to enhance the aroma. After a further two weeks the pot-pourri will be ready for use.

SPICY ORANGE POT-POURRI

DRY METHOD

25g/1oz coriander seeds

25g/1oz whole cloves

50g/2oz star anise

15g/½oz cinnamon bark, crumbled

15g/½oz allspice berries

dried rind of 2 oranges, crumbled

1tbsp ground cinnamon

1tbsp ground orris-root powder

Mix all the ingredients together and set them aside in a lidded container for four weeks, stirring daily to blend the aromas.

ROSE PETAL AND LAVENDER POT-POURRI

DRY METHOD

2 cups dried rose petals

1 cup dried lavender flowers

1 cup dried herb leaves such as pineapple mint, thyme, lemon verbena

1tbsp ground cinnamon

1tbsp ground allspice

2tbsp ground orris-root powder

2 drops lavender oil

Mix ingredients as for Spicy Orange Pot-pourri.

OPPOSITE: To make pot-pourri by the moist method, partially dried petals and small flowers are layered in a shallow dish with salt, which acts as a desiccant and draws out the moisture. Rose petals, marigold petals and larkspur (delphinium) flowers make a colourful blend.

Dry Pot-pourri

Pot-pourri made by the dry method is a blend of pre-dried flowers, petals and leaves with the ground spices, fixatives and oils mentioned above. To make pot-pourri in this way you can dry plant materials over an extended period and spanning several seasons, or use dried-flower off-cuts from your collection.

Pot-pourri recipes are infinitely variable and you can compose mixtures biased towards sweet, citrus or pungent aromas to suit your personal preference. As a general guide, to every 4 cups of dried plant material allow 2–3tbsp powdered spices, 2tbsp ground orris-root powder or other fixative, a strip of dried citrus fruit peel, and 2 drops of an essential oil. Place the dried plant materials, spices and fixative in a lidded container and stir them daily with a spoon or with your fingers – the therapeutic part of the process – for six weeks. Add the oil and set aside, stirring every day or two, for another two weeks.

POT-POURRI POWER

A dried-flower arrangement with the lasting aroma of pot-pourri – give as a gift, or give the components for the recipient to make themselves.

1 *Cut the foam to fit the container, leaving a gap of 1.5cm/¹⁄₂in all round, and extending about 2.5cm/1in above the container. Place a piece of adhesive clay on the bottom of each prong; set the prongs in the container, and position the foam securely on top of the prongs.*

2 *Spoon the pot-pourri mixture into the gaps on all sides, and to conceal all but the top of the foam. Position the selection of dried flowers and herbs throughout the foam, ensuring that the design is well-rounded, and does not present a flat plane with the front of the container.*

EQUIPMENT
* glass container
* scissors
* dry stem-holding foam
* florists' adhesive clay
* plastic prongs
* knife

DECORATIVE MATERIALS
* about 125g/6oz pot-pourri, depending on size of container
* selection of dried flowers and herbs, such as roses, carnations, peonies, statice, cornflowers, marjoram and purple sage

ORCHID BLEND

DRY METHOD

This is a romantic and pretty way to preserve the memory of a special gift of orchids or other luxury flowers.

1 cup dried orchid flowers
1 cup dried carnation petals
1 cup dried peony petals
1 cup dried marjoram leaves
1 tbsp ground ginger
1 tsp ground cloves
2 tbsp ground orris-root powder
2 drops carnation oil

Mix ingredients as for Spicy Orange Pot-pourri.

MARIGOLD MIXTURE

MOIST METHOD

2 cups partially-dried rose petals
1 cup partially-dried marigold petals
1 cup partially-dried larkspur (delphinium) flowers
about 50g/2oz salt
1 tbsp ground coriander
1 tsp grated nutmeg
1 tsp ground cloves
2 tbsp ground orris-root powder
2 drops oil of cloves

Mix the petals and salt, and leave in a moisture-proof lidded box for 10 days. When the mixture has formed a solid block, break up, and mix with the spices and orris-root powder. Leave for 6 weeks, and add a few drops of essential oil. Leave for another 2 weeks before using.

RIGHT: Rose Petal and Lavender Pot-pourri (left) and Marigold Mixture (right).

POT-POURRI HOBBY BASKET

COMPOSING A Christmas gift basket for a friend or relation could be the start of something big by inspiring a new and absorbing hobby for the recipient. The basket shown here is filled with a selection of ingredients that could be combined to create a variety of aromatic pot-pourri blends, a 'scroll' of suggested recipes and a decorative rosebud pomander, scented with cloves in the traditional way. To complete the floral theme, there are jars of rose-petal jelly, decorated inside and out with more petals.

Other 'ingredients' baskets could be made up of the materials needed for a friend new to the art of flower arranging. This could include wires and scissors, with dried flowers for a decorative touch.

ROSE PETAL JELLY

Make the jelly in a similar way to the lavender jelly shown on the previous pages, using the same proportion of apples and sugar. In place of the lavender flowers, add a cup of scented rose petals such as those plucked from red or cerise damask roses. Wash the petals and pull off the white tips which can give a bitter flavour. Add another handful of rose petals when you boil the strained fruit juice and sugar and remove them before the preserve reaches setting point.

Make your gift as delightful to look at as it is to taste. Pour it into inexpensive glasses instead of preserve jars (warm them first) and press fresh rose petals onto the surface. Glue pressed petals to the glass and add a ribbon bow as a finishing touch.

LEFT: Packed in vibrant pink tissue paper with a scattering of rose petals, this gift basket has the makings of many an aromatic pot-pourri blend. It has decorative elements, too, a rosebud pomander, ribbon-tied glasses of preserve, and a dried full-blown peony.

ROSEBUD POMANDER

Encourage the recipient to get into the pot-pourri mode by including a pretty rosebud pomander.

EQUIPMENT

* 7.5cm/3in dry foam ball
* whole cloves
* dried rosebuds
* florists' scissors
* 1.5cm/¾in-wide bow
* scissors
* stub wires (floral pins)
* wire cutters

1 *Stud the dry foam ball with cloves, to give the decoration the authentic aroma of a medieval pomander. Cut the rosebud stems to equal lengths, about 5cm/2in, and press them into the foam so that the flowers just touch.*

2 *Tie the ribbon into a bow. Bend half a stub wire to make a U-shaped staple, thread it through the back of the loop and press it into the foam.*

3 *If you have to keep the pomander any length of time before Christmas, put it in a bag with a few cloves and a crumbled cinnamon stick to retain and even intensify the aroma.*

POT-POURRI HEART

Pour out your heartfelt feelings with a gift of a pretty pot-pourri heart. No-one would guess its humble beginnings!

1 *Cut the foam block in half lengthways and stick the two halves together with hot glue. Draw the shape of the heart and cut it with a sharp knife. Working on small sections at a time, cover the top and sides with glue and press on the pot-pourri.*

2 *When the shape is covered, tie a bow with the unfurled paper ribbon and fix it to the heart with a bent stub wire. Stick a peony in place and stick the rose in its centre.*

EQUIPMENT

* block of dry stem-holding foam
* hot glue gun
* pencil
* knife
* half stub wire

DECORATIVE MATERIALS

* pot-pourri, about 100g/4oz/ ½ cup
* dried peony
* dried rose

ALL SET FOR CHRISTMAS!

THIS THEME basket holds a quartet of country preserves, the ideal gift at Christmastime. There is Cranberry Preserve to enjoy with everything from muffins to meats; Yellow Pepper Relish to serve with cold poultry or fish; Mint Jelly to serve with lamb and add to sauces, and Scented Geranium Leaf Jelly to enhance rich meats from pork and ham to goose and duck, and to serve on buttered teacakes, scones and muffins.

But that's not all – on the following pages there are recipes for Quince Paste, known in Spain as *pasta de membrillo*, which is cut into diamonds, sprinkled with icing sugar and studded with cloves, and Turkish delight, flavoured with rosewater and decorated with sugared rose petals. With these preserves and candies in your repertoire, you will be all set for Christmas giving.

MINT JELLY

Fill an attractive container with mint jelly for a delightful and welcome gift.

INGREDIENTS

*1.5kg/3¼lb cooking apples,
roughly chopped
1.75 litres/3pt/7½ cups water
juice of 2 large lemons
about 20 stalks of young, fresh
mint leaves
sugar (see method)
8tbsp chopped mint*

1 Put the apples in a large pan with the water, lemon juice and mint leaves stripped from the stalks. Bring to the boil, and simmer until the fruit is tender.

2 Strain the fruit and liquid through a jelly bag suspended over a large bowl and leave for at least 2 hours. Do not squeeze the bag, or the juice may be cloudy.

3 Measure the juice and pour it into the cleaned pan. Add 450g/1lb sugar to each 600ml/ 1pt/2½ cups juice. Stir over a low heat to dissolve the sugar, then bring to the boil. Fast-boil for about 10 minutes, until setting point is reached (see cranberry preserve method). Stir in the chopped mint, allow to cool slightly, then stir again.

4 Pour into clean, warm jars or glasses, cover with waxed circles and transparent paper covers, and label.

Makes about 1.5kg/3¼lb

LEFT: A shallow basket holds four tumblers of assorted preserves – an ideal gift to take if you are a house guest over the Christmas holidays.

CRANBERRY PRESERVE

INGREDIENTS

450g/1lb cranberries
1kg/2¼lb cooking apples, peeled,
cored and chopped
350ml/12fl oz/1½ cups water
1.5kg/3¼lb sugar

1 Put the cranberries and apples in a pan with the water, bring to the boil and simmer gently until the fruit is tender, stirring occasionally.

2 Add the sugar and stir over a low heat to dissolve. Bring to the boil, and fast-boil, stirring frequently, until setting point is reached. This is when a small amount of preserve left to cool on a saucer wrinkles when pushed with a finger. Pour into clean, warm jars or glasses, cover and label.

Makes about 2.5kg/5½lb

SCENTED GERANIUM LEAF JELLY

INGREDIENTS

1.5kg/3¼lb cooking apples,
roughly chopped
1.75 litres/3pt/7½ cups water
juice of 2 large lemons
about 20 large scented geranium
leaves, plus extra to garnish
sugar (see method)

1 Make the jelly in the way described for mint jelly, substituting the scented geranium leaves for the mint.

2 Pour the preserve into clean, warm jars or glasses and place a washed scented geranium leaf on each. Cover with waxed circles and transparent paper covers and label.

Makes about 1.5kg/3¼lb

YELLOW PEPPER RELISH

INGREDIENTS

3 large yellow peppers, core and
seeds removed, chopped
450g/1lb cooking apples, peeled,
cored and chopped
600ml/1pt/2½ cups cider vinegar
675g/1½lb/3 cups sugar
juice of 1 large lemon

1 Place the peppers, apples and vinegar in a large pan and bring to the boil. Simmer slowly for 20 minutes.

2 Add the sugar and lemon juice and stir over a low heat to dissolve. Bring to the boil and fast-boil for about 5 minutes, stirring frequently until setting point is reached. Pour into clean, warm jars, cover and label.

Makes about 1.25kg/3lb

ABOVE: The four preserves, left to right, are Cranberry Preserve, Mint Jelly, Scented Geranium Leaf Jelly and Yellow Pepper Relish. The glasses, covered with yellow and green gingham circles, are tied with raffia and decorated with herbs.

QUINCE PASTE

This is known in Spain as *pasta de membrillo*, where it is decorated with icing sugar and sometimes cloves, and served after meals or to garnish desserts. To pack the paste as a gift, layer it in a box between sheets of non-stick baking paper.

INGREDIENTS
1kg/2¼lb quinces
1 litre/1¾pt/4⅓ cups water
1kg/2¼lb/4¼ cups sugar
vegetable oil, for brushing
icing (confectioners') sugar, for dusting
whole cloves, to garnish

1 Wash and slice the quinces and put them into a large pan with the water. Bring to the boil, then simmer for about 45 minutes, until the fruit is soft.

2 Mash the fruit against the sides of the pan, then spoon it and the liquid into a jelly bag suspended over a large bowl. Leave to drain for at least 2 hours, without squeezing the bag.

3 Pour the strained juice into the cleaned pan, add the sugar and stir over a low heat to dissolve. Cook over a low heat for about 2 hours, stirring frequently, until a spoon drawn through the paste parts it into 2 sections.

4 Lightly brush a Swiss roll tin (jelly roll pan) with oil, pour in the preserve and leave to set. When it is cool, cut it into diamonds or other shapes, brush with icing sugar and stud each piece with a clove. Store between layers of non-stick baking paper in an airtight container.

Makes about 1.25kg/2½lb

TURKISH DELIGHT

INGREDIENTS
300ml/½pt/1¼ cups hot water
25g/1oz/1 tbsp powdered gelatine
450g/1lb/2 cups sugar
scant ½tsp citric acid
130ml/2tbsp rosewater
50g/2oz/¼ cup icing (confectioners') sugar
25g/1oz/1 tbsp cornflour (cornstarch)

1 Pour the water into a pan, sprinkle on the gelatine and stir in the sugar and citric acid. Stir over a low heat until the sugar dissolves. Bring to the boil, and boil for 20 minutes. Remove the pan from the heat and set aside for 10 minutes without stirring. Stir in the rosewater.

2 Rinse a Swiss roll tin (jelly roll pan) in cold water, then pour in the mixture. Level the top and leave in a refrigerator for 24 hours.

3 Sift together the icing sugar and cornflour and sprinkle on a piece of non-stick baking paper. Turn the sweetmeat onto the paper and cut into squares with a sharp knife. Toss the pieces in the sugar mixture to coat them on all sides. Pack the pieces between layers of non-stick baking paper and store in an airtight container.

Makes about 600g/1¼lb

OPPOSITE: Tangy Quince Paste.

ABOVE LEFT AND BELOW: Turkish Delight.

DELICIOUS GIFTS

Take a selection of fresh and dried fruits, dip them in chocolate or fondant (sugarpaste) and transform them into colourful and delectable *petits fours*. For the prettiest effect, only partially cover the fruit so that you have an irresistible visual combination – the contrasting textures and colours of the fruit and the sweet coating.

You can use almost any firm fruits of your choice, with strawberries perhaps making the prettiest presentation. Dip them chevron style, first into the bitter chocolate and then, when that has set, in white chocolate for a dramatic three-colour effect. Other delicious possibilities are fresh dates, pitted and filled with marzipan; kumquats, which look like sugar-coated acorns; orange and tangerine segments; cherries; and Cape gooseberries (physalis) released from their papery cases.

Among dried fruits you can choose prunes, dramatic when coated with either white chocolate or fondant (sugarpaste); apricots; semi-dried figs (do not use the sugar compressed ones in this way); and whole dates.

Crystallized (candied) fruits such as orange segments and mango slices can be enhanced with a chocolate coating. Covering them with fondant (sugarpaste) may seem, in terms of sweetness, like gilding the lily.

ABOVE: Make the wrappings as stylish as the contents for an irresistible gift. This box is wrapped in gold paper and tied with a black and gold ribbon.

RIGHT: Prunes dipped in pink fondant (sugarpaste), and fresh dates dipped in green make a colourful combination.

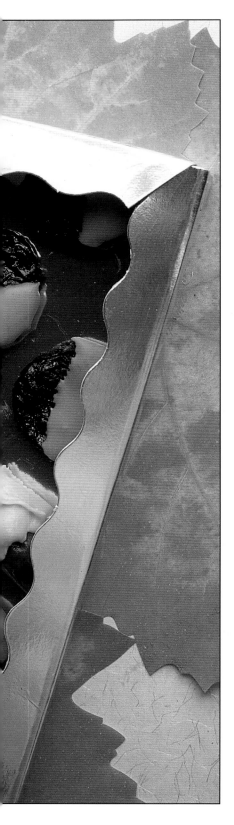

CHOCOLATE COATING

Use a good quality Swiss or Belgian chocolate when making home-made treats.

1 Melt bitter (semi-sweet) chocolate and white chocolate separately in bowls over a pan of simmering water. Do not allow the water to reach the bowl, or the chocolate may overheat.

2 Holding each piece of fruit on a toothpick, partially dip it in the chocolate. Place the fruits in rows on non-stick baking paper and leave them in a dry place – not a hot, steamy kitchen – to set. Dried crystallized (candied) fruit will keep well for several weeks in an airtight container. Fresh fruits will last only for their normal shelf life.

LEFT: Kumquats in green fondant (sugarpaste) take on the shape of acorns. The tanginess of the fruit contrasts well with the sweet covering.

FONDANT (SUGARPASTE)

With one batch of fondant (sugarpaste) you can make a seasonal crop of holly leaves and berries — a mouthwatering gift in themselves — and have enough left to dip a selection of fruits.

INGREDIENTS
450g/1lb/2 cups sugar
150ml/¼pt/⅔ cup water
25g/1oz/2tbsp powdered glucose
colouring (see method)

1 Put the sugar and water into a pan and stir over a low heat until the sugar it dissolves. Bring to the boil, add the glucose and boil until the mixture reaches 125°C/240°F, the stage described as 'soft ball'. This is reached when a small amount of the mixture forms a soft ball when dropped into a cup of cold water.

2 Sprinkle a little cold water onto a cold surface such as a marble slab and pour on the syrup. Leave it for a few minutes to cool, until a skin begins to form round the edges.

3 Using a spatula, turn the mixture over and over, sides to the middle, in a figure-of-eight movement, until it becomes opaque and grainy. Scrape the mixture into a ball, knead it until it is smooth and leave it to cool.

4 Divide the mixture into portions and add colouring as you wish. A teaspoon of concentrated blackberry or blackcurrant juice will give an attractive pink colour; redcurrant or cranberry juice may be used to obtain a clear red.

5 If you wish to make fondant (sugarpaste) shapes such as holly leaves, cut them out with a confectionery cutter, place them on a board or flat plate, mark 'vein' lines with a sharp knife and leave them for 24 hours. Roll the berries from a small piece of fondant coloured red.

6 You can use the 'off-cuts' left after cutting the shapes to coat fresh, dried and crystallized (candied) fruits. Place the fondant (sugarpaste) in a bowl over a pan of simmering water, or in a double boiler, until it has melted. Hold the fruits on a wooden toothpick and dip them into the warm fondant. Place the dipped fruits on non-stick baking paper and leave them to dry.

7 Pack the dipped fruits in airtight boxes. If fresh fruits are included, it would be thoughtful to mark the box with an 'eat by' date.

Makes 450g/1lb fondant (sugarpaste)

ABOVE LEFT: *Holly leaf shapes cut from green fondant (sugarpaste) and berries rolled from red mixture make a festive gift.*

FRUITFUL GIFTS

GATHER THE pick of the crop of each season and you can crystallize (candy) a tempting variety of fruits to make the most irresistible gifts ever. Choose from kumquats and cranberries, clementines and cherries, prunes and plums, oranges and grapefruits, apricots, pineapples and more.

Select your fruits with a view to their eye appeal, blending colours, shapes and textures to make the most dramatic arrangement, and include some, like grapefruit and cranberries, that retain a hint of sharpness.

The method could not be simpler, so do not be put off by instructions that stretch ahead to 'Day 18'. Five minutes a day is a small price to pay for candies that are this good, and so expensive to buy!

CANDIED PEEL

Candied citrus peel has many uses at Christmastime, in cakes, puddings, biscuits (cookies) and candies; and that does not include just eating it whole!

INGREDIENTS
450g/1lb citrus peel; orange, lemon, grapefruit, tangerine and citron are all suitable
600ml/1pt/2½ cups water
350g/12oz/1½ cups granulated sugar

1 Wash or scrub the fruit, halve it and remove the flesh. Simmer the peel in the water until it is tender.

2 Remove the peel with a draining spoon and arrange it in a single layer in a shallow dish. Measure the poaching liquid and, if necessary, make it up to 300ml/½pt/1¼ cups with more water.

3 Pour the liquid back into the pan, add 225g/8oz/1 cup of the sugar and bring it slowly to the boil. Pour the hot syrup over the peel, cover and leave for 2 days.

4 Drain the syrup into the pan, add the remaining 100g/4oz/½ cup of sugar and bring it slowly to the boil. Add the peel and simmer until it is semi-transparent.

5 Pour the peel and syrup into a dish, cover and leave for 2–3 weeks. Drain off any remaining syrup, place the peel on a wire rack and leave in a dry, warm place to dry. Store in airtight jars.

RIGHT: A luxurious present deserves stylish wrapping. A round box of crystallized (candied) fruits, covered with transparent paper, is wrapped in a richly-patterned table napkin. The gold beads are looped around the top.

CRYSTALLIZED FRUIT

INGREDIENTS

450g/1lb fruit, or fresh root
ginger
300ml/½ pint/1¼ cups water
approx. 675g/1½lb/3 cups
granulated sugar
caster (superfine) sugar

1 Prepare the fruit according
to type. Peel clementines
and leave them whole. Peel and
segment oranges and grapefruits.
Slice pineapple, carefully cut
away the skin and halve or
quarter the slices. Halve large
figs. Peel, core and halve or
quarter apples and pears. Prick
apricots and plums all over with
a darning needle.

2 Put the fruit in a pan with
the water, bring to the boil
and simmer until it is just tender.
This may be from 2–15 minutes,
according to type. Lift out the
fruit with a slotted spoon and
arrange it in a single layer in a
shallow heatproof dish.

3 Add 175g/6oz/¾ cup of
the sugar to the poaching
liquid and dissolve it over a low
heat. Pour the hot syrup over the
fruit and leave it for 24 hours.

4 The next day, pour the
syrup into a pan, add 50g/
2oz/¼ cup of the sugar and
dissolve slowly. Pour this
thickened syrup over the fruit,
cover and leave for 24 hours.

5 Repeat this process 5 times
more. The next day, Day
8, pour off the syrup, dissolve
50g/2oz/¼ cup of sugar in it,
pour over the fruit, cover and
leave for 2 days. Repeat this
process twice more until Day 14.
This time leave the fruit to soak
for 4 days, until you reach Day
18, when the process will be
almost complete.

6 Lift the fruit from any
remaining syrup and
arrange it on a wire rack placed
over a dish or baking sheet.
Leave it in a dry, warm place
until the surface is dry.

7 For a glacé finish, dip the
pieces of crystallized
(candied) fruit quickly in and out
of boiling water, drain off excess
moisture and roll in the caster
(superfine) sugar. Pack the fruit
between layers of waxed paper in
a box to store.

Makes 450g/1lb

**LEFT: A glass pedestal dish
makes an appropriate
container for a gift of colourful
crystallized (candied) fruits.
Wrap it in shiny transparent
paper and tie it with a bow.**

CRANBERRY FUDGE

This recipe comes from Scotland, where it is called 'Butter tablet'. You can make a variety of flavours — colours, too — by replacing the cranberries with chopped pecans, walnuts or hazelnuts, crystallized (candied) ginger or other candied fruits.

INGREDIENTS

900g/2lb/4 cups granulated sugar
50g/2oz/¼ cup unsalted butter
175ml/5½fl oz/⅔ cup milk
1 tbsp golden (corn) syrup
200g/7oz can full-cream condensed milk
100g/4oz/¾ cup fresh cranberries

1 Place the sugar, butter, milk and golden (corn) syrup into a heavy saucepan and bring slowly to the boil, stirring constantly. Add the condensed milk, return to the boil and boil for 20 minutes, still stirring, until the mixture reaches 130°C/250°F, or the 'hardball stage', when a spoonful of the mixture dropped into a cup of cold water sets hard.

2 Remove the pan from the heat, stir in the cranberries or other flavourings and pour into a well-greased Swiss roll tin (jelly roll pan). Mark the candy into squares just before it hardens. When the candy is cold, break it into pieces and store in an airtight container.

Makes approximately 900g/2lb

GOURMET PICKLES

G IVE SOMEONE a jar layered to the brim with vegetables, olives and small hard-boiled eggs and you give
them one of the most appetizing and colourful gifts of the
season. It is an ideal present for someone who has everything, or one to take to your host if you are invited away over
Christmas. Take also, perhaps, one or two small whole local
cheeses and you give them the ingredients for a drinks party
with style.

Since the beauty of a gift like this is that it looks as good
as it tastes, choose vegetables and fruits such as green and
black olives that retain their colour well.

PICKLED VEGETABLES

INGREDIENTS
assorted fresh, bottled, canned or
dried vegetables
black or green olives
shelled hard-boiled eggs
coarse salt
virgin olive oil
spices such as peppercorns, mustard
seed, coriander seed, cardamom
seeds
bay leaves, fresh or dried
anchovy fillets

1 Prepare the ingredients according to type and arrange in layers in a lidded jar or pot. Add bay leaves and a sprinkling of spices such as red, black, white or green peppercorns, coriander, mustard and, sparingly, cardamom seeds. If they are not among the main ingredients, you can add a few small dried red or green chillies. For an Italian-style pickle, you can also add a few anchovy fillets as a seasoning.

2 Fill the jar with virgin olive oil. Bang it firmly on the work surface to ensure that the oil fills all the gaps, and fill the jar to the top again. Close the lid and store in a cool, dry place away from strong light. The pickle should keep well in good storage conditions for up to 6 months.

ABOVE: Filled to the top with vegetables and olive oil, the jar is ready for presentation – if you can bear to part with it.

RIGHT: The colourful line-up in the dish is, from left to right, capers, garlic cloves, black olives, chillies, shelled hens' eggs and green olives.

PREPARING VEGETABLES FOR PICKLING

Aubergines (eggplants) Cut aubergines into slices, place them in a colander and sprinkle them with salt in the proportion of 50g/2oz/¼ cup to each 450g/1lb vegetable. Leave for 2 hours while the salt draws out the excess moisture. Rinse and drain the slices, pat them dry with paper towels and shallow fry them in olive oil until they are brown on both sides.

Eggs Choose small hens' eggs or use quails' eggs. Hard-boil them, then shell them and leave them whole.

Garlic Peel garlic and cut the cloves in slices or leave them whole.

Onions Skin and slice onions into rings. Sprinkle them with salt and leave them for about 1 hour, then rinse and drain them.

Peppers Grill red, green, yellow and orange peppers until the skins turn black. Plunge them into cold water and skin them. Slice the peppers and remove the core and seeds.

Pickled and dried vegetables Rinse and drain olives and capers that have been pickled in brine. Slice dried vegetables such as large chillies. Leave small ones whole.

Root vegetables Slice vegetables such as carrots and turnips thinly and blanch them in boiling, salted water for 2–3 minutes, until they are just becoming tender.

Sweetcorn Blanch sweetcorn heads in boiling, salted water until the kernels are nearly tender, then strip them from the cob with a sharp knife. You can leave baby sweetcorn whole.

HARLEQUIN BASKET

BLACK AND white with a dash of orange – that is the recipe for the harlequin gift basket full of delicious surprises. It is packed with tasty gifts, from Pickled Walnuts in Spiced Vinegar to Fruit Liqueurs. Triangles of melt-in-your-mouth Coconut Ice are added for sheer indulgence.

BELOW: The deep, tall-handled basket is painted with two coats of emulsion (latex) paint and packed with crisp white tissue paper.

FRUIT LIQUEURS

Bullaces, sloes and rowanberries were used in this recipe, but you can make other liqueurs in a similar way using blackcurrants, blackberries, raspberries and other soft fruits. Keeping the fruit, spirit and sugar in similar proportions, adjust the quantities according to your budget. Some of the spirit-soaked fruits such as blackberries and raspberries may be served over ice-cream.

INGREDIENTS
500g/1lb fruit (see above)
75–100g/3–4oz/⅓–½ cup sugar, to taste
600ml/1pt/2½ cups gin or vodka

1 Prick the skins of fruits such as bullace, sloe and rowanberry (mountain ash) with a darning needle. Pack them, each type separately, to half-fill clean bottles. Add the sugar and fill up the bottle with spirit. Close the bottle, shake it well and leave it in a dark place for 3 months to mature.

2 Strain off the fruit and pour the liqueur into clean bottles. Cover with decorative paper tops.

Makes about 900ml/1½pt/3¾ cups liqueur

PICKLED WALNUTS

Gather the walnuts before the shells begin to form. After that, it is too late to pickle them, and you should leave them to develop fully.

INGREDIENTS
immature walnuts
coarse salt (see method)
water
spiced vinegar

1 Wearing rubber gloves to protect your hands from the black dye, prick the walnuts with a sterilized needle and put them in a bowl. Make a brine to cover them, using 100g/4oz/½ cup coarse salt to 1 litre/1¾pt/4⅓ cups water. Pour the brine over the walnuts, cover and leave for 5 days.

2 Pour off the brine, rinse the bowl and replace the walnuts. Cover them with fresh brine and leave for a further 7 days.

3 Drain the walnuts, place them on a wire rack and leave them for about 36 hours, until they turn black. Pick them up with a spoon or tongs and pack them into clean jars with vinegar-proof caps. Cover with cold spiced vinegar, seal and cover with decorative papers.

COCONUT ICE

INGREDIENTS
225g/8oz/1 cup granulated sugar
5tbsp milk
60g/2½oz/1¼ cups desiccated coconut
oil, for brushing

Brush a shallow 12.5cm/5in-square tin (pan) with oil. Put the sugar and milk into a pan and dissolve over a low heat. Bring to the boil and boil gently for 10 minutes, when the temperature of the mixture should be 120°C/240°F, or at the 'soft ball' stage. Remove from the heat and stir in the coconut at once. Pour the mixture quickly into the tin (pan). Leave until nearly set, then mark into diamonds. Break into pieces when cold and store in an airtight container.

Makes about 325g/11oz

SPICED VINEGAR

Use good-quality malt or white wine vinegar and add mixed spices in the proportion of 25g/1oz/1tbsp to each 600ml/1pt/2½ cups. A mixture of dried chillies, mustard seed, black peppercorns and coriander is traditional. Bring the vinegar and spices to the boil, simmer for 5 minutes, then cool and strain. You can keep the vinegar indefinitely in a stoppered jar before using.

ABOVE LEFT: *Diamonds of Coconut Ice look dramatic on black. The marigold is an optional extra.*

RIGHT: *Turn fruits into potent liqueurs and give small bottles as delicious digestifs.*

CHRISTMAS CARDS AND WRAPPING

Take the most utilitarian brown wrapping papers and you can give them a new life with the luxury look of burnished gold. Sheets of coloured tissue can be transformed into gift wrappings that would seem fit for a king to open. Take a few pieces of card (posterboard) and scraps cut from used greetings cards and shape them into stylish and matching gift tags. Trace a traditional outline from a Christmas card onto embroidery cloth and sew greetings cards of your own. Look at the following suggestions for wrappings, cards and trims and let your creative ideas flow.

CUSTOMIZED TISSUE PAPER

TISSUE PAPER is relatively inexpensive, readily available and it comes in a spectrum of colours, but it is undeniably plain. With a can or two of spray-paint you can soon alter that, creating fantastic all-over patterns that take plain ordinary tissue paper into the luxury class. Crêpe paper, another familiar yet unexciting wrapping, can be treated in similar ways – with style.

THE TIE-DYE TECHNIQUE

The technique used to dye fabrics with exotic sunburst designs can be adapted to give tissue and crêpe paper a colourful face-lift. Scrunch up small areas of the paper into a series of tight peaks (there is no need to use rubber bands, as with fabric) and spray over them with gold, silver or another colour. Repeat the process at intervals across the whole sheet of paper – the closer together the peaks, the more sunburst patterns will result. Leave the paper to dry, then open out the scrunches to reveal a series of shimmering patterns.

LEFT: Wrap a bottle in stiff card to make a neat cylinder and then wrap in tie-dyed tissue paper secured with double-sided adhesive tape. A band of pink-toning glitter ribbon and a cascading bow complete the trimmings.

ABOVE: Two special effects in process: tissue paper scrunched into peaks and sprayed with gold paint for a sunburst effect, and black crêpe paper crumpled into a ball for a crackled-metal finish.

RIGHT: Silver-sprayed black crêpe paper conceals a round Christmas pudding. The gift is placed in the centre of a square of decorated paper, the sides are drawn up over the pudding – the creases in the paper make this easier to do neatly – and tied around with silver thread. A design of fruit and leaves cut out of silver foil stuck onto a card makes a glittering tag.

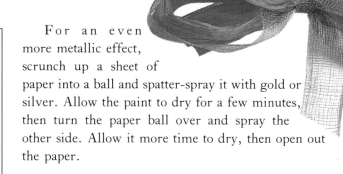

WRAPPING TIP

If you wish to restore tissue paper to its original, pristine and uncreased state you can place it on a sheet of plain paper and press it with a very cool iron on the unsprayed side. But this is not necessary. Creased paper which has been spray-painted has a certain style, and is much easier to wrap neatly around awkward parcel shapes such as spheres, and round or oval boxes.

For an even more metallic effect, scrunch up a sheet of paper into a ball and spatter-spray it with gold or silver. Allow the paint to dry for a few minutes, then turn the paper ball over and spray the other side. Allow it more time to dry, then open out the paper.

RANDOM STRIPES

Tissue and crêpe paper patterned with gold and silver random stripes are equally dramatic, but in a completely different way. To achieve this gold-and-silver-dagger effect, cover a work surface or floor area with protective newspapers or scrap paper and place a piece of tissue paper or crêpe paper flat on top of it. The brighter or darker the colour of the paper to be decorated, the more outstanding the pattern will turn out to be.

Cut long, narrowly angled strips from newspaper or scrap paper and place them at random over the paper surface, angling them in any way you please. Secure the masking strips with double-sided adhesive tape, or hold them in place with the fingers of one hand.

Spray the unmasked areas of the tissue or crêpe paper with gold and silver paint so that the finished design will have a three-colour effect. Leave the paper to dry – you can hang it on a clothes line if you wish – and use the masking strips in random order to decorate other pieces of paper.

ABOVE: A boxed parcel shows off the striped paper to maximum effect. For added glamour, trim it with a double red and silver bow and glass baubles.

RIGHT: Tissue paper masked with randomly cut strips of newspaper is sprayed with gold and silver paints to create a dramatically modern look.

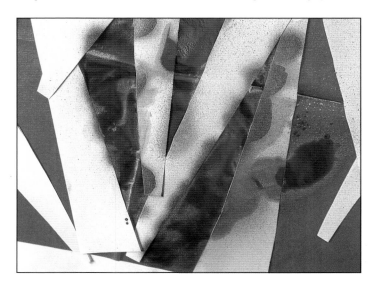

GIFT TAGS AND PLACE CARDS

Making your own gift tags and place cards is an important part of pre-Christmas activity. You can not only save a significant sum of money by making these at home but also create a completely co-ordinated look for gift-wrapped presents and decorations. If you have chosen a particular colour scheme, especially if it is not a traditional one, you could spend fruitless time trying to buy the right shade and style of tags. By making these small but significant items yourself, you can be sure of making a perfect match.

Choose your wrapping paper first. It may be tissue paper, art paper with a marbled look, or crêpe paper scrunched into a ball and sprayed. Buy good-quality writing paper or plain postcards in appropriate colours for the gift tags. Look through any of last year's greetings cards you may have kept, and select motifs or panels to cut out. The used cards on these pages provided strips of gold for the abstract designs and the edgings, and a gold felt-tipped pen was used to outline some of the motifs.

Left: A golden bird motif cut from a used Christmas card decorates a plum-coloured gift tag. Gilded hydrangea florets echo the Midas look.

LEFT: Traditional holly and bell shapes; abstract designs; motifs cut from used Christmas cards and gilded flower petals demonstrate the variety of designs that can be achieved with name tags created in a combination of three colours.

LEFT: Select cords and ribbons in colours and textures which harmonize or contrast with the cards. Both approaches are effective.

ABOVE: Horizontal place cards with a variety of motif decorations – a cut-out bird shape, a fresh pansy and a nursery-rhyme illustration. The napkin is wrapped with shiny cord in criss-cross formation.

CINDERELLA STORY

Take the most utilitarian and basic wrapping paper imaginable, plain brown parcel wrapping; take a can of gold spray-paint and a little imagination and you can achieve a design transformation of fairy-tale proportions.

THREE-DIMENSIONAL STENCILS

Use shapely leaves, nuts, shells, spices and other items from around the home as three-dimensional stencils. You could use a collection of varied items, some leaves, some shells, some nuts and so on, but using shapes of the same kind will give a more readable and recognizable pattern.

Cover a large, flat surface – a work table or even the floor – with newspaper or scrap paper and place a sheet of brown paper on it, right side up. Arrange a few of the 'stencils' either in rows or at random and using a can of gold spray-paint, spray lightly over the items. Leave them to dry partly for a minute or so, then move the stencils over the paper and spray over them again. Continue in this way until the paper is decorated all over. Leave it for about 30 minutes to dry. The completed design of gilded images makes wonderful wrapping paper.

ABOVE: A gold-stencilled brown paper parcel to the right of an evergreen arrangement forms part of a gold-accented still-life group.

RIGHT: Plain brown wrapping paper and a collection of natural stencils that could be used to decorate it. Leaves, nuts, shells and spices offer a wide variety of pattern shapes.

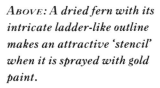

ABOVE: A dried fern with its intricate ladder-like outline makes an attractive 'stencil' when it is sprayed with gold paint.

RIGHT: Three parcels wrapped in gold-sprayed brown paper have a touch of class and individuality in the trims. A gingerbread tree dusted with gold powder and with false-berry candles tops a parcel that is tied around with red ribbon. Gilded hydrangea flowers add to the glitter and texture (top right). A stencil cut to a holly leaf shape and sprayed with gold makes the central feature of this parcel. The theme is echoed in the gold-sprayed holly leaf and the trim is completed with a raffia band (bottom). A length of gold beads becomes a parcel tie, with a pair of gold-sprayed vine leaves and a glittering star providing even more glamour (top left).

BELOW: A utilitarian brown paper bag undergoes a complete transformation when it is spatter-sprayed with both gold and silver paint. Here it is decorated with a trio of candies wired to the ribbon and with gilded hydrangea heads stuck onto one side.

EMBROIDERED CARDS

Embroidered christmas card designs are surprisingly simple to make, whether you are an embroidery enthusiast or have little or no experience with a needle, thread and canvas.

Card blanks with cut-out panels are available from hobby shops, or can be made at home. Cut a piece of stiff card (posterboard) to the required size. The cards illustrated on these pages range from 26 × 11cm/10½ × 4½in to 30 × 15cm/12 × 6in in size. Measure the card lengthways, divide it into three equal sections and fold it along the vertical lines. Cut a rectangular or oval panel from the centre section, which will become the frame for the embroidered design.

EMBROIDERED GIFT-WRAPPING

An embroidered stocking shape edged with red velvet and backed with red cotton makes a delightful tree decoration, or a miniature surprise to be brought down the chimney on Christmas Eve. Small in stature it may be (the stocking measures 14cm/5½in from the top to the toe) but there is room enough for a galaxy of gifts. The toe is packed with wrapped candies and kumquats – scaled-down versions of the traditional orange – and a candy stick, a toy musical instrument and a miniature Christmas cracker peep enticingly over the top.

Above: A plainly-wrapped parcel is transformed by the addition of a double bow in toning colours. An embroidered greetings card does double duty as a gift tag.

Left: Christmas cards can provide ideas and outlines for embroidery designs of all kinds.

Use Christmas cards as inspiration for simple motifs — trees, churches, a pair of holly leaves or perhaps a manger scene. Attractive composite designs might include a group of candles, a small galaxy of stars, a pair of bells — the possibilities are endless.

Transfer the design onto graph paper, where each square will represent one cross-stitch. Cut a piece of embroidery canvas with space to spare, and, if you wish, mark the design with felt-tipped pens in the appropriate colours. This simple expedient will prevent you having to count stitches or cross-refer to the graph-paper pattern and will save time.

Stitch the design in cross-stitch, using double embroidery thread, and outline it in black, if desired. The holly and manger designs were both emphasized in this way. When the design is complete, cut the canvas slightly larger than the open panel and stick it, face outwards, onto the back of the panel. Fold over the left-hand section of the card and stick it to cover the back of the canvas. A seasonal message can then be written on the inside of the card.

ABOVE: Four Christmas cards embroidered with seasonal motifs, from a sprig of holly with bright red berries to a church with colourful stained-glass windows.

MAKING CHRISTMAS CARDS

Making your own Christmas cards can be an absorbing project to occupy family members of all ages through many a long winter evening. Hand-made cards convey a more personal and meaningful message than bought cards ever can, and when the children become involved, the cards become even more precious. Cards such as these are destined to be pasted lovingly into a family memento album.

STENCILLED CARD

The Christmas tree card is made from a simple stencil and painted in three seasonal colours, green, red and gold. You can trace an outline from an old Christmas card, or draw it freehand. Symmetry of line and branch is not important. Children should not use a sharp craft knife to cut the stencil.

1 Cut plain card (posterboard) to make the Christmas card blanks. Fold the cards in half along the long sides. Trace or draw the tree outline onto a small piece of card (posterboard) and cut out the shape with a craft knife.

2 Dampen a sponge and dip it into green paint. Place the stencil centrally on the front of the card blank and dab on the green paint. It is more effective if the paint is not applied too evenly. Colour the rest of the cards and leave to dry.

3 With a small paintbrush and red paint, fill in the outline for the tree trunk and pot, and paint shapes to represent bells hanging on the tree branches. Wash the brush and paint gold stars on the tree shape and a crescent moon or star above it.

CUT-OUT MANGER CARD

Children can help by tracing the template outline on the card blanks, but the design itself should be cut out by adults or older children.

EQUIPMENT

* stiff card (posterboard)
* pencil
* ruler
* tracing paper
* craft knife
* envelopes
* silver felt-tipped pen

1 *Cut the card blanks to measure 19 × 13.5cm/7½ × 5¼in. Measure the centre along the 2 long edges and draw a thin pencil line from top to bottom. Measure the centre of both the left-hand and right-hand sections and draw thin pencil vertical lines. The card will now be marked into 4 equal sections. Trace the outline of the cut-out section from the template. Place the tracing in the centre section of the card, with the base of the tracing 4.5cm/1¾in from the base of the card. Draw over the traced outline onto the card.*

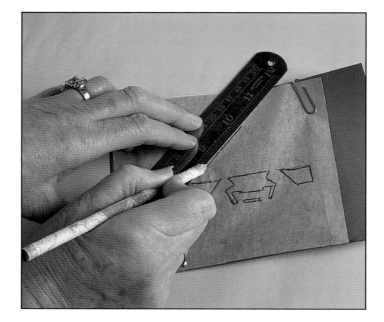

2 *Using the craft knife, cut around the imprinted outlines on the card. As the shapes are cut out, the outline of the Holy Family in the manger will appear. Measure and mark a point on the centre line 4cm/1½in above the top of the cut-out. This will form the roof of the manger. Draw a thin pencil line from this point to the top of the cut-out section on each side.*

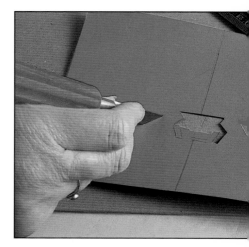

3 *To construct the manger, fold the 2 outside lines inwards to the centre. Fold the top and the bottom sections of the centre line in the opposite direction. The card will now fold into a long narrow strip. Fold the 2 diagonal lines marking the stable roof outwards and the centre line between them inwards.*

CHRISTMAS PARTIES

Christmas is a time for parties of all kinds. This section will help you to plan a party that fits in with your life-style and the time you have available. There are ideas and recipes for all kinds of occasions from a leisurely brunch to an impromptu meal for unexpected guests, from a hot buffet meal to a coffee party to raise funds for charity. There is even advice on how to prepare rooms and look after your house guests to make sure that their stay is as comfortable and easy-going as possible, both for them and for yourself.

PARTY TIME!

WHATEVER THE scale of the party you decide to give, whether it involves inviting a few neighbours in for a festive drink or half the neighbourhood for a buffet supper, meticulous planning is essential.

Decide first on the type of party you wish to give. The suggestions and recipes on the following pages may fire your enthusiasm for a theme gathering such as a pie and pâté or a cheese and wine party, or may help you to decide whether a hot or a cold buffet is more practical in your circumstances.

Once you have chosen the style of your party, think carefully about the date, to ensure it doesn't clash with other people's commitments. Then issue your invitations as soon as possible; three weeks before the party is not too early at this time of year.

Make an inventory of the glasses, cutlery and china, and the cooking and serving dishes you have, so that you are alerted well in advance to any shortfall. If there are only a few items you need, you could probably borrow from a friend, otherwise you would be best advised to use an outside supplier. In some countries, wine merchants will lend glasses to a customer who places even a moderate order, and some also offer a sale-or-return service. If your stock of tableware is inadequate for the numbers involved, you could consider good-quality disposable plates and bowls as an alternative to hiring (renting).

Calculate the quantities of food you will need, and check that your pantry is adequately stocked with the dried herbs and spices, gelatine and bottled flavourings, dried fruits and canned fish. Then make a shopping list of the fresh foods and other ingredients you will need, and the flowers and foliage to compose any decorations.

Clean and defrost (if necessary) your refrigerator days in advance and, as far as possible, clear space for the party food, soft drinks and wines. Make quantities of ice cubes and fancy ice shapes, store them in plastic bags in the freezer and then make some more. You can never have too much ice!

If it is to be a large gathering and 'reception room' space is limited, pack away any valuable ornaments and trinkets to avoid damage and embarrassment and, on the day, rearrange or move back the furniture to make easy traffic routes.

Set out the drinks on a table – a trestle table even – at one end of the room and organize a table with the food at the other end, or in a separate room.

With your plans made well in advance and put into operation with military precision, remember to build in enough time to dress and get ready for your own party. It is your welcoming and relaxed smile that will set the tone of the event and put your guests immediately at their ease.

LEFT: A luxurious-looking table fit for a banquet. Frosted grapes and sugared fruits are decorative in themselves. An arrangement of dried flowers and Christmas baubles complement the scene.

OPPOSITE: A festive table in pink is scattered with orchids and Amaretto biscuits (cookies). Pink candles cast a warm glow.

DINNER ON CHRISTMAS EVE

CHRISTMAS EVE is one of the most enchanting and significant days of the Christian festival. In many Christian countries throughout the world, Christmas Eve is celebrated as *the* feast day, with the most lavish and elaborate meal served by candlelight. You could serve a menu including Whole Baked Salmon with orange, 'Royal Pyes' – a mincemeat flan topped with soft meringue – and in the Scandinavian tradition, Redcurrant and Blackcurrant Kissel.

BAKED SALMON

INGREDIENTS

40g/1½oz/3tbsp butter, melted
juice of 1 orange
*1 whole salmon, about 1.75kg/
4lb, cleaned, washed and dried*
fresh fennel or parsley sprigs
salt and pepper

75g/3oz/6tbsp butter, softened
grated rind of 1 orange
large pinch of curry powder
*750g/1½lb new potatoes,
scrubbed*
2tbsp olive oil
rock salt
1 orange, peeled
1 egg yolk
*5-cm/2-in piece cucumber, to
garnish*
watercress, to garnish

1 Heat the oven to 200°C/400°F/Gas 6. Brush a large piece of foil with melted butter. Sprinkle 1tbsp orange juice inside the fish and place the herb sprigs in the cavity. Season the fish with salt and pepper.

2 Blend the softened butter with the orange rind and curry powder and spread half of it over both sides of the salmon. Wrap the fish loosely in foil so that air can circulate inside the parcel.

3 Place the fish on a baking sheet and cook it in the oven for 30–35 minutes, until the fish feels firm when pierced with a skewer.

4 Cook the potatoes in boiling, salted water for 10 minutes, then drain and dry them. Drizzle them with olive oil and sprinkle with rock salt. Place them on a baking sheet and cook them in the oven for the last 15 minutes while the fish is cooking.

5 Thinly slice the orange and cut the slices in half.

6 When the salmon is cooked, transfer it to a warm serving dish. Cover with foil and keep it warm. Drain the cooking juices into a small pan and add the remaining orange juice. Poach the orange slices for 2 minutes, remove with a draining spoon and keep hot. Whisk the egg yolk and the remaining butter and curry mixture into the hot orange juice. Heat gently, whisking until the sauce thickens slightly. Pour into a sauce boat or jug.

7 Skin the salmon and cover the top with the cucumber slices. Arrange the orange slices along the centre. Garnish the fish with watercress and arrange the potatoes around the outside of the dish. Serve at once, accompanied by the sauce. Cooked in this way, the fish is equally good served cold, and may be garnished with the cucumber and orange slices once it has cooled.

Serves 6

'ROYAL PYES'

INGREDIENTS

225g/8oz/2 cups plain (all-purpose) flour
125g/5oz/½ cup butter cut into pieces
50g/2oz/¼ cup caster (superfine) sugar
1 tsp grated orange rind
1 egg yolk, lightly beaten
3 tbsp orange juice
milk, for brushing

FOR THE FILLING

2 cooking apples, peeled, cored and thickly sliced
3 tbsp water
1 tbsp clear honey
5cm/2in cinnamon stick
150g/6oz/1 cup mincemeat
40g/1½oz/3 tbsp butter, melted
2 tsp grated orange rind
2 tbsp rum or brandy

FOR THE TOPPING

2 egg whites
100g/4oz/½ cup caster (superfine) sugar

1 Sift the flour into a bowl and rub in the butter until the mixture is like fine breadcrumbs. Stir in the sugar, orange rind and egg yolk and enough of the orange juice to make a firm dough. Wrap the dough in foil and chill for 30 minutes.

2 Put the apple slices, water, honey and cinnamon in a pan over a low heat, and simmer until the fruit is barely tender.

RIGHT: 'Royal Pyes', an apple and mincemeat flan with a soft meringue topping, contrasts well with tangy Redcurrant and Blackcurrant Kissel.

3 Heat the oven to 190°C/375°F/Gas 5. Roll out the pastry on a lightly floured board and use to line a flan tin (spring form pan). Brush the rim of the pastry with milk. Cut out holly leaves and other fancy shapes from scraps of pastry and arrange them around the rim. Brush these, too, with milk.

4 Spread the mincemeat over the base of the pastry case, sprinkle with orange rind and rum or brandy. Arrange the apple slices evenly on top, and brush them with the melted butter. Bake in the oven for 25 minutes.

5 Whisk the egg whites until they are stiff. Sprinkle on half the sugar and whisk again until the meringue is stiff and glossy. Fold in the remaining sugar. Take the flan from the oven and spread the meringue over the apples. Swirl the top with a knife.

6 Lower the heat to 180°C/350°F/Gas 4 and bake the flan for 15 minutes, until the meringue is evenly pale brown. Serve hot or cold.

Serves 6–8

REDCURRANT AND BLACKCURRANT KISSEL

INGREDIENTS

450g/1lb redcurrants
450g/1lb blackcurrants
150ml/¼pt/⅔ cup water
5 tbsp clear honey
2 tbsp cornflour (cornstarch)
berries and leaves, to garnish (optional)

1 Put the fruit into a large pan with the water and honey. Bring just to the boil over a low heat, stirring occasionally. Put the cornflour into a small bowl and stir in about 3 tbsp of the juice from the fruit. Pour the mixture into a pan and stir over a low heat until it thickens and becomes translucent and glossy. Allow to cool slightly, then pour into a serving dish.

2 Decorate the top if you wish with seasonal berries and washed leaves.

Serves 8

POT-LUCK PARTY

CHRISTMAS is a time for informal gatherings of family and friends. If your holiday schedule is already packed, consider asking your friends to share the joy of cooking and come to a pot-luck party. The following recipes would be welcome at any gathering.

TOFFEE COOKIES

INGREDIENTS
175g/6oz/¾ cup unsalted butter, melted
200g/7oz/1 cup instant porridge (rolled) oats
100g/4oz/½ cup soft light brown sugar
100ml/4fl oz/½ cup corn syrup
2tsbp vanilla extract
large pinch of salt
200g/6oz/¾ cup plain (semi-sweet) chocolate, grated
40g/1½oz/⅓ cup chopped walnuts

BELOW: Toffee Cookies.

1 Heat the oven to 200°C/400°F/Gas 6.

2 Mix together the butter, oats, sugar, syrup, vanilla and salt and press into a greased 37.5 × 25cm/15 × 10in baking tin (pan). Bake in the oven for about 15–18 minutes, until the mixture is brown and bubbly. Remove from the oven and immediately sprinkle on the chocolate. Set aside for 10 minutes, then spread the chocolate over the base. Sprinkle on the nuts. Cool on a wire rack. Cut into squares.

Makes 36 squares

ALMOND MACAROONS

INGREDIENTS
3 egg whites
200g/7oz/1¾ cups sifted icing (confectioners') sugar
150g/6oz/1½ cups blanched almonds, chopped
2 drops almond or ratafia essence (extract)
edible rice paper
about 45 blanched almond halves

1 Whisk the egg whites until they are stiff, gradually sprinkling on half the sugar. Fold in the remaining sugar and the chopped almonds.

ABOVE: Almond Macaroons.

2 Line a baking sheet with edible rice paper. Using 2 teaspoons, drop heaps of the mixture well apart on the paper. Press an almond half on each macaroon and set aside to dry for about 2 hours.

3 Heat the oven to 150°C/300°F/Gas 2.

4 Bake the macaroons in the centre of the oven for 30 minutes, until they are lightly browned on top and still soft in the centre. Cool the macaroons on a wire rack, then peel off the surrounding paper.

Makes about 45 macaroons

LEMON CHEESE BARS

INGREDIENTS

100g/4oz/1 cup plain (all-purpose) flour
50g/2oz/⅓ cup chopped walnuts
75g/3oz/⅓ cup soft light brown sugar
75g/3oz/⅓ cup unsalted butter
juice and grated rind of 1 small lemon
225g/8oz/1 cup full-fat cream cheese
50g/2oz/¼ cup granulated sugar
1tbsp milk
½tsp vanilla extract
1 large egg

1 Heat the oven to 180°C/ 375°F/Gas 4.

2 Beat together the flour, walnuts, brown sugar and butter and form it into a soft crumbly dough. Divide the dough into 2. Press 1 piece of the dough into a greased pan 22.5cm/9in square. Bake in the oven for 12–15 minutes, until lightly browned. Remove from the oven.

3 Beat together the lemon juice and rind, cheese and sugar, then beat in the milk, vanilla and egg.

4 Spoon the cheese mixture over the partly cooked pastry and sprinkle the remaining mixture evenly over the top. Bake for a further 25 minutes, until the top is golden. Cool on a wire rack, then chill. Cut into bars.

Makes 24 bars

CITRUS SPICE BARS

INGREDIENTS

100g/4oz/¾ cup candied orange peel, chopped
50g/2oz/⅓ cup seedless raisins
5tbsp rum
50g/2oz/¼ cup clear honey
50g/2oz/¼ cup molasses
1 egg
100g/4oz/1 cup ground almonds
150g/6oz/1½ cups wholewheat flour
½tsp baking powder
large pinch bicarbonate of soda (baking soda)
1tsp ground cinnamon
½tsp ground ginger
100g/4oz/1 cup unblanched almonds, chopped
butter for greasing

FOR THE ICING

50g/2oz/½ cup sifted icing (confectioners') sugar
about 3tbsp orange juice

ABOVE: Citrus Spice Bars.

LEFT: Lemon Cheese Bars.

1 Heat the oven to 200°C/ 400°F/Gas 6.

2 Place the orange peel, raisins and rum in a bowl, cover and set aside for 1 hour.

3 Place the honey and molasses in a pan and bring to the boil. Set aside to cool, then beat in the egg. Mix together the ground almonds, flour, baking powder, soda and spices and stir into the mixture. Stir in the chopped almonds and the rum mixture and form into a dough.

4 Lightly grease a baking tin (pan) 33 × 23cm/13 × 9in and press in the dough. Bake for about 20 minutes. Cool .

5 Place the icing (confectioners') sugar in a bowl and stir in just enough orange juice to make a spreading consistency. Set aside for 1 hour.

6 Spread the icing over the cake. Cut into bars.

Makes 50 bars

WINTER WARMER BUFFET

IF YOU, your family and friends come in from a long walk in the country or a sports event, or if you would like to give an informal supper party for a group of friends and neighbours, this is the perfect menu. All the dishes can be made in advance and, where appropriate, reheated at the last moment.

APPLE AND PARSNIP SOUP

INGREDIENTS
50g/2oz/¼ cup unsalted butter
2 large onions, sliced
1 clove garlic, chopped
2 large parsnips, scrubbed and cubed
450g/1lb cooking apples, peeled, cored and cubed
2tsp medium curry powder
1.5 litres/2½pt/6¼ cups chicken stock
300ml/½pt/1¼ cups single (light) cream
salt and pepper

FOR THE TOPPING
100g/4oz/1 cup pecans, chopped
25g/1oz/1tsp unsalted butter
150ml/¼pt/⅔ cup crème fraîche or soured cream

1 Melt the butter in a large pan and sauté the onions and garlic over a moderate heat until the onions are translucent. Stir in the parsnip and apple and sauté for about 3 minutes, stirring once or twice. Stir in the curry powder and cook for 1 minute. Pour on the stock, bring to the boil, cover the pan and simmer for 20 minutes.

2 Purée the soup in a processor and return it to the pan. Stir in the cream, season and heat gently.

3 Melt the butter in a small pan and sauté the pecans over a moderate heat for 5 minutes. Swirl the crème fraîche on top and sprinkle with pecans.

Serves 8–10

GRAPE CHEESECAKE

INGREDIENTS
50g/2oz/¼ cup butter
50g/2oz/¼ cup caster (superfine) sugar
125g/5oz/1 cup digestive biscuits (Graham crackers), crushed
225g/8oz/1 cup full-fat soft cream cheese
2 eggs, separated
100g/4oz/½ cup caster (superfine) sugar
grated rind of 1 lemon
3 drops vanilla extract
150ml/¼pt/⅔ cup double (heavy) cream
2tbsp lemon juice
11g/scant ½oz/1tbsp powdered gelatine (1 sachet)

FOR THE TOPPING
150g/6oz/¾ cup black grapes, halved and seeded
small spray of scented geranium leaves

1 Melt the butter and sugar in a pan over a low heat and stir in the biscuit (cracker) crumbs. Press the mixture evenly into the base of a flan dish (spring-form pan) and place in the refrigerator to set.

2 Beat together the cheese, egg yolks, 50g/2oz/¼ cup of the sugar, the lemon rind, vanilla extract and cream. Put the lemon juice into a small bowl, sprinkle on the gelatine crystals and place in a bowl of hot water. Stir to dissolve then remove from the heat.

3 Whisk the egg whites until stiff then whisk in the remaining sugar. Fold lightly into the cheese mixture. Spoon the mixture onto the cheesecake base and level the top. Chill for about 3 hours, until the filling is set.

4 Arrange the halved grapes, cut sides down, on top of the cheesecake and decorate with the scented geranium leaves. Serve the cheesecake chilled.

Serves 8

BUTTERSCOTCH PEACHES

INGREDIENTS

8 large, ripe peaches
225g/8oz full-fat soft cream cheese
3tbsp orange liqueur
scented geranium leaves, to decorate

FOR THE SAUCE

200g/7oz/1 cup soft light brown sugar
25g/1oz/2tbsp unsalted butter
2tbsp milk

1 Dip the peaches into boiling water, then remove the skins. Halve the fruit and remove the stones (pits).

2 Beat together the cream cheese and orange liqueur. Spoon the mixture into the peach cavities and sandwich the halves together. Secure each reassembled peach with a wooden toothpick.

3 To make the sauce, place the sugar, butter and milk in a small pan and stir until the sugar dissolves. Bring to the boil and simmer for 7 minutes. Beat until the mixture starts to thicken.

4 Arrange the peaches in a serving dish and pour over the sauce, which will become hard as it cools.

Serves 8

ABOVE: The tempting array of desserts includes Butterscotch Peaches (left) and Grape Cheesecake (centre front). Mincemeat Slice and sugared Mince Pies are in the background.

115

BRUNCH PARTY

S OMEWHERE BETWEEN a leisurely breakfast and an informal lunch, a brunch party is a fun way to entertain family and friends. There can be tempting semi-sweet dishes like Waffles and Griddle Cakes to enjoy with Rosemary Honey and a range of other preserves; fork foods like Rumbled Eggs, shrimps, crispy Corn Fritters, fried bananas and braised ham to give ample choice and substance as the meal progresses, and berry-bright Cranberry Flan with fruit salad and yoghurt or fromage frais to follow.

ABOVE: A plain tumbler wrapped around with large ivy leaves and tied with raffia makes an attractive holder for a stubby candle. The napkin, *decorated in a similar style, strikes a note of equal informality.*

GRIDDLE CAKES

These cakes are traditional to Wales, where they used to be made on black iron griddles. They can be made in any heavy frying pan or in an electric pan.

INGREDIENTS
1¹/₂tsp baking powder
¹/₂tsp salt
¹/₂tsp ground ginger
225g/8oz/2 cups plain (all-purpose) flour, plus extra for dusting
100g/4oz/¹/₂ cup granulated sugar
150g/6oz/³/₄ cup unsalted butter, cut into small pieces
150g/6oz/1 cup sultanas (golden raisins)
2 large eggs
3–4tbsp milk

1 Sift the flour, baking powder, salt and ginger into a bowl and stir in the sugar. Rub in the butter until the mixture is like fine breadcrumbs. Stir in the sultanas. Beat the eggs and stir in just enough to make a firm but sticky dough.

2 Turn the dough onto a floured board, sprinkle it with flour and roll it to a thickness of 1.5cm/¹/₂in. Cut it into rounds with a 6.5-cm/2¹/₂-in cutter. Re-roll the trimmings and cut out more rounds.

3 Brush a heavy frying pan (skillet) with oil and heat it over a medium heat. Fry the cakes for about 5 minutes on each side until they are well browned. Serve warm, with butter and preserves.

Makes about 16 cakes

CRANBERRY FLAN

INGREDIENTS

150ml/¼pt/⅔ cup water
3 sachets (33g/1.2oz) gelatine crystals
750g/1½lb fresh or frozen cranberries, thawed
350g/12oz/1½ cups redcurrant jelly
225g/8oz/1 cup granulated sugar
2tbsp brandy
2 20-cm/8-in shortcrust pie shells, baked

1 Pour the water into a small bowl, sprinkle on the gelatine and stand the container in a pan of hot water. Stir occasionally until the crystals have dissolved.

2 Put the cranberries, sugar and jelly in a pan over a low heat for 10 minutes, until the fruit is just tender but not bursting. Remove from the heat and cool slightly. Stir in the gelatine and brandy.

3 Cover the top of the filling with a piece of wetted non-stick baking paper to prevent a skin forming. Set aside to cool.

4 Stir the filling and pour into the 2 pie shells. Chill before serving. You could decorate the flan with whole geranium leaves and, if you wish, a fresh flower.

Makes 2 20-cm/8-in flans

ROSEMARY HONEY

INGREDIENTS

4–5 sprays fresh rosemary
2 sprigs fresh thyme
3–4 strips dried orange peel
2tsp lemon juice
900g/2lb/6¾ cups clear honey

1 Place the rosemary, thyme, orange peel and lemon juice in a large heatproof jar and pour on the honey. Cover the jar with plastic wrap and place in a pan with cold water to come almost to the top. Bring the water to the boil, remove the pan from the heat and leave to cool.

2 Set aside for 1 week. Strain the honey into a clean jar (it may be necessary to warm the honey first) and cover. Serve with scones, waffles, teacakes or toast.

Makes 900g/2lb/6¾ cups flavoured honey

RUMBLED EGGS

INGREDIENTS

8 eggs

pinch of salt

black pepper, freshly ground

2tbsp water

75g/3oz/⅓ cup butter

150g/6oz smoked salmon, cut into
strips

2tsp lemon juice

2tbsp chives, chopped, to decorate

1 Beat the eggs in a bowl.
Season with salt and pepper
and beat in the water. Melt half
the butter in a heavy pan and
when it is hot, but not turning
brown, pour in the eggs and stir
over a low heat, gradually
adding the remaining butter.

2 Gently heat the smoked
salmon and lemon juice in a
small pan. Turn the eggs onto a
warm dish, arrange the smoked
salmon on top and garnish with
the chives. Serve warm.

Note: You can serve the
Rumbled Eggs in pre-baked
individual tart shells, or in a
pre-baked pastry case (pie shell).

Serves 8

WAFFLES

INGREDIENTS

100g/4oz/½ cup plain (all-
purpose) flour

pinch of salt

1tsp baking powder

1 egg

200ml/6fl oz/¾ cup milk

1tbsp caster (superfine) sugar

50g/2oz/¼ cup butter, melted,

1 Sift together the flour, salt
and baking powder. Beat in
the egg and gradually beat in the
milk. Stir in the sugar. Add the
melted butter just before cooking.

2 Heat the waffle iron and
brush with melted butter.
Pour on enough mixture to cover
the base plate. Close the iron and
cook for two minutes on each side
over a high heat. Serve warm
with melted butter or maple
syrup.

Makes about 8 waffles

CORN FRITTERS

INGREDIENTS

225g/8oz/2 cups frozen sweetcorn
kernels, thawed

100g/4oz/1 cup plain (all-
purpose) flour

1tsp salt

1 egg

100ml/4fl oz/½ cup milk

2tsp chopped parsley

butter for frying

1 Sift together the flour and
salt. Gradually beat in the
egg, and then the milk. Stir in
the sweetcorn and the parsley.

2 Melt a small knob of butter
in a heavy pan. Drop
tablespoons of the batter well
apart in the hot pan. When the
underside is brown, flip the
fritters over and fry on the second
side. Serve warm.

Makes about 16 fritters

*ABOVE: Hollowed-out fruits
containing a fruit salad, an
arrangement of fruit, foliage
and flowers, and spring-like
posies of violets set the scene
for a stylish brunch party. The
pineapple shell in the centre
has been fitted with a block of
absorbent stem-holding foam
soaked in water, and arranged
with dried leaves and many-
coloured freesias. Small
bunches of grapes and a
clementine are mounted on
stub wires which are then
pushed into the foam.*

*The cubes of pineapple cut
from the two fruits, and the
orange segments, form the
basis of the fruit salad piled
into the other shell.*

*OPPOSITE: Crispy Corn
Fritters (in the foreground) are
served hot with Rumbled Eggs.*

COME FOR COFFEE!

AN INVITATION to coffee can be all things to all people on all occasions. It can represent a short break in the middle of a busy day when friends and neighbours get together for a chat; a no-fuss way of inviting acquaintances to raise funds for a favourite charity – perhaps to buy toys for a children's hospital ward at Christmas – or it can be a leisurely event to be enjoyed to the full.

This last situation is a common occurrence in Greece, where an invitation to drink a cup of coffee and enjoy a 'spoon sweet' is part of a deeply-rooted tradition of friendship and welcome. So what better time for the rest of us to follow suit than at Christmas.

In Greece, it is customary for the host or hostess to offer each guest a cup of coffee, some fruit preserved in thick syrup – it may be anything from kumquats, cherries, pumpkin, figs, grapes or plums, according to local availability – a glass of iced water and, sometimes, a small glass of *raki*, a colourless spirit distilled from wine. The guest, according to tradition, eats the fruit, the 'spoon sweet', drinks the coffee and lastly, if it is offered, the spirit. Custom dictates that this is enjoyed in one swallow, but hosts and hostesses tend to be flexible on this point.

The recipes on these pages would be suitable for just such an occasion, or for a less formal invitation to coffee.

PRESERVED KUMQUATS

INGREDIENTS
1kg/2¼lb/4½ cups sugar
450ml/¾pt/¾ cups water
1kg/2¼lb kumquats (or other suitable fruit)
juice of two lemons
strip of thinly pared lemon rind
3–4 drops vanilla extract

1 Put the sugar in a large pan, pour on the water and dissolve over a low heat, stirring occasionally.

2 Remove the stems from the kumquats and prick the fruit all over with a darning needle. Add the fruit, lemon juice, lemon rind and vanilla essence to the syrup, bring to the boil and boil for 5 minutes.

3 Pour the fruit syrup into a bowl, cover and leave it overnight.

4 The next day, return the fruit and syrup to the pan, bring to the boil and simmer for 1 hour, or until the kumquats are soft.

5 Lift out the fruit with a draining spoon and pack it into warm, sterilized jars. Boil the syrup until thick, when a teaspoon of it dropped onto a cold plate will hold its shape and not spread. Pour the syrup over the fruit, close the jars with screw caps or clip-on lids and store in a cool, dry place.

Makes about 1kg/2¼lb

LEFT: Preserved Kumquats are a traditional Greek 'spoon sweet' served with coffee as a symbol of friendship and welcome.

HONEY PUFFS

INGREDIENTS

225g/8oz/2cups plain (all-purpose) flour
7g/¼oz/½tbsp dried yeast
1tsp sugar
150ml/¼pt/⅔ cup warm milk
150ml/¼pt/⅔ cup warm water
vegetable oil, for deep frying

SYRUP

6tbsp honey
200ml/7fl oz/¾ cup water
1tbsp lemon juice
1tbsp rosewater

1 Sift the flour into a bowl. Dissolve the yeast and the sugar in the warm milk and water and leave in a warm place until it froths. Make a well in the flour, pour in the yeast mixture and mix to form a smooth, soft batter. Cover and leave to rise in a warm place for 1 hour.

2 Beat the mixture well and leave to rise again.

3 Meanwhile, make the syrup. Put the honey, water, lemon juice and rosewater into a small pan and stir over a low heat until it has blended. Set aside to cool.

4 Heat the oil for deep frying to 190°C/375°F, when a cube of day-old bread browns in 50 seconds. Scoop out the dough with a wet dessert spoon and drop a few spoonfuls at a time into the oil. When they rise to the surface and are crisp and golden on all sides, remove them with a slotted spoon and drain them on paper towels. Cook the remaining mixture in the same way.

5 Arrange the honey puffs in a shallow dish, pour on the cooled syrup and roll them over to cover them completely. Place them on a wire rack to drain. Pile the cakes onto a dish and, if you like, decorate them with a fresh flower.

Makes about 16–20 cakes

LEFT: The perfect ending to an invitation to coffee – a dish of fresh and dried fruits dipped in bitter and white chocolate, nuts and festive candies.

ABOVE: Honey Puffs and crystallized ginger are suitable delicacies to serve with coffee in the Greek style.

TEENAGE PARTY

WHEN YOU have invited the younger generation to a party, the food needs to be filling, easily assembled and not too expensive. Pizzas and a salad, Banulfi Pie and Peanut Butter Brownies make an appetizing spread.

You can make the pizza bases using an easy-rise dough made with quick-blending yeast or, if you prefer, buy uncooked, ready-made bases from a supermarket. Create different toppings, the ingredients for which can be chopped, grated, and sautéed and set out ready to assemble just before the party starts. Then simply place the pizzas on baking sheets and cook.

PIZZA BASE

This is a good basic recipe for pizza dough which will make three 20-cm/8-in bases. If it is more convenient, you can freeze the shaped and unbaked dough well in advance of the party.

INGREDIENTS

about 450g/1lb/4 cups strong white bread flour
1 tsp salt
7g/¼oz dried yeast
⅛ tsp sugar
350ml/12fl oz/1½ cups water

1 Place 350g/12oz/3 cups of the flour in a bowl with the salt, yeast and sugar and gradually pour on the water. Mix into a sticky dough and turn out onto a well-floured board.

2 Knead the dough lightly, adding more of the remaining flour until the dough is smooth and elastic.

3 Form the dough into a ball, place it in a bowl and cover with a cloth. Leave it in a warm place to rise for about 1 hour, when the dough should have doubled in size.

4 Remove the dough from the bowl and knead it again. Divide it into 3 pieces and roll each one on a lightly floured board to a 20-cm/8-in circle.

LEFT: Three sizzling hot pizzas and a bowl of crunchy salad await teenage guests at an informal supper party.

To Cook the Pizzas

Heat the oven to 220°C/425°F/Gas 7. Place each pizza on a baking sheet and bake in the oven for 15–18 minutes, until the cheese topping is golden brown and sizzling. Sprinkle with chopped parsley if you wish.

Each 20-cm/8-in pizza serves 2–4, depending on the appetite of the guests.

Alternative Toppings

- Sliced ham, topped with sliced red and green peppers and black olives, and sprinkled with grated Parmesan
- Sliced Cheddar cheese, topped with thinly-sliced courgettes (zucchini) and mushrooms, and sprinkled with grated Parmesan
- Canned artichoke hearts, drained and thinly sliced, topped with anchovies and crumbled feta cheese
- Thinly-sliced cooked chicken, topped with sliced leeks and sprinkled with crumbled Stilton cheese
- Left-over chilli con carne sprinkled with grated Cheddar cheese
- Left-over spaghetti Bolognese sauce sprinkled with grated Cheddar and Parmesan cheese

TOMATO SAUCE

This sauce can be used as a base for all types of toppings.

INGREDIENTS
4tbsp olive oil
2 large onions, finely chopped
2 large cloves garlic, crushed
400g/14oz can chopped tomatoes
1tsp dried oregano
1tsp dried thyme
salt and freshly ground black pepper

1 Heat the oil in a pan and fry the onions and garlic over a moderate heat for 3–4 minutes, until the onions are soft.

2 Add the tomatoes and herbs and season with salt and pepper. Bring the mixture to simmering point and cook, uncovered, for about 20 minutes until it forms a thick, spreading paste. Taste and add more seasoning if needed.

3 Set aside to cool, then spread the sauce over the pizza bases.

TUNA AND OLIVE TOPPING

INGREDIENTS
2tbsp plus 2tsp olive oil
1 large onion, thinly sliced
Tomato Sauce
175g/6oz can tuna in brine, drained and flaked
2 hard-boiled eggs, thinly sliced
3 tomatoes, thinly sliced
1tsp dried oregano
salt and freshly ground black pepper
4tbsp grated Parmesan cheese
25g/2oz/1/2 cup Gruyère cheese, grated
12–16 black olives

1 Heat 2tbsp of the oil in a pan and fry the onion over a moderate heat for 3–4 minutes, until it is soft.

2 Lift out the onion with a draining spoon, drain off any excess oil and scatter over a pizza base spread with Tomato Sauce.

3 Cover the onion with a layer of flaked tuna, then with the egg and tomato slices. Sprinkle on the oregano and season with salt and pepper. Sprinkle on the cheeses and dribble on the extra olive oil.

4 Arrange the olives around the edge of the pizza.

ABOVE: *The principal ingredients you will need to make pizza toppings.*

PEANUT BUTTER BROWNIES

These chewy brownies have the rich, familiar taste of peanut butter. Cut them in squares or fingers to serve with soft drinks or coffee, or as a dessert with ice-cream.

INGREDIENTS

75g/3oz/³/4 cup plain (all-purpose) flour
1tsp baking powder
¹/4tsp salt
225g/8oz/1 cup soft light brown sugar
50g/2oz/¹/4 cup coarse peanut butter
¹/2tsp vanilla extract
1 large egg
100g/4oz/²/3 cup walnuts, chopped

1 Heat the oven to 180°C/ 350°F/Gas 4. Sift together the flour, baking powder and salt. Beat in the sugar, peanut butter, vanilla and egg until the mixture is well blended. Stir in the walnuts and pour the mixture into a well-greased 20-cm/8-in square baking tin (pan). Level the top with a spatula.

2 Bake in the oven for 25 minutes until a skewer inserted in the centre comes out clean. Place the tin (pan) on a wire rack to cool, then cut into 8 fingers while still in the pan.

3 To store, leave the cake in the tin (pan), cover with foil and leave in a cool place. It will keep fresh for up to 1 week.

Makes 8 fingers

LEFT : Peanut Butter Brownies, arranged on a pottery dish ringed with pine branches, and ready to be cut into fingers before eating.

MUSHROOM AND MOZZARELLA TOPPING

INGREDIENTS

Tomato Sauce
175g/6oz mozzarella cheese, thinly sliced
2 tomatoes, thinly sliced
150g/6oz button mushrooms, thinly sliced
2tsp dried oregano
3tbsp grated Parmesan cheese
2tsp olive oil
salt and freshly ground black pepper

1 Arrange the mozzarella slices over a pizza base spread with Tomato Sauce.

2 Cover the cheese with the tomato slices and then with the mushroom slices, and sprinkle with the oregano and grated Parmesan cheese.

3 Sprinkle on the olive oil and salt and pepper.

BANULFI PIE

Deliciously gooey and delightfully sticky, Banulfi pie has layers of sliced banana and butterscotch topped with whipped cream and sugared cranberries.

INGREDIENTS
175g/6oz digestive biscuits (Graham crackers), crushed
75g/3oz/¹/₃ cup butter, melted
40g/1¹/₂oz/3tbsp demerara (light brown) sugar

FOR THE FILLING
175g/6oz/¹/₂ cup dark brown sugar
4tbsp cornflour (cornstarch)
2 large eggs, beaten
600ml/1pt/2¹/₂ cups milk
50g/2oz/¹/₄ cup butter, cut into pieces
¹/₂tsp vanilla extract
2 bananas, thinly sliced
150ml/¹/₄pt/²/₃ cup double (heavy) cream, whipped

1 To make the case, stir together the biscuit (cracker) crumbs, melted butter and sugar and press the mixture into a 22.5-cm/9-in spring-clip flan case. Chill while you make the filling.

2 Place the sugar, cornflour and eggs in the top of a double boiler or a bowl placed over a pan of simmering water. Do not allow the water to touch the base of the upper pan or bowl. Stir well, then gradually pour on the milk and stir constantly for 10–15 minutes, until the custard is smooth and thick enough to retain the trace of the spoon.

3 Remove the upper container from the heat and beat in the butter a little at a time. Stir in the vanilla extract. Cover the surface with a piece of wetted non-stick baking paper to prevent a skin from forming, and set aside to become cold.

4 Arrange the sliced bananas in the pie case. Stir the butterscotch and pour it over.

5 Fit a piping bag with a 1.5-cm/¹/₂-in star nozzle and pipe whirls of cream around the edge and in the centre of the pie. Serve chilled.

Serves 6–8

An Invitation to Tea

An invitation to afternoon tea may be a rare occurrence for most of us these days, a treat to be enjoyed perhaps only in the holidays. For the rest of the year the afternoon may rush by in a turmoil of work or other activity, but at Christmastime when family, friends and neighbours are at home for a few days, many of us have the opportunity to slow down and enjoy a relaxing afternoon break.

With so many rich foods on offer throughout the festive days, it may be a welcome idea to revert to 'good plain cooking' when inviting friends for tea. Scones of all kinds, a favourite in Victorian times, are a perfect choice. You can flavour a basic mixture with cinnamon, ginger and other spices, grated orange rind, sunflower or pumpkin seeds, chopped nuts, dried fruits or chocolate chips and serve them with preserves as varied as Rosemary Honey, Cranberry Conserve and Scented Geranium Jelly.

Apricot Meringue Bars are sheer indulgence, and certain to be a favourite. A melt-in-your-mouth base is spread with apricot jam, and topped with nutty meringue – a wonderful holiday treat which is sure to appeal to young and old alike.

LEFT: Cinnamon Scones and Chocolate Drop Scones are an irresistible treat.

TEATIME SCONES

You can vary these traditional favourites by adding 1–2 tbsp of chocolate drops (chips) or 1–2 tsp ground cinnamon.

INGREDIENTS
225g/8oz/2 cups plain (all-purpose) flour, plus extra for dusting
¼tsp salt
½tsp bicarbonate of soda (baking soda)
1tsp cream of tartar
25g/1oz/2tbsp butter
about 150ml/¼pt/⅔ cup milk or buttermilk

1 Heat the oven to 220°C/425°F/Gas 7. Sift the flour, salt, soda and cream of tartar into a bowl. Rub in the fat until the mixture is like fine breadcrumbs, and gradually pour on just enough milk to make a light, spongy dough.

2 Turn the dough onto a lightly-floured board and knead until smooth. Roll it to a thickness of 2.5cm/1in. Cut into rounds with a 5-cm/2-in cutter (or a 4-cm/1½-in cutter for cocktail savouries). Place the scones on a floured baking sheet and brush the tops with milk. Bake in the oven for 7–10 minutes, until the scones are well risen and golden brown.

Makes about 16 scones

SAND TARTS

These tarts are traditionally served at Christmastime by the Moravian community in Pennsylvania, USA. It is a tradition which has its roots in Germany.

INGREDIENTS
100g/4oz/½ cup unsalted butter, at room temperature, plus extra for greasing
½tsp vanilla extract
large pinch of salt
125g/5oz/scant ¾ cup caster (superfine) sugar
1 large egg
100g/4oz/1 cup plain (all-purpose) flour
¼tsp bicarbonate of soda (baking soda)
1½tsp ground cinnamon
1 small egg white, lightly beaten
about 35 pecan halves

1 Cream the butter, vanilla, salt and 100g/4oz/½ cup of the caster (superfine) sugar until it is light and fluffy, then gradually add the beaten egg, beating constantly. Sift together the flour, soda and ½tsp of the cinnamon and stir it a little at a time into the butter mixture. Form the mixture into a dough, wrap it in plastic wrap and chill it in the refrigerator overnight.

2 Remove the dough from the refrigerator and set it aside for about 30 minutes until it becomes pliable.

3 Heat the oven to 180°C/350°F/Gas 4. Roll out the dough on a lightly floured surface until it is about 3mm/⅛in thick. Cut the dough into rounds with a 5-cm/2-in cutter. Re-roll the trimmings and cut more rounds.

4 Place the rounds on a lightly greased baking sheet and brush the tops with the egg white. Mix the ground cinnamon with the remaining caster (superfine) sugar. Sprinkle over the rounds and press a pecan half into each centre. Bake in the oven for 8–10 minutes until golden brown and just beginning to turn brown at the edges. Cool on a wire rack and store in an airtight container.

Makes about 35 biscuits (cookies)

APRICOT MERINGUE BARS

INGREDIENTS
50g/2oz/½ cup plain (all-purpose) flour
50g/2oz/½ cup butter
½tsp vanilla extract
large pinch of salt
1 large egg, separated
100g/4oz/½ cup caster (superfine) sugar
50g/2oz/⅓ cup chopped walnuts
50g/2oz/⅓ cup chopped pecans
100g/4oz/½ cup apricot jam

1 Heat the oven to 180°C/350°F/Gas 4. Beat together the flour, butter, vanilla, salt, egg yolk and 50g/2oz/¼ cup of the sugar. Spread the mixture evenly over the base of a greased 20-cm/8-in baking tin (pan), prick it all over with a fork and bake it in the oven for 10 minutes.

2 Beat the egg white until stiff. Gradually beat in the remaining 50g/2oz/¼ cup sugar until the mixture is smooth and glossy. Gently fold in the chopped walnuts and pecans, but do not over-mix.

ABOVE: Sand Tarts decorated with pecan halves are the perfect complement to Apricot Meringue Bars.

3 Remove the tin (pan) from the oven, spread the apricot jam over the base and spread the meringue mixture to cover it evenly. Bake in the oven for 20 minutes, until the meringue is crisp and light brown. Cool on a wire rack, then cut into 10 × 2.5cm/4 × 1in bars. Apricot Meringue Bars may be stored in an airtight container for up to 3 days.

Makes 16 bars

A PLEASANT SURPRISE

WHEN FRIENDS announce over the telephone that they will unexpectedly be passing by around lunchtime tomorrow, most people experience twin reactions. Their first thoughts are at the pleasure of a surprise visit, renewing old acquaintanceships, exchanging news and gossip. Their second thought is usually 'What shall I give them to eat?'

At this time of year, the problem is unlikely to be a lack of provisions. Before Christmas the cupboards, refrigerator and freezer will be crammed with food – but much of it is destined for the Christmas dinner or a planned party. And after Christmas, it is satisfying if you can avoid serving obvious left overs.

Here is a quick, easy, colourful and appetizing stir-fry of duck or chicken breasts and fresh, crispy vegetables, followed by a dried-fruit *Rumtopf* which you can prepare in advance for just such an occasion. It has all the concentrated sweetness of mixed dried fruits blended with the tang of alcohol. You can use rum or brandy, as you wish.

SURPRISE STIR-FRY

Oyster sauce, a distinctive flavouring used in Chinese dishes, is made from oysters and soy sauce. Dark soy sauce may be used instead.

INGREDIENTS
450g/1lb boneless duck or chicken breasts, skinned
2tbsp peanut oil
2 stalks tender celery, thinly sliced
1 green pepper, cored, seeded and cut into matchstick strips
1 yellow pepper, cored, seeded and cut into matchstick strips
1 orange pepper, cored, seeded and cut into matchstick strips
150g/6oz mange-tout (snow) peas, trimmed
100g/4oz button mushrooms, thinly sliced
100g/4oz fresh beansprouts

FOR THE MARINADE
2tbsp light soy sauce
2tbsp peanut oil
3tbsp dry white wine, or dry sherry
3tbsp oyster sauce

1 Mix the marinade ingredients together.

2 Cut the meat diagonally into 3mm/⅛in strips. Place the meat in a bowl, pour on the marinade and mix well. Cover the bowl and set aside for up to 2 hours.

3 Heat the peanut oil in a wok or heavy frying pan. Lift out the meat with a straining spoon, reserving the marinade, and stir-fry it for 2 minutes. Add the celery, peppers and mange-tout (snow) peas and fry for 1 minute. Then add the mushrooms and beansprouts and stir-fry.

4 Pour the marinade into the wok or pan and heat through. Serve with rice.

Serves 4

LEFT: *Surprise Stir-fry glistens with marinade.*

DRIED-FRUIT
Rumtopf

Make this preserve at least 4 weeks before the holidays to allow the flavours to blend. Then keep on hand for a quick and easy dessert.

INGREDIENTS
225g/8oz/2 cups dried apricots, soaked and drained
225g/8oz/2 cups dried apricot halves
100g/4oz/²⁄₃ cup dried pitted prunes
100g/4oz/²⁄₃ cup semi-dried figs
100g/4oz/½ cup dried apple rings
225g/8oz/1 cup dried orange rings
1tsp cloves
3 sticks cinnamon, halved

FOR THE SYRUP
100g/4oz/½ cup granulated sugar
250ml/8fl oz/1 cup water
about 350ml/12fl oz/1½ cups dark rum or brandy

1 First make the syrup. Put the sugar and water into a small pan over a low heat. Stir occasionally until the sugar has dissolved, then bring to the boil and boil for 5 minutes. Remove the mixture from the heat and set aside to cool.

LEFT: Soaked and drained Hunza apricots, dried orange rings and semi-dried figs with, left to right, dried orange peel, apple rings, cloves, cinnamon, dried apricots and prunes – the fruit components of a **Rumtopf**.

BELOW: The fruit is served in straight-sided glasses, still in layers, with an orange 'butterfly' and a sprig of apple mint to decorate. Plain yoghurt is a good accompaniment to this sweet and rich dessert.

2 Pack the fruits into 3 clean, dry 450-g/1-lb jars, arranging them in layers to alternate colours, textures and flavours. If you position the orange rings upright round the edge of the jars, they make a decorative 'lining'. Divide the cloves, cinnamon sticks and syrup between the jars and top them up with rum or brandy. Cover the jars and tip them from side to side to blend the liquids. The exact amount of spirit you will need will depend on the capacity and shape of the jars.

3 Cover and seal the jars and store in a cool, dry place. The fruit should keep well for up to 6 months.

Fills 3 450-g/1-lb jars

PIE AND PÂTÉ PARTY

INVITING GUESTS to a 'theme' party makes the occasion even more special. Guests have an idea what to wear and what to expect – though exactly what pies and pâté you will serve may remain a close secret.

It is probably not a good idea to carry the theme through to the dessert course and serve fruit pies to follow. Add a little variety to the dishes, or your guests may have too much of a good thing.

Recipes are given for a coarse Pork and Pheasant Pâté and that most decorative of vegetable flans, Pissaladière, followed by Apple and Kumquat Compote intriguingly flavoured with star anise. The apple motif – which has age-old associations with the celebrations of the winter festival, and with Christianity – may be carried through in the decorations. You could decorate Christmas crackers with dried apple rings dusted with gold craft powder and centred with star anise pods.

LEFT: Apple and Kumquat Compote is cooked in honey and fruit juice and flavoured with star anise.

APPLE AND KUMQUAT COMPOTE

INGREDIENTS
225g/8oz/1 cup clear honey
juice of 2 oranges
juice of 2 lemons
5 or 6 star anise seedpods
225g/8oz kumquats
1kg/2¹/₂lb cooking apples, peeled, cored and quartered

1   Place the honey, orange juice, lemon juice and star anise in a small pan over a low heat. Stir occasionally until the honey has melted, bring to the boil and remove from the heat. Set aside to cool.

2   Prick the skins of the kumquats with a needle and place them in a large, shallow baking dish with the apples. Pour on the honey mixture and bake, uncovered, for 20 minutes. Turn the fruit carefully once or twice, taking care not to break them. Remove from the oven and allow to cool, but do not chill. Remove the star anise pods and replace them with others.

Serves 6

PORK AND PHEASANT PÂTÉ

INGREDIENTS
1 pheasant, about 1kg/2¹/₄lb, dressed weight
1 onion, sliced
1 carrot sliced
1 bouquet garni
water to cover
1 tsp meat or yeast extract
5 tbsp hot water
2 tsp gelatine crystals
2 bay leaves
1 dried apple ring
1 olive
225g/8oz belly of pork, bones and rind removed, cut into pieces
225g/8oz bacon, rind removed, cut into pieces
3 cloves garlic
100g/4oz/1 cup dry white bread, cut into pieces
1 tsp dried thyme
¹/₂tsp dried oregano
1 tsp ground mace
¹/₂tsp grated nutmeg
2 tsp salt
1 tsp black pepper, freshly ground
2 eggs, beaten
sliced peppers and tomatoes

1   Place the pheasant in a pan, add the onion, celery, carrot and bouquet garni and cover with water. Bring to the boil, skim off any foam that rises to the surface, cover and simmer for 1¹/₄ hours. Remove from the heat and set aside to cool.

2 Meanwhile, stir the meat or yeast extract into the hot water, sprinkle on the gelatine crystals and stand in a pan of simmering water until the crystals have dissolved. Arrange the bay leaves, apple ring and olive in the base of a 1-litre/³/4-pint/1-quart loaf tin (pan). Pour on the gelatine mixture and place in the refrigerator to set.

3 Heat the oven to 170°C/ 325°F/Gas 3. Remove the pheasant from the bones, discard the skin and roughly chop the meat. Reserve the bones and stock for soup. Place the pheasant, pork, bacon, garlic and bread in a food processor and grind them in several batches to a coarse texture. Turn the mixture into a bowl, add the seasonings and stir to mix well. Stir in the beaten eggs until well blended.

4 Spoon the mixture into the prepared tin (pan) and cover with a double thickness of foil. Stand the tin (pan) in a baking dish half-filled with hot water and cook in the oven for 2½ hours. Allow to cool, turn out onto a serving dish and garnish with sliced peppers and tomatoes.

Serves 10–12

RIGHT: A taste of things to come – the ingredients to make Pissaladière.

PISSALADIÈRE

INGREDIENTS

1 green pepper
1 red pepper
4tbsp olive oil
450g/1lb tomatoes, peeled and chopped
½tsp dried oregano
½tsp sugar
pinch of salt and freshly ground black pepper
3 onions, peeled and thinly sliced
1 22.5-cm/9-in shortcrust pie shell, baked
3tbsp grated Parmesan cheese
1 can anchovies in oil, to garnish
about 12 black and green olives, to garnish

1 Heat the grill to medium and grill (broil) the peppers, turning them frequently, until the skins are black on all sides. Place them in cold water and rub off the skins. Halve the peppers, remove the cores and seeds and pat dry with paper towels. Slice the peppers thickly and set aside.

2 Heat 2tbsp of the oil in a heavy pan, add the chopped tomatoes and sprinkle with the oregano and sugar. Season to taste with salt and pepper and cook over a low heat, uncovered, for about 15 minutes, stirring occasionally, until the mixture has formed a thick purée. Turn into a bowl and set aside to cool.

3 Heat the remaining 2tbsp oil in the cleaned pan and fry the onions over a medium heat until they are translucent. Set aside to cool.

ABOVE: Pissaladière, a vegetable flan layered with cheese, onions, tomatoes and peppers, makes a suitable contrast to the rich pâté and can be adapted to serve to vegetarians.

4 Heat the oven to 180°C/ 350°F/Gas 4. Cover the base of the pie shell with the cheese, onions and tomato paste. Arrange the pepper slices on top, make a lattice pattern with the anchovies and garnish with the olives. If the pie is to be served to vegetarians, reserve strips of pastry to make the lattice topping, in place of anchovies. Bake in the oven for 30 minutes. Serve hot.

Serves 6

CHEESE AND WINE PARTY

A CHEESE AND wine party must be high on the list of no-frills, no-fuss events, with a gratifying ratio of enjoyment over workload. It is the perfect format for busy hosts and hostesses who enjoy company more than cooking, and for a spur-of-the-moment get-together. It is even possible to have a selection of mature, ripened and prime-condition cheeses, and cheese savouries, in the freezer ready and waiting for just such an occasion.

Unless you plan your party as a cheese and wine tasting, when you may want to shop around for rare and palate-teasing examples, it is best to limit the cheeses to a few widely differing types. Make your selection as interesting as possible, including some well-known (and always popular) types as well as any local specialities or favourites of your own. Take into account the balance of flavours – mild and mature, salty and 'sweet'; textures – hard, semi-hard, soft and creamy; and colour. It is important to remember that the cheeseboard will be seen before it is tasted, and a selection of cheeses that are all visually similar will do little to excite the tastebuds.

THE WINES

As a general rule, the more mature the cheese, the more assertive the wine should be. A well-flavoured mature Cheddar is complemented by a medium-bodied red wine such as St Emilion or Pomerol or even by a sweet white wine such as Monbazillac. Blue cheeses stand up well to full-bodied red wines, sweet wines and all but the driest sherries. Soft cheeses such as Brie and Camembert go well with red, fruity wines such as Crozes-Hermitage, Fleurie or Fitou.

CYPRIOT CHEESE PIES

INGREDIENTS

450g/1lb/4 cups plain (all-
purpose) flour, plus extra for
dusting
1tsp salt
100ml/4fl oz/½ cup corn oil
1tbsp lemon juice
100ml/4fl oz/½ cup water
butter, for greasing

FOR THE FILLING

50g/2oz/¼ cup butter
3tbsp plain (all-purpose) flour
6tbsp milk
300ml/½pt/1¼ cups single
(light) cream
450g/1lb/2 cups feta cheese,
crumbled
100g/4oz/¼ cup Gruyère cheese,
grated
4 eggs, beaten
4tbsp chopped flat-leaved parsley
freshly ground black pepper
grated nutmeg

1 Sift the flour and salt into a
bowl, make a hollow in the
centre and pour in the oil. Mix
until it is thoroughly blended,
then gradually pour on the lemon
juice and water.

2 Knead the mixture to form
a firm dough, then cover it
with a cloth and leave it to rest
for about 45 minutes.

3 Meanwhile, make the
filling. Melt the butter in a
small pan and stir in the flour.
Cook over a low heat, stirring,
for 1 minute. Gradually pour on
the milk and cream, still
stirring, and simmer over a low
heat for 3 minutes. Do not boil.
Set aside to cool.

4 Stir the cheeses, eggs and
parsley into the sauce and
season with pepper and nutmeg.
Beat until the mixture is well
blended. Heat the oven to
200°C/400°F/Gas 6.

5 When the dough has rested,
knead it again on a lightly
floured board and cut it into 4
pieces. Roll each piece to a
thickness of 4mm/⅛in and, using
a saucer or a template, cut
rounds 15cm/6in in diameter.
Re-roll the trimmings and cut
more shapes.

6 Lightly brush the dough
rounds with cold water and
place about 2tbsp of the cheese
filling on each. Fold over the
dough circles and pinch the edges
firmly to close.

7 Place the pies on greased
baking sheets and bake them
in the oven for 20 minutes until
they are just beginning to turn
light golden brown. Serve hot.

Makes about 25 pies

*OPPOSITE: A selection of fancy
breads, a choice of mature,
hard cheeses displayed with a
cascade of grapes, and a dish
of Cypriot Cheese Pies set the
scene for a stylish cheese and
wine party.*

*ABOVE: Fruit salad makes a
light and refreshing end to a
simple meal of bread, cheese
and pastries. Grapes, melon
balls, sliced apples and kiwi
fruits are blended in lime syrup
and decorated with star fruit
and Sharon fruit (persimmon).*

AFTER-CAROLLING PARTY

BESIDES THE fun of singing and the satisfaction of collecting money for a church or charity, part of the pleasure of carolling is being welcomed into a warm home afterwards, offered a hot drink – mulled wine or a wassail cup are traditional – and a hearty casserole.

If it is your turn to entertain the group, prepare Spiced Lamb to serve with haricot beans, Old English Trifle topped with crystallized (candied) fruits and, as an alternative dessert or a sauce to serve with the trifle, a mixed fruit *Rumtopf*. The spirit content is guaranteed to revive the coldest of guests!

SPICED LAMB WITH HARICOT (NAVY) BEANS

This dish can be made in advance and reheated, or left in the oven at a low temperature while you are out carol-singing.

INGREDIENTS

225g/8oz/1⅓ cups dried haricot (navy) beans, soaked and drained (see method)
1.5kg/3¼lb boned shoulder of lamb
6tbsp sunflower oil
2 large onions, sliced
1 large aubergine (eggplant), cut into 2.5-cm/1-in cubes
1tsp ground ginger
1tsp turmeric
1tsp ground cinnamon
3 × 225g/8oz cans chopped tomatoes
2 cloves garlic, chopped
1tbsp dried thyme
salt and pepper
300ml/½pt/1¼ cups plain yoghurt
fresh coriander or mint, to garnish

1 Place the haricot beans in a pan, pour on boiling water to cover and set aside for 2 hours. Alternatively, soak the beans in cold water overnight. Drain the beans, put them in a pan with fresh, cold water and bring them to the boil for 45 minutes–1 hour until they are tender. Drain the beans and set them aside.

2 Meanwhile, trim any excess fat from the meat and cut it into cubes. Heat the oil in a large, heavy frying pan (skillet) and fry the meat in batches over a high heat to brown it on all sides. Remove the meat with a draining spoon and set it aside.

3 Add the onion and
aubergine (eggplant) to the
oil in the pan and fry, stirring
occasionally, until the onion is
translucent. Stir in the ginger,
turmeric and cinnamon and cook
for 1 minute to allow the spices to
blend. Add the tomatoes, garlic
and thyme and season with salt
and pepper. Return the meat to
the pan, bring to simmering
point, cover and simmer for
about 1½ hours, stirring
occasionally, until the meat is
tender.

4 Stir in half the yoghurt and
4 tbsp of the haricot beans
and heat gently. Taste and adjust
the seasoning if necessary.

5 Spoon the remaining
yoghurt and beans into a
small pan and heat gently.
Season with salt and pepper.

6 Transfer the lamb to a
warmed serving dish and
the beans to a smaller one and
garnish with herbs. Serve hot.

Serves 8–10

OLD ENGLISH TRIFLE

INGREDIENTS
*1 packet trifle sponge cakes, or 2
× 17.5cm/7in fatless sponge cakes
450g/1lb/2 cups apricot jam or
quince jelly
200ml/8fl oz/1 cup sweet sherry*

FOR THE CUSTARD
*600ml/1pt/2½ cups single (light)
cream
vanilla pod
50g/2oz/¼ cup caster (superfine)
sugar
1 tsp cornflour (cornstarch)
5 eggs*

FOR THE TOPPING
*600ml/1pt/2½ cups double
(heavy) cream, whipped
crystallized (candied) fruits, sliced
a few split almonds, toasted
holly or other leaves, to decorate
(optional)*

1 First make the custard.
Pour the cream into a pan,
add the vanilla pod and bring it
to the boil. Mix together the
sugar and cornflour, beat in the
eggs and beat until smooth.
Remove the vanilla pod, and
strain the cream onto the egg
mixture, beating constantly.

2 Return the custard to the
rinsed pan and stir it over a
very low heat until it thickens.
Remove from the heat.

3 Split the sponge cakes in
half horizontally and
spread them with the jam or
jelly. Sandwich them together
and arrange them in a serving
dish. Pour on the sherry and then
the hot custard. Set aside to cool.

4 Spread the whipped cream
thickly over the custard.
Decorate the top with
crystallized (candied) fruits,
toasted almonds, and, if you like,
pairs of holly leaves.

Serves 8–10

NEW YEAR'S EVE BUFFET

It is New Year's Eve. There's a mood of joyous optimism, of hopeful anticipation and of friendships renewed and reavowed. It is time for a party, a buffet that can be prepared in advance so that the host and hostess can enter into the relaxed and happy mood.

The suggested menu includes one substantial meat dish, Spiced Beef; one fish dish, a delicious and unusual Prawn (Shrimp) Cheesecake, and a choice of simple but spectacular desserts. Add baked potatoes and two or three salads and you have a feast worthy of the year to come.

LEFT: *A tempting buffet to ring out the old year, and ring in the new. Spiced Beef and Prawn (Shrimp) Cheesecake are served with a variety of salads.*

PRAWN (SHRIMP) CHEESECAKE

INGREDIENTS
75g/3oz/1/2 cup butter, plus extra for greasing
175g/6oz water biscuits (unsalted crackers), finely crushed
grated rind of 1/2 lemon
1 tbsp sesame seeds
salt and freshly ground black pepper

FOR THE FILLING
225g/8oz/1 cup soft cream cheese
2 eggs, separated
grated rind and juice of 1/2 lemon
150ml/1/4pt/2/3 cup soured cream or crème fraîche
225g/8oz/1 cup frozen prawns (shrimp), thawed and chopped
large pinch of cayenne
11g/scant 1/2oz/1 tbsp gelatine crystals (1 sachet)
2 tbsp orange juice

FOR THE TOPPING
150ml/1/4pt/2/3 cup soured cream
thinly sliced cucumber
small sprigs parsley
8 whole prawns (shrimp)

1 *Melt the butter in a pan over a low heat. Remove from the heat and stir in the biscuit (cracker) crumbs, lemon rind and sesame seeds and season lightly with salt and pepper. Press the mixture into the base of a greased, loose-bottomed 20-cm/ 8-in round cake tin and level the surface. Chill while you make the filling.*

2 *Beat the cream cheese until it is soft. Beat in the egg yolks, lemon rind and lemon juice, soured cream and chopped prawns (shrimp) and season with salt and pepper and cayenne. Sprinkle the gelatine crystals over the orange juice in a small bowl, stir well and place it in a pan of simmering water to dissolve. Stir in the prawn (shrimp) mixture and set aside until it is on the point of setting.*

3 *Whisk the egg whites until stiff and fold into the prawn (shrimp) mixture. Spoon into the tin and level the top. Chill for about 3 hours, until the filling is set.*

4 *Run a knife around the edge of the cheesecake to loosen it, and then lift it out of the tin, still on the base. Spread the soured cream on top and garnish with the cucumber, parsley and prawns (shrimp).*

Serves 8

SPICED BEEF

This dish is an excellent choice for a New Year's party, contrasting with the rich foods enjoyed at Christmas. You need to start the preparation at least 16 days in advance. Calculate the cooking time at 50 minutes per 450g/1lb raw meat. After this time, the meat should be tender but still pink in the centre.

INGREDIENTS
2.5kg/5lb rolled topside or silverside of beef
1 large onion, sliced
2 carrots, sliced
4 stalks celery, sliced
600ml/1pt/2½ cups beef stock
150ml/¼pt/⅔ cup port or red wine

FOR THE MARINADE
1tsp black peppercorns
1tsp mustard seeds
3–4 mace blades
½tsp grated nutmeg
large pinch of powdered cloves
1tbsp dried rosemary, crumbled
1tsp thyme
225g/8oz/1 cup soft dark brown sugar
225g/8oz/1 cup coarse salt
8 bay leaves, crumbled
1tbsp juniper berries, crushed

1 Crush the peppercorns, mustard seeds and mace with a pestle and mortar, or put them into a paper bag and lightly crush them with a rolling pin. Mix the spices with the nutmeg, powdered cloves, rosemary, thyme and sugar.

2 Place the beef in a shallow earthenware or pottery (not metal) dish and rub the sugar and spice mixture into the meat on all sides. Spoon up any mixture that does not adhere to the meat at first and rub it well in. Cover the dish and set aside in the refrigerator.

3 After 3 days, mix half the salt with the bay leaves and juniper berries and rub the mixture all over the meat, basting the meat with the marinade (which will now be moist) in the dish. Cover the dish and set it aside for 24 hours, then rub in the remaining salt. Cover and set aside again for 11 days, turning the meat and basting it with the brine every day.

4 At the end of this time, on the 15th day, remove the meat from the brine, wipe off all the spices and wipe it all over with a damp cloth.

5 Heat the oven to 140°C/275°F/Gas 1. Place the meat in the rinsed dish, arrange the onion, carrot and celery around it and pour on the stock and port or red wine. Cover the dish with a lid if it has one, and with a double thickness of foil pressed tightly around the rim.

6 Cook the meat in the bottom of the oven for 4 hours 10 minutes. Remove it from the oven and, without uncovering the dish, leave the meat to cool in the liquor. Remove the meat, place it on a flat board or dish with another one on top and place heavy weights (such as cans of food) on top of that. Leave it to press in this way for 24 hours.

7 Remove the meat, wrap it in foil and keep it in the refrigerator until it is needed. Having been marinated in this way, it is partially preserved and may be kept chilled for up to 14 days. This means that you can start the preparation well before Christmas. Serve thinly sliced.

Serves 14–16

PEARS IN GRENADINE

The sunset colour of this dessert makes it a delightful attraction on the buffet table.

INGREDIENTS

10 cooking pears
150g/6oz/3/4 cup caster (superfine) sugar
600ml/1pt/2 1/2 cups water
thinly pared rind and juice of 1 lemon
1 small cinnamon stick
5 tbsp grenadine syrup
1 tbsp cornflour (cornstarch)
2 tbsp cold water
4 tbsp redcurrant or raspberry jelly

1 Peel the pears, leaving the stalks intact.

2 Place the sugar, water, lemon rind and lemon juice in a large pan, add the cinnamon and grenadine and stir over a low heat until the sugar has dissolved. Bring to the boil, add the pears and spoon the liquid over them. Reduce the heat, cover the pan and simmer for 15–20 minutes, turning the pears until they are just tender. Lift out the pears and arrange them in a dish.

3 Blend the cornflour and water, spoon on a little of the syrup and pour into the pan. Stir over moderate heat until the mixture thickens. Discard the cinnamon and lemon rind, stir in the jelly and pour over the fruit. Do not chill.

Serves 10

*OPPOSITE: **Pears in Grenadine** and **Orange Posset** are shown on a dessert table decorated with orchids.*

ABOVE: Stylish decorations fit for the New Year – the printed table napkins are bound with gilt beads.

ORANGE POSSET

This is a traditional English recipe which was popular in the London gentlemen's clubs in the eighteenth century. Served icy cold with oranges in jelly it is especially refreshing.

INGREDIENTS

600ml/1pt/2 1/2 cups double (heavy) cream
grated rind and juice of 2 oranges
grated rind and juice of 1 lemon
150ml/1/4pt/2/3 cup dry white wine
100g/4oz/1/2 cup caster (superfine) sugar, plus 2 tbsp
3 large egg whites
julienne strips of peel of 1 orange
whipped cream, to decorate (optional)

1 Beat the double (heavy) cream with the grated rind of the oranges and lemon until it is stiff. Gradually beat in small amounts of the orange juice, lemon juice and white wine, beating between each addition so that the cream completely absorbs the liquid. This will prevent the cream curdling.

2 Beat in 100g/4oz/1/2 cup of the sugar until the mixture is stiff enough to form soft peaks and hold its shape.

3 Beat the egg whites until they are stiff and fold in the 2 tbsp of sugar. Fold the whites into the cream mixture and spoon it into a serving dish. Decorate with orange strips and swirls of whipped cream if you wish.

Serves 10

THE PERFECT HOST OR HOSTESS

HAVING GUESTS to stay over the Christmas holidays is a special pleasure. But there is no denying that it involves extra work and responsibility for the host and hostess, who will want to ensure that guests not only enjoy the highlights of their stay, but the quiet moments too.

For your own busy schedule and peace of mind, prepare guest bedrooms well in advance. Check that there are plenty of basic requirements such as fluffy towels, tissues, cotton wool (absorbent cotton) and guests' soap. If you plan well ahead you can delight visitors with sticks of your own handmade lavender-scented soap. They are sure to appreciate such a luxury.

If you have the facilities, it is a good idea to take a leaf from the hoteliers' book and provide coffee- and tea-making equipment, something that is especially welcomed by those who wake up at unsociably early hours. Arrange a tray with an electric kettle, a small cafetière and a jar of ground coffee (or just supply instant coffee, if it's easier), a teapot and a choice of two tea blends. Add wrapped sugar and a decora-

tive tin of biscuits (cookies), with milk and fresh fruit to be replenished daily.

Make a small selection of books and general-interest magazines for friends who like to travel light, and may not bring their own reading material. Check that there are bulbs in the reading lamps and provide an electric torch (flashlight) or plug in extra nightlights to help night-time navigation to the bathroom.

Flowers help to make a room more welcoming. If there are plenty of Christmas decorations in the other rooms, flowers can bring a breath of spring or summer to the guest rooms. Dried flower arrangements are a pretty option that prevent the need for last-minute preparation.

When guests arrive be sure to show them such essentials as where the light switches and plug sockets are and which cupboard space is available. Such extra thoughtfulness has an advantage for the host and hostess too, giving you a chance to do some household tasks surreptitiously, while guests enjoy the warmth of your hospitality.

ABOVE: A plate is fitted with stem-holding foam for this pretty arrangement. Freesias should be used in moderation in arrangements intended for bedrooms – their heavy scent, though lovely, may be oppressive to some guests.

RIGHT: Dried-flower arrangements are a bonus to a busy host or hostess because they can be arranged ahead of time and can include out-of-season flowers. Here, small baskets are filled with rosebuds and gypsophila (baby's breath).

OPPOSITE: Spoil your guests with breakfast in bed. Although the preparation is simple (coffee, orange juice and croissants warmed in the oven) the presentation is cheerful and welcoming – bright blue china is offset by flowers in complementary yellow.

PARTY GAMES

Christmas may be the one time of year when the extended family gets together purely for pleasure. In this section there are groups of guessing games to test ingenuity and judgement; pencil and memory games to demonstrate powers of deduction and concentration; word and card games, some of which will amaze and delight the assembled company; noisy games to enable guests of all ages to let off steam, and team games to encourage a little good-humoured competitiveness. And, to complete the package, there are ideas for inexpensive prizes to be awarded for merit and talent, and hilarious forfeits (penalties) to be paid.

GUESSING GAMES

GUESSING GAMES are perhaps the most enthralling of all family-fireside games, since they involve an element of intrigue. The rest of the group has to use skill and judgement to unravel a secret known only to one person, or to members of the opposing team. It is a challenge that is eagerly taken up by young and older guests alike, and the challenge may come in many guises.

CHARADES

This is a mime game that can be both fun and frustrating. Each person in the group thinks up the name of a book, a play, a TV show, a song, or a film, and writes it on a slip of paper. One player picks a title from the pack at random and without saying a word, tries to mime it as a whole, in separate words, or in syllables for the others to guess. The first person to get it right takes the centre stage and performs his or her own title mime.

To indicate the category of the title, the player opens out his palms like the pages of a book; mimes drawing back the

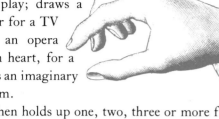

curtains for a play; draws a square in the air for a TV screen; mimes an opera singer, hand on heart, for a song; and winds an imaginary handle for a film.

He or she then holds up one, two, three or more fingers to indicate the number of words in the title and then indicates which of those words he intends to mime by holding up the appropriate number of fingers. If the mime represents a syllable of the word, then he places one, two, three or four fingers on the forearm. If the title were *A Christmas Carol*, the player would hold up three fingers. Then to mime the syllable 'mas', he would hold up two fingers followed by placing two fingers on his forearm.

The word 'the' is indicated by making the letter T with both forefingers, and 'a' or 'an' by holding up an index finger and thumb together. If he intends to mime a 'sounds like' word, 'time' instead of 'lime', for example, he cups one ear with his hand.

LEFT: Ribbons galore, from colourful paper ones to shiny raffia, comprise a teaser for 'How long is a piece of string?'

How Many, How Long?

This is an interlude game which you can pass from hand to hand in a group, or set out on a table with a notebook and pencil for guests to enter their guesses.

To prepare the game, gather together as varied and colourful a collection of bits and pieces of ribbon or string. Carefully measure each piece, add up the total, write it on a card and put it in a sealed envelope. Tie the ribbons into double and multi-bows, joining them together in one long, complicated-looking string. The answers to how long is that piece of string are likely to vary wildly from a couple of yards to half a mile! The same game can be played with a jar full of candies, as everyone guesses the number in the jar.

What Manners!

This is a game that allows the cheekiest of questions to be met by the most tantalizing responses.

One person in the group thinks up an adverb. It can be a simple one like 'happily' or 'sadly' or a more obscure one like 'self-effacingly' or 'bookishly'. The others take it in turn to ask the key player to respond to questions or perform certain activities in the manner of that adverb. 'Tell me what you thought of the Christmas present I gave you', asks an intrepid player. One can only hope that the chosen adverb wasn't 'frankly'! The first one to guess the adverb takes over the key role.

ABOVE: For 'How many in a jar' choose the most colourful candies you can find and decorate the jar with a ribbon and a sprig of greenery. Provide paper and pencil for the estimates.

Silence, Please!

The players are seated in a circle, on chairs or on the floor. Each one in turn whispers to his left-hand neighbour telling him to do some absurd thing. When the instructions have gone full circle, everyone stands up and takes a vow of silence. Each player in turn rises and performs his given task and sits down only when someone in the group has guessed his mime. Anyone who speaks or laughs, pays a forfeit (penalty).

PENCIL AND MEMORY GAMES

IN THEORY, pencil and memory games provide a quiet interlude between, say, lunch and tea, or tea and television, or between noisy team games. But it does not always work out like that, especially when the answers or results are read out or scrutinized.

PELMANISM

This game requires a little preparation on the part of the host or hostess, so have everything ready to bring in when you judge the moment is right.

Collect 40 or 50 small items from around the home, and place them on a tray. There may be a candle and a coin, a nut and a nail, a key and a kumquat, a cone and a stone, a leaf and a lime, a pottery cat and a cork or any other easily forgettable selection you care to make. Give each player a paper and pencil, and bring in the tray covered with a cloth. Remove the cloth and give everyone, say, 1 minute to study the tray, then 3 minutes to write down as many items as they can remember. Have small prizes such as chocolate bars ready to reward the most accurate memories.

MY AUNT WENT CHRISTMAS SHOPPING

This is another lazy-afternoon game. No-one needs to move! One player starts by saying 'My aunt went Christmas shopping and she bought . . .' It may be that her purchase was a pair of look-alike fun-fur zebras. The next player repeats the line about his aunt's expedition, and her first purchase, and then adds his own. Her next good buy might be a second-hand pink and blue feather boa. And so it goes on. As each player's memory fails or even an adjective is forgotten, he drops out of the game until eventually the only niece or nephew who accurately repeats the list wins.

BEETLE GAME

This is such an old favourite that some families organize beetle-drives on a similar principle to whist drives, four to a table with the winner moving onto the next. The game can be played by three or more players; everyone needs their own pencil and paper. The aim is to complete a drawing of a beetle.

This is purely a game of chance, the outcome being determined by the luck of the dice.

Each player takes it in turn to throw the die and cannot start his drawing until he has thrown a six, for the body. With this oval drawn, he can complete the beetle outline, in any order, when he throws a five for the head, a four for each of six legs, a three for each of two antennae, a two for the tail, and a one for each of the two eyes. The player who completes his insect first cries 'Beetle!'.

THE MINISTER'S CAT

This is a memorizing-out-loud game. It is up to the organizer to keep the game moving at a steady pace. Too many long pauses and the hesitant player is out!

The first player announces that the minister's cat is an awkward, or an awesome, or an Alpine cat. The next player repeats the 'a' adjective and adds one of his or her own, beginning with the letter 'b', and so it goes on, round the circle and through the alphabet. Anyone who remembers that the minister's cat is an awesome, batty, cantankerous, dowdy, eclectic, fastidious, gregarious, horrendous, indigenous, jumpy, kinky, lazy, mischievous, notorious, opulent, pernicious, quiet, rowdy, sleepy, tortoiseshell, undisciplined, violent, wayward, xenophobic, yellow, zany cat – starts again! Anyone who does not, is out.

IT'S IN THE BAG

Children love this rummaging game. Collect a number of small and unlikely items together and put them in a thick pillowcase, cushion cover or even a Christmas stocking. Give each player about 30 seconds to rummage in the bag without looking. Each one then writes down what he or she felt in the bag. Whoever comes up with the most complete list claims a small prize for the most accurate or the most humorous list.

LEFT: A tray of small items can tax the most alert mind in the Pelmanism game.

RIGHT: Fill a Christmas stocking with an assortment of objects for the memory game 'It's in the Bag'.

PICTORIAL SEQUENCES

This is a game that can verge on the bizarre – if it is to be the greatest fun. Divide the company into groups of four and give each player a paper and pencil or felt-tipped pen.

Each player draws a human, animal or fantasy head at the top of the paper, folds it over to leave just the neck showing and passes it to the player on the left. He or she draws down to the waist, folds it and passes it on. The next person draws the figure from the waist to the knees and passes it on to the fourth player to add the feet.

Word and Card Games

Some word games seriously tax the lexicographers among the group, while others encourage hilarity and deviousness. There is a place at a family party for both types. And Christmas wouldn't be Christmas without a few card games and tricks.

The Mad Maharajah

This game gives children a chance to act up. They can be theatrically sick, writhe about in seemingly grievous pain and even dramatically drop down dead. But before that they have to remember to spell.

One player stands in the middle of the circle, points to another player, and announces, 'I, the mad Maharajah, do not like the letter (for example) P. What will you give me to eat? The player indicated must offer the Maharajah a food that will not, by including the letter P, poison him. He might serve up a flan but not a pie, an orange or lemon but not an apple or pear, and so on. Easy? Not when the Maharajah demands more and more food as he points to other players and warns them of one poison letter after another. Each successive food offered must contain none of the poison letters. If it does, the Maharajah drops down dead, the player who poisoned him is out, and someone else takes the crown.

Chinese Whispers

The chances of the original whisper going full circle around the group are remote enough, without the wiles of mischievous players who deliberately muddy the waters!

The first player whispers a message close to the ear of his or her neighbour in the circle. That person passes it on, to the next person, who whispers it to the next until in theory the message should return unscathed – this rarely happens – to the first player. He calls out the message he has just received, and everyone falls about laughing at how the message has changed since they passed it on.

Olders players may remember the legendary story of the World War I message which was transmitted as 'Send reinforcements, we're going to advance', and was ultimately received as 'Send three-and-fourpence, we're going to a dance'.

Bank Robbers

This trick relies on a confident smile and a ready line of patter if it is to astonish your audience – younger children are more likely to be amazed.

Take the pack of cards and remove, publicly, the four jacks and, stealthily, four other cards. Fan out the jacks with the other four cards hidden behind them.

Place the remaining 44 cards on a table in front of you and hold up the four jacks, explaining that they are robbers who are going to break into a bank and steal its gold. Then place the jacks and, again stealthily, the other four cards face down on top of the pack.

Take the top card, concealing its face, and place it into the pack, saying that this is the first robber entering the bank. Take the second, third and fourth cards and place them one by one in the pack. These will of course be the 'innocent' cards, not the robbers.

Now tap the pack with a very knowing air and produce the four jacks from the top of the deck as if by magic.

Take a bow, to delighted applause.

OLD MAID

Remove the Queen of Hearts from the pack
of cards and deal the remainder to the players.
Each player sorts his or her hand into pairs, two
cards of equal numbers or court (face) value, places
them face down on the table. The first player offers
one of his cards to the player on his left. If that
player can match it with a card he holds, he discards
the pair and anyway passes a card to the player
on his left and so on round the table.
Players who run out of cards just pass a
card from the player on their right to
the one on their left. As there is an
uneven number of queens, the last card is
certain to be one of them.

BEGGAR YOUR NEIGHBOUR

Don't despair! Someone who seems to be winning this game
hands down could be declared out in a matter of minutes.

Deal two packs of cards, face down, between the players
who stack them in neat piles in front of them. The player on
the dealer's left turns over the card on the top of his pack and
puts it in the centre of the table. The next player puts his top
card face up on the first one and so on round the table.

If a court (picture) card is turned over the player has to
pay a forfeit, placing four cards on the central pile for an ace,
three for a king, two for a queen and one
for a jack. If, when paying a forfeit
(penalty), the player turns over a
court card, his punishment stops
and the player on his left pays
the appropriate new forfeit.
If only numbered cards are
turned over when paying a
forfeit, the player takes all the
cards in the central pile and
places them beneath his own.
He turns up the first card in
the next round, and so it
goes on. Players drop out of
the game when they have
run out of cards.

BALANCING ACT

This is another way to amuse the assembled company. Take
a card in your hand and attempt to balance an unbreakable
glass on its rim. The glass will fall off. Now tell your
audience that with a little concentration you can perform
this seemingly impossible balancing act.

This time take the two prepared cards in your
hand. One has been folded lengthways and one half
pasted to the back of the other to create a flap.
Show the audience both sides of the apparently
single card, making sure that the flap is closed.

Work up the anticipation in the audience and,
with a deft movement, open the flap towards you
so that the two cards present (only to you) a T-shaped
edge. Balance the tumbler on this edge with a look of
studied nonchalance.

BOISTEROUS GAMES

THERE ARE times in every family party when the older members have to put their fingers in their ears and grin and bear the noise made by the youngsters. And there are times when they can't resist joining in!

FARMYARD NOISES

The title speaks for itself!

The players form a circle with one of their number, the farmer, blindfolded in the centre. The players walk round him and, when the 'farmer' taps his foot on the ground, they stop. He points at a player (whom he cannot see of course) and asks him to make the noise of a farmyard animal, such as a cow, a pig or a horse. The farmer has to guess who the animal is. If he guesses correctly, the two players change places. If not, the circle moves round again and he points to another player with a request for another impersonation.

MUSICAL MINDREADING

You need someone playing a piano or controlling the volume of a recorded piece of music. One player goes out of the room and the others decide on a simple act he has to do. This may be rearranging the fruit in a bowl, cracking a nut and so on. The music starts and the player enters and walks around the room. The nearer he gets to his goal the louder the music plays. The further he gets, the softer the music. As the player approaches his goal, the music becomes deafening. The player must guess what the task is and perform it.

AND THE BAND PLAYED ON

This game is noisy in the extreme, but all the more fun for that.

Divide the group into orchestras of four or five players and supply a selection of household items and utensils which they can use as improvised musical instruments. These items could include empty 'mixer' bottles, a jug of water, metal skewer, rubber bands, combs, spoons, rulers and tissue paper. Tell the orchestras to select and create their musical instruments, and give them about 5 minutes to rehearse a tune. This could be an earsplitting time! Then each band gives a polished performance to the others, and everyone votes for the best one. Voting for one's own band is not allowed.

Primitive music can be made in primitive ways. Bottles filled to different levels will produce different notes when struck by a metal skewer or spoon. Rubber bands stretched around a ruler at different tensions will produce a variety of notes when plucked. Paper wrapped tightly around a comb will make an instrument with some of the characteristics of a mouth-organ, and the rounded sides of spoons tapped together sound like castanets, to the untutored ear. Good listening!

FAN RACE

You need a good, clear space to play this game. It could even be played outside on a still, dry afternoon.

Each player is given a small fan and a feather. Everyone stands in a row, toeing the line, with his or her feather on the ground in front of him. At a given signal, the fun begins. Players have to fan their feathers to the finishing line. Anyone who touches his feather with his hands, or blows it, is disqualified. Anyone not taking part in the race is encouraged to pick a winner and cheer his 'horse' to the finishing post.

SPOON A BALLOON

This is a game of gamesmanship. The players each have a spoon, and stand in a circle with about a metre (a yard) between each of them. A balloon is placed on one spoon and is then tossed from spoon to spoon around the circle. The other players, without moving from their posts, do all they can, in the way of verbal discouragement, to make the receiving player lose concentration. Any player who fails to catch the balloon on his spoon is out, and the others close ranks.

BALLOON RACE

This game can be played in heats, the winners of each event meeting in the semi-finals and the finals. Each heat consists of three or four players – more if space and the number of participants permit. Each player is given a balloon and a short, thin stick with which he has to pat it across the room and into a bowl on the other side. If he touches the balloon or it falls to the ground the player is disqualified. Onlookers will no doubt wish to cheer on their chosen contestants.

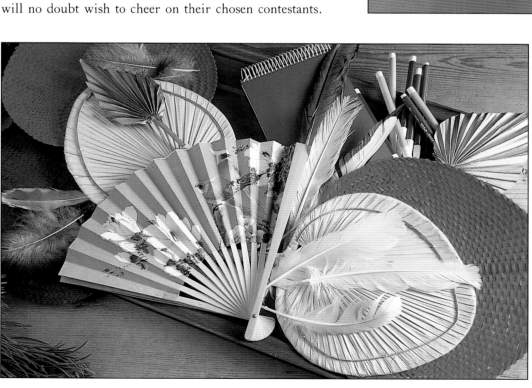

ABOVE: Spoons at the ready for the Spoon a Balloon Game in which the players' natural dexterity is foiled by verbal discouragement from the opposition.

LEFT: An assortment of feathers and coloured fans for a Fan Race. A notepad and coloured pens are on hand to keep score.

Team Games

Bring a little competitive spirit to the party by introducing a few team games. You don't need a full-size Olympic stadium for these family favourites.

Orange Relay

Divide the group into two teams, and then each team into two sections, one at each end of the room. Provide each team leader with an orange wrapped around with an elastic band, and each player with a skewer.

The two team leaders hold the orange on a skewer, threaded through the band, and run to the next member of their team at the other end of the room. They transfer the orange to that player's skewer without using their hands. The two new runners rush to the other end of the room, pass on the orange, and so the game continues until one team has successfully completed the race. If the orange falls to the ground at any stage, that team starts again.

Rope Race

The players divide into two teams. Each team is given a length of rope knotted into a large circle (make sure the knot is secure and cannot be 'slipped'). On the word 'go' the first player in each team passes the rope circle over his or her head, over his shoulders and down to the ground. It is picked up by the next player who does the same, and so on down the line and back again, to the first player in each team. The side which finishes first celebrates vociferously.

The Chocolate Race

You will have to shop in advance for this game, for two large bars of chocolate.

Divide the group into two teams and ask each one to form a circle. Place a chair in the middle of each group, with an unbreakable plate, a large chocolate bar, a knife and fork, a hat and a scarf.

Give each team a die and a die shaker. The first one on each side to throw a six rushes to the chair, dons the hat and scarf, cuts off a piece of chocolate with the knife and conveys it to his or her mouth with the fork. The next person to throw a six grabs the hat and scarf from his team-mate, puts them on and proceeds to devour another piece of chocolate in the same way.

The Orange Race

This game is all the more fun if you divide the group into two teams evenly balanced with small children and tall grown-ups.

The two teams stand in line. Each team leader is given an orange, which he or she tucks under the chin. On the word 'go', the two players attempt to transfer the orange to the chin of the next two players in line. Touching the orange with the hands is the worst form of cheating, punishable by returning the orange to the first in line and starting all over again. The same fate befalls a team if the orange falls to the ground.

The winning team is the one which successfully manoeuvres the orange from the first to the last in line.

OBSTACLE RACE

This is a race for two players, and a heap of fun for everyone else. Two players go out of the room while the others prepare two identical obstacle courses, placing two piles of books, heaps of cushions, empty boxes and so on in two lines down the room. The two contestants are brought in, led to the start of the course and told to memorize it. They are then blindfolded, and the rest of the group, the conspirators, silently remove the obstacles.

On the word 'go', the two contestants climb and clamber over obstacles that are no longer there, while the conspirators fall about laughing. The first competitor to reach the finishing line with success, claims a prize.

TREASURE HUNT

This game involves some preparation by the host and hostess, and a polite request to observe that some rooms are out of bounds, if this is the case.

Divide the party into teams of three or four players, and give each of them a different list of 'treasure' to be unearthed, and a box to put it in. Give the teams, say, 10 minutes to go on the hunt. The prize goes to the team who gets closest to finding all the items on their list within the time limit.

Make up the lists with some items that players are likely to have in their pockets or handbags and others which may be found without too much disruption in the kitchen and dining room. Suitable treasure might include a railway season ticket, a bus ticket, a library card, a driving licence, a foreign coin, a lipstick, a teaspoon, a saltcellar, a pecan, a book of matches, a used envelope and so on.

Children especially enjoy this game, and sharing any 'treasure' given as a prize to the winning team.

YOU WIN!

Although it is not absolutely necessary to award prizes for individual or team success, a small token is always appreciated, especially by children.

For children
chocolate bar; candies; wrapped gingerbread men and other shapes; wrapped home-made biscuits and small cakes; coat badge; Christmas tree ornament.

For adults
chocolate bar; miniature chocolate liqueur; individually wrapped truffles or pralines; miniature pot of preserve; scented drawer sachet; bath cube; packet of bath pearls.

YOU LOSE!
Sometimes the forfeits (penalties) that players are asked to pay are as much fun (for the rest of the company!) as the games themselves. Here are some suggestions that should help to spark off other ideas.

- Kiss everyone in the room of the opposite sex.
- Dance gracefully to some imaginary ballet music.
- Whistle the national anthem.
- Mime a given task, such as getting dressed in the morning, or having a shower.

CHILDREN'S CHRISTMAS

Probably nothing can quite match the joy and excitement that children feel as Christmas approaches. This section of the book is designed to turn that excitement into creative energy, with projects for the children to make themselves. There are fully illustrated step-by-step instructions for gingerbread house biscuits (cookies), popcorn and candy garlands, table decorations and tree trims; projects for younger children to create bright and beautiful paper flowers and for older ones to cut out stained-glass patterns from card (posterboard) and tissue paper. All the projects are simple to make, and are certain to appeal to children of all ages.

DECORATING WITH CANDIES

LIGHT-AS-AIR and irresistible popcorn and brightly-wrapped candies come together to make the tastiest decorations ever. Let the children string popcorn and candies onto a thread to make garlands for the tree or to loop from side to side on a wall. Thread popcorn onto flexible wires to make pretty loops tied onto the tree branches with bright lengths of ribbon. And combine wired popcorn and threaded candies with two-colour holly leaves for a children's party centrepiece. They really are sweet ideas!

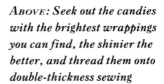

ABOVE: Seek out the candies with the brightest wrappings you can find, the shinier the better, and thread them onto double-thickness sewing thread. Take the needle through the candies for the long strips, through one end of the wrapping papers for the bunches at the side.

ABOVE: A wooden toy train can be used as the base of a flower arrangement for a children's party. Fix a plastic foam-holding saucer on the top, insert a cylinder of absorbent foam soaked in water and arrange a flurry of brightly coloured flowers and dried or evergreen leaves. The orange gerbera, like a giant daisy, has special child-appeal rivalled only by the toffee apples.

LEFT: A garland of candies and popcorn is a pretty and unusual tree trim that is becoming increasingly popular.

POPCORN AND CANDY RING

This is a design that older children can make by themselves, as a party centre-piece. Younger ones will need help in cutting the stub wires.

EQUIPMENT

* stub wires (floral pins)
* wire cutters
* 20cm/8in diameter pre-formed dry foam ring

DECORATIVE MATERIALS

* popcorn
* brightly wrapped candies
* variegated holly, or other evergreens such as ivy, cypress or pine
* 5cm/2in-wide ribbon

1 Cut the stub wires in half. Thread popcorn onto the wires to within 2.5cm/1in of the end. Push the threaded wires into the foam ring well spaced out all around. Bend some of the wires so that they face different ways.

2 Push a half-wire through one end of the candy wrapping, but not through the candy. Bend the ends of the wire downwards to make a U-shape, and twist the ends together.

3 Push the wired candies into the ring, mixing the colours and arranging the candies so that some face inwards and others outwards. Cut the holly or other evergreens into short sprays and press them into the foam ring to fill the gaps.

4 Tie the ribbon into a bow and thread a wire through the loop at the back. Twist the wire ends together and press it into the ring. Be sure to tell your guests that the candies are not for eating until after the party!

BRIGHT AND BEAUTIFUL

CHILDREN LOVE all things bright and beautiful, especially at Christmastime, when they are asked to play their part in decorating the home. Give them a specific project, beyond their naturally enthusiastic involvement in trimming the tree. It may be a garland made from threaded popcorn and candies; a group of pine-scented Christmas-tree candles, which older children could manage safely or a dish of Christmas-pudding-shaped candles ringed around at a safe distance with sprays of red-berried holly. Children will also enjoy making the following papercraft ideas created with jewel-bright tissue paper and paper glue.

PAPER FLOWERS

When bright colours are the order of the day realism is not important, as the paper flowers shown here demonstrate. Each petal is made of two circles of paper, folded, twisted into a cone and then glued edge-to-edge to its neighbour.

EQUIPMENT

* saucer or bowl 10cm/4in in diameter, or a pair of compasses
* pencil
* paper scissors
* paper glue

DECORATIVE MATERIALS

* tissue paper in various colours such as lime green, dark green and bright red

FOR A VASE OF FLOWERS

* narrow canes or strong wheat stalks
* jug or other tall container

FOR A GARLAND

* darning needle
* fine twine or strong thread
* 5cm/2in-wide ribbons (optional)
* 1 stub wire (floral pin), cut in half (optional)

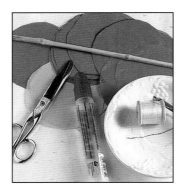

1 Trace around the saucer or bowl (or use the compasses) and cut out a number of 10cm /4in-circles in 3 colours of tissue paper. Make some flowers in a single colour and others in all 3 shades. Each flower needs about 14 petals, each one cut from 2 thicknesses of tissue paper. Taking 1 double circle, fold it once into a semicircle and again into quarters.

2 Holding the paper shape by the point, between the thumb and first finger of one hand, put your other thumb and first finger into the cone and twist it sharply to open it out. It should be tightly twisted at the base so that it holds its shape.

3 When you have made several petals, stick them together by gluing along the length of one petal, from top to bottom, and pressing it to another one. Hold the joined edges for a few seconds while the glue sets. Continue gluing more and more petals to make a ball shape. Eventually, when you have come full circle, you will be gluing the first petal to the last one.

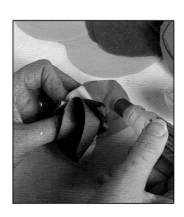

4 To make a vase of flowers, push a cane into the centre of each flower. If it does not stay firm, spread glue inside the lowest petal and wrap it around the stick. Arrange the flowers in a jug or other container and stand them in a place of honour. They make a lovely welcoming group in a hall or a bright feature in a room corner.

5 To make the garland, thread a darning needle with fine twine or strong thread and string the flowers together, mixing the colours as much as possible. If you wish, you can finish the design with ribbon bows at each end. To do this, push half a stub wire (floral pin) through the loop at the back, bend it to make a hook, and hook it over the garland.

NEW-LOOK BAUBLES (GLASS BALLS)

Give the children a few plain baubles from last year's tree-trim box, a tube or two of glitter glue and a free hand in the design. They may come up with some works of art.

Encourage them to go for snappy colour contrasts — silver on red and deep pink baubles, red on silver ones, gold on dark green and so on.

Squiggle designs are interesting and fun, though the children's artistic flights of fancy may take in funny faces, names and seasonal messages.

'STAINED GLASS' PAPERCRAFT

Take a lead from the craftsmen and women who create wonderful patterns in stained glass and try your hand at this brilliant form of papercraft. Use black paper for the outlines and coloured tissue paper to fill in the shapes. Apart from that, all you need is a pair of paper scissors, a tube of paper glue and a little patience.

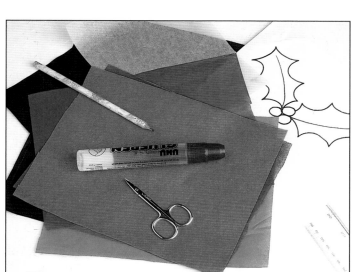

EQUIPMENT

* tracing paper
* pencil or ball-point pen
* ruler
* paper scissors
* paper glue
* patterns

DECORATIVE MATERIALS

* black art paper
* coloured tissue papers

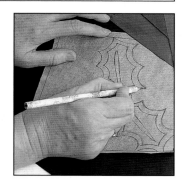

1 Trace the design. Cut a piece of black art paper to the size of the panel and place the tracing paper over it. Trace over the outlines with a pencil or ball-point pen so that it leaves an impression on the black paper.

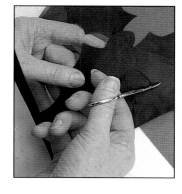

2 Look at the finished designs in the photograph as a guide to the shapes which are to be cut out of the black paper and which ones will remain, to represent the leading in the window panels. Mark the areas to be cut out with a pencil or pen and cut around the outlines.

3 Cut tissue paper in the appropriate colours a little larger than the spaces which will be covered. Place it on the back of the black card design and draw the shape on the tissue paper, allowing a narrow overlap all round. Cut out the tissue paper and stick each piece on the back of the black panel, over the appropriate cut-out shape.

4 The candle panels are designed to be wrapped around straight-sided tumblers, or you could make them to decorate preserve jars. You can use any colourful tissue paper scraps you have, in any order. The candle flames are made in 2 colours, pale orange and red, for variety.

5 Make the candle panels to fit tumblers or preserve jars. Put a nightlight inside each one, and you have brilliant tablelamps that will be the stars of your Christmas party.

6 When the lights are turned down low the lamps look even more dramatic.

GINGERBREAD TREATS

YOUNG COOKS love to make treats that can be used to decorate the Christmas tree, become the centre of attraction on a party table, or be given as delicious take-home gifts to visitors of all ages. These gingerbread house biscuits (cookies) meet all these demands, and more.

The house shapes can be decorated in any way the young cooks like, with plain white and coloured icing to outline the roofs, doors and windows; and small coloured candies. They should be wrapped in transparent paper or plastic wrap if they are intended as gifts.

One batch of the mixture makes two house-shaped cookies and about 20 small shapes to trim the tree.

GINGERBREAD HOUSES

If these houses are to be given as gifts, write the name or house number of the recipient in icing.

INGREDIENTS
225g/8oz/2 cups plain (all-purpose) flour, plus extra for dusting
pinch of salt
1tsp baking powder
2tsp ground ginger
1/2tsp ground cinnamon
125g/5oz/1/2 cup unsalted butter at room temperature, cut into small pieces, plus extra for greasing
100g/4oz/1/2 cup caster (superfine) sugar
2tbsp golden (dark corn) syrup
1 small egg, beaten, to mix

DECORATION
50g/2oz/1/2 cup icing (confectioners') sugar
about 2tsp water or lemon juice
2–3 drops edible food colouring (optional)
chocolate drops and candies (optional)

EQUIPMENT
* weighing scales
* large spoon
* teaspoon
* sieve (sifter)
* mixing bowl
* cup or small bowl
* fork
* pastry board
* plastic bag
* piece of white stiff card (posterboard)
* ruler
* pencil
* rolling pin
* knife
* spatula
* baking sheet
* small bowl
* icing bag
* small plain icing nozzle to pipe lines

DECORATIVE MATERIALS
* star-, tree- and heart-shaped biscuit (cookie) cutters
* skewer
* wooden toothpick
* small icing nozzle to pipe stars
* narrow ribbon or cord for hanging

LEFT: Stars, Christmas trees, hearts and other shapes cut out with cookie cutters and decorated with icing make pretty tree ornaments.

1 Sift together the flour, salt, baking powder, ground ginger and ground cinnamon into the mixing bowl. You will have to do this in several batches. Using your fingertips, rub in the butter until the mixture looks like breadcrumbs. Add the sugar and golden (dark corn) syrup and mix it well. Add just enough of the egg to make a stiff dough.

2 Sprinkle a little flour onto a pastry board, turn out the gingerbread dough and knead it with your hands until there are no more cracks. Put the ball of dough into a plastic bag and leave it in the refrigerator for about 30 minutes.

3 While the dough is chilling, make the template to cut out the house shapes. On a piece of white stiff card (posterboard), draw a rectangle 20 × 10cm/8 × 4in and cut it out. Measure and mark the centre of one of the short sides. Measure 7.5cm/3in down from the top on each long side and make marks. Draw lines from those marks to the centre top and cut along them. That represents the roof line.

4 Take out the dough. Sprinkle a little more flour onto the pastry board and roll out the dough until it is about 3mm/ 1/8in thick. Set the oven to 180°C/350°F/Gas 4.

5 Use the card template to make the house shapes, cutting round the outline with the points of a knife. ▶

ABOVE: Gingerbread House cookies line up along the most exciting street ever. A slice of orange completes the picture.

163

6 Carefully, lift up the dough houses with a spatula and place them well apart on the baking sheet.

7 Using the cookie cutters, cut out star, heart and other shapes from the rest of the dough. Gather up the pieces left over, roll them into a ball, sprinkle a little more flour onto the pastry board and roll them out to the same thickness as before. Cut out as many shapes as you can. Push a hole near the top of each with the skewer and lift them onto the baking sheet.

8 Bake the gingerbread in the oven for 12–15 minutes, until it is pale golden brown and just beginning to darken at the edges. Take the baking sheet from the oven and leave the gingerbread to cool thoroughly on the sheet.

9 Use the spatula to transfer the shapes to the cleaned pastry board.

10 Sift the icing (confectioners') sugar into a small bowl, and add just enough water or lemon juice so that it makes a stiff paste when you mix it. If you want to add food colouring (an adult should help children with this) divide the mixture into two or three and add 1 drop of each colour to each. It is easiest to do this accurately by dipping a toothpick into the bottle of colouring, and shaking a drop off the end of it and into the bowl. Mix well, to achieve an even colour.

11 Put the plain nozzle into an icing bag, spoon some of the icing mixture into it and pipe the detail on the house shapes.

12 Use a little of the icing to stick chocolate drops or other candies to the house shapes, if you use them.

13 Wash the icing bag and put in the star nozzle. Pipe blobs of icing onto the star, tree and heart shapes. When it is dry thread narrow ribbon through the holes in the cookies to hang them on the tree.

RIGHT: A Gingerbread House cookie makes a lovely, if breakable, take-home present after a party. Wrap each one in cling film (plastic wrap) and tie it with pretty ribbons.

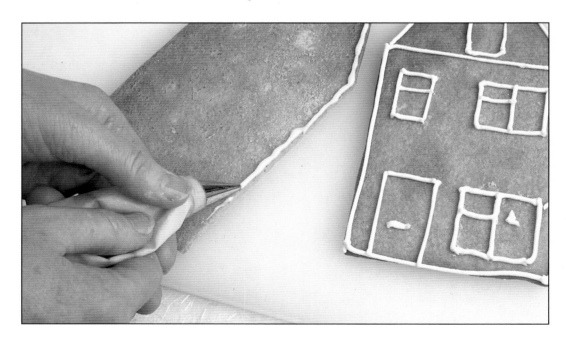

FOR THE GRAVY

giblets from the bird, washed
1 onion, skinned and quartered
4 cloves
1/2 lemon, roughly cut
slice of orange peel
1 stalk celery, sliced
1 carrot, sliced
1 litre/1³⁄₄pt/4¹⁄₃ cups water
1tbsp plain (all-purpose) flour
3tbsp red wine
salt and freshly ground black
pepper

1 Remove the goose from the refrigerator about 3 hours before cooking.

2 Wash the bird thoroughly inside and out and dry it with paper towels. Pull off any loose pieces of fat. Rub the bird inside and out with the cut lemon. Mix the salt and pepper and rub it well into the skin of the bird.

3 Spoon the stuffing into the neck end to plump out the shape of the goose. Tuck the neck flap over the stuffing and secure the flap underneath with a wooden skewer, or sew it in place with a darning needle threaded with fine twine. Pack the stuffing into the tail end of the bird. Truss the bird by tying the legs and wings together with fine string.

4 Prick the skin with a fork many times all over, inserting the prongs at a narrow angle so that you do not pierce the flesh, to release the succulent meat juices.

5 Calculate the cooking time at 20 minutes for each 450g/1lb, including the stuffing. Heat the oven to 230°C/450°F/Gas 8.

6 Place the goose, breast-side up, on a wire rack in a large roasting pan and cook it at a high temperature for 20 minutes. Pour off the melted fat.

7 Reduce the temperature to 180°C/350°F/Gas 4, then turn the bird breast-side down and continue cooking for 1¹⁄₂ hours. Turn the bird breast-side up again and continue cooking for the remainder of the calculated time. To test that the bird is cooked, pierce one of the thighs with a fine skewer at the thickest part; the juice should run clear and not be pink.

8 To cook the whole apples, slit the skins all around with a sharp knife. Pack the cavity with cranberries and place the fruit in a shallow baking dish. Dot the apples with half the butter and sprinkle with 1tbsp of the sugar. Cook the apples in the oven with the goose for the last 20 minutes of the cooking time. Do not allow them to become overcooked or they will collapse.

Alternatively, place the apples in a microwave-safe dish, cover them with plastic wrap and cook them in the microwave on High for 5–6 minutes.

9 To make the giblet gravy, put the giblets, the onion quarters stuck with cloves, the lemon, orange peel, celery and carrot into a large pan and pour on the water. Bring to the boil and skim off the foam that rises to the surface. Cover the pan and simmer for 1 hour.

10 When the goose is cooked, transfer it to a heated serving dish, cover it loosely with foil and keep it warm until needed.

11 Heat the remaining butter in a pan and fry the apple slices for 4–5 minutes on each side. Arrange them along the centre of the goose, sprinkle with the sugar and place a star anise pod in the centre of each.

12 Pour off the goose fat from the pan, reserving the juices, and stir in the flour over a low heat until it forms a roux. Strain the stock from the pan and gradually stir it into the roux. Add the wine and stir until the gravy is smooth, glossy and thickened.

Serves 8

ABOVE: Silver-sprayed nuts, fruits and pine cones have a distinctly Medieval quality, suitable for a banquet in which goose is served.

RAISIN AND PECAN STUFFING

INGREDIENTS

1 large onion, chopped
6 stalks celery, finely chopped
3tbsp water
150g/6oz/1½ cups fresh white
breadcrumbs
100g/4oz/⅔ cup seedless raisins
125g/5oz/1 cup pecans (or
walnuts), chopped
grated rind and juice of 1 orange
2 eggs, beaten
grated nutmeg
salt and freshly ground black
pepper

1 Place the onion and celery
in a small pan with the
water and simmer for about 5
minutes, or until the vegetables
are tender.

2 Turn the vegetables into a
bowl and stir in the
breadcrumbs, raisins, nuts,
orange rind and juice and the
eggs. Season to taste with
nutmeg, salt and pepper.

3 Allow to cool, then pack
into the goose.

Makes about 450g/1lb

APPLE SAUCE

INGREDIENTS

2 large cooking apples, peeled,
cored and chopped
2tbsp apple juice or dry cider
15g/½oz/1tbsp butter
1tbsp soft light brown sugar
1 star anise seedpod, plus 1 to
decorate
salt and freshly ground black
pepper

1 Place the apples in a pan
with the apple juice or
cider, the butter, sugar and one
of the star anise pods. Cook over
a moderate heat, uncovered, for
15 minutes, stirring from time to
time, or until the fruit is soft.

2 Remove the star anise and
pureé the fruit in a food
processor or blender. Season with
salt and pepper.

3 You can store the sauce in a
lidded container in the
freezer or refrigerator. Serve
hot, garnished with the
remaining star anise pod.

Serves 8

PRUNE SAUCE

INGREDIENTS

350g/12oz/2½ cups pitted, no-
soak prunes, chopped
1 medium cooking apple, peeled,
cored and chopped
grated rind and juice of ½ lemon
3tbsp red wine
5cm/2in cinnamon stick
salt and freshly ground black
pepper
fresh herb leaves, to garnish

1 Put the prunes, apple,
lemon rind and juice and
cinnamon stick in a pan and pour
on the wine. Cover the pan and
cook over a moderate heat until
the fruit is soft.

2 Remove the cinnamon and
pureé in a food processor or
blender. Season with salt and
pepper.

3 You can store the sauce in a
lidded container in the
refrigerator or freezer. Serve
hot, garnished with herb leaves.

Serves 8

*LEFT: Apple Sauce and Prune
Sauce are both tasty
accompaniments which offset
the richness of goose meat.*

ROAST BEEF

FOR MANY people, roast beef is a popular alternative to turkey or goose for the Christmas dinner. It may be one of the few times of the year when the number of family and friends gathered around the table makes it practicable to enjoy a large rib of beef or rolled sirloin; when it is possible to appreciate both the appearance and the flavour of such a succulent treat.

ROAST RIB OF BEEF

INGREDIENTS

2.5kg/5lb forerib of beef, on the bone
flour, for dredging
75g/3oz/1/2 cup dripping, melted and strained, or lard
salt and freshly ground black pepper

FOR THE GRAVY

1tbsp plain (all-purpose) flour
300ml/1/2pt/1 1/4 cups meat or vegetable stock, or water
5tbsp red wine

1 Heat the oven to 230°C/450°F/Gas 8. Dust the meat on all sides with flour but not, at this stage, with salt which would draw out the juices.

2 Place the dripping in a roasting pan and, when it is hot, stand the joint upright and roast it for 10 minutes. Baste it well with the hot dripping and reduce the heat to 180°C/350°F/Gas 4. Continue cooking, basting the meat frequently, for 1 3/4 hours for rare meat or 2 1/4 hours for well-done meat. If you have a meat thermometer, this should register 60°C/140°F for rare,

68–70°C/154–158°F for medium and 75–77°C/167–170°F for well-done meat.

3 When the joint is cooked to your satisfaction, remove it from the oven and transfer it to a warmed serving dish. Season the meat on all sides with salt and pepper and leave it in a warm place to 'rest' for 10–15 minutes while the juices settle.

4 To make the gravy, pour off most of the fat from the roasting pan (this will become dripping in which to cook another joint) and sprinkle the flour into the pan. Set it over a medium heat, stir until it forms a roux, then gradually pour on the stock or water and the wine. Bring to the boil, stirring, and season with salt and pepper. Serve hot.

5 Carve the meat in thin slices, asking guests whether they prefer a cut from the outside or from the inside which will be more rare. Serve the beef with Yorkshire Pudding. A sauce made of horseradish is another traditional accompaniment.

Serves 8

ABOVE: *Roast beef is a popular choice for Christmas dinner. Serve it with potatoes, Yorkshire pudding (popovers) and horseradish sauce.*

YORKSHIRE PUDDING (POPOVERS)

INGREDIENTS

*100g/4oz/1 cup plain (all-
purpose) flour
large pinch of salt
freshly ground black pepper
1 egg
250ml/8fl oz/1 cup milk
about 40g/1½oz/3tbsp dripping
or lard (shortening)*

1 Sift the flour and salt into a
bowl and stir in a few
grindings of pepper. Make a well
in the centre and add the egg.
Beat in half of the milk, drawing
the flour in from the sides of the
bowl, and beat until the mixture
is smooth.

2 Stir in the remaining milk,
and mix to a smooth batter.

3 Heat the oven to 220°C/
425°F/Gas 7. Put 1tsp of
fat into each of 8 deep muffin tins
or flat Yorkshire pudding tins
and place them in the oven until
the fat begins to smoke.

4 Stir the batter well and
pour it into the pans. Bake
in the oven for 20–25 minutes,
until the puddings (popovers) are
well risen and almost hollow.

Makes 8 puddings (popovers)

**BELOW: Individual Yorkshire
Puddings (Popovers)
accompany a medium-rare rib
of beef.**

THAWING TIMES FOR FROZEN BEEF

Bring the beef to room temperature before cooking it. If it
has been frozen, calculate the thawing times as follows:

Weight	*Thawed at room temperature – 18°C/65°F per 450g/1lb* hours	*Thawed in refrigerator 4°C/40°F per 450g/1lb* hours
joints under 1.5kg/3¼lb	1–2	3–4
joints over 1.5kg/3¼lb	2–3	6–7

ROASTING TIMES FOR BEEF JOINTS

There are several ways of achieving a perfectly-roasted
joint, and the recipe for Roast Rib of Beef is only one. It
may, for example, be more convenient for you to roast a
joint by the 'slow' method. Calculate the cooking times
according to the table below.

Joints	**Quick roasting** *230°C/450°F/Gas 8 for 10 minutes then reduce to 180°C/ 350°F/Gas 4 for:*	**Slow roasting** *170–180°C/ 325–350°F/ Gas 3–4*
Beef on the bone, e.g. rib and forerib	15 minutes per 450g/1lb, plus 15 minutes extra for rare; 20 minutes for medium; 25 minutes for well-done	25 minutes per 450g/1lb, plus 25 minutes extra for rare; 30 minutes for medium; 35 minutes for well-done
Beef without bone, e.g. rolled sirloin	20 minutes per 450g/1lb, plus 20 minutes extra for rare; 25 minutes for medium; 28 minutes for well-done	30 minutes per 450g/1lb, plus 30 minutes extra for rare; 33 minutes for medium; 38 minutes for well-done

HONEY-ROAST HAM

A ROAST BACON joint (cured ham roast) can be a succulent addition to the Christmas turkey or goose. Glazed with honey and mustard and studded with cloves, the joint is equally good served cold. It would be a substantial addition to a brunch party menu, would enhance a New Year buffet, and provides a satisfactory meal in moments when unexpectedly guests call.

HONEY-ROAST HAM

INGREDIENTS

2kg/4½lb boned gammon joint
(cured ham, leg or shoulder roast)
1 onion
cloves
2 bay leaves
few black peppercorns
twist of orange peel
small piece of fresh ginger
½ cinnamon stick
few stalks of parsley

FOR THE GLAZE

cloves
6tbsp clear honey
2tbsp whole grain mustard

1 Weigh the ham and calculate the cooking time at 20 minutes per 450g/1lb, plus 20 minutes extra.

2 Place the ham in a large pan and cover with cold water. Bring to the boil and remove from the heat. (This process is instead of soaking the joint overnight to draw off some of the salt used in curing the meat.) Pour off the water, rinse the pan and replace the joint. Cover it with cold water and add the onion, quartered and

stuck with cloves, and the remaining flavouring ingredients to taste. They give a slightly spicy flavour to the meat. Bring slowly to the boil, cover the pan and simmer for the calculated cooking time less 15 minutes. In the case of a ham weighing 2kg/4½lb, this would be 1 hour 35 minutes.

3 Remove the ham from the pan (reserve the stock for soups, casseroles and sauces) and allow it to cool slightly. Cut off the rind as evenly as possible and score the fat in a diamond pattern with a sharp knife. Heat the oven to 180°C/350°F/Gas 4.

4 Press the cloves into the fat at intervals. Mix together the honey and mustard and spread it over the skin. Wrap the ham in foil, leaving only the glazed area uncovered.

5 Place the ham, glazed-side up, in a roasting tin (pan) and bake in the oven for 15 minutes. Serve hot or cold.

Serves 8–10

ABOVE: The glazed joint is equally good hot or cold. It may be served with cranberry conserve, pineapple sauce or its traditional accompaniment, Cumberland sauce.

CUMBERLAND SAUCE

This is the traditional accompaniment to both hot and cold ham.

INGREDIENTS

150ml/¼pt/⅔ cup port
juice and grated rind of 1 orange
225g/8oz/1 cup redcurrant jelly
1tsp mustard powder
1tbsp water
salt and freshly ground black pepper

1 Put the port, orange juice, orange rind and redcurrant jelly into a small pan and bring to simmering point.

2 Mix together the mustard powder and water and stir into the sauce.

3 Season and simmer for 5 minutes. Do not allow to boil. Serve hot or cold.

Serves 6–8

LEFT: These decorations would benefit any holiday table. Tumblers are filled with cranberries, evergreens and candles.

ALTERNATIVE GLAZES AND COATINGS

Cranberry glaze Mix together 6tbsp Cranberry sauce, 2tbsp orange juice and 1tsp grated orange rind and spread over the diamond-cut fat on the ham.

Marmalade glaze Mix together 6tbsp coarse-cut chopped marmalade, 1tbsp whisky and 1tsp lemon juice and spread over the diamond-cut fat on the ham.

Sweet ginger glaze Mix together 150g/6oz/¾ cup demerara (light brown) sugar, 1tsp ground ginger and 2tbsp ginger syrup from a jar of preserved ginger and spread over the diamond-cut fat on the ham.

Sweet and sour glaze Mix together 4tbsp clear honey and 3tbsp red wine vinegar and spread over the diamond-cut fat on the ham.

Nuts and breadcrumb coating Mix together 150g/5oz/½ cup dry breadcrumbs, 2tsp chopped parsley, 2tbsp finely chopped walnuts or pecans, a pinch of salt and freshly ground black pepper and press firmly into the fat while it is still warm. Do not cut the fat into diamond shapes.

Scottish mealy coating Mix together 6tbsp fine oatmeal, 25g/1oz/2tbsp melted butter and 2tbsp chopped parsley and pat onto the fat. Do not cut it into diamond shapes.

Spiced crumbs Mix together 150g/5oz/½ cup dry breadcrumbs, 1tsp ground mace and 2tbsp demerara (light brown) sugar and pat onto the fat on the ham. Do not cut into diamond shapes.

A VEGETARIAN MEAL

Cooking for a vegetarian guest at Christmastime need present no problems. These two suggested recipes can be prepared at least partially in advance and served with style. Both would make an admirable post-Christmas meal for other poultry-weary appetites.

FOUR-VEGETABLE PEPPERS

INGREDIENTS

225g/8oz/2 cups lentils or split peas, soaked and drained
6tbsp olive oil
1 large onion, chopped
2 large cloves garlic, chopped
350g/12oz tomatoes
boiling water
2tbsp tomato purée
2tbsp dried oregano
1tbsp fresh chopped coriander
1 medium aubergine (eggplant), cut into 2.5cm/1in cubes
1/2tsp turmeric
1/2tsp paprika
salt and freshly ground black pepper
1/2 small cauliflower, cut into small florets (flowerets)
1 each large red, yellow, orange and green pepper

1 Cook the lentils in boiling, unsalted water in a covered pan for 30 minutes, or until they are just tender. Remove from the heat, drain and set aside.

2 Heat 2tbsp of the oil in a pan and fry the onion and garlic over moderate heat until the onions are translucent.

3 Dip the tomatoes into boiling water, remove them with a draining spoon and peel off the skins. Roughly chop the tomatoes and add them to the onions and garlic. Stir in the tomato purée, oregano, coriander and aubergine (eggplant) and season with turmeric, paprika, salt and pepper. Bring the mixture to the boil, lower the heat and simmer, stirring occasionally, for about 20 minutes, until the mixture forms a thick paste.

4 Steam or boil the cauliflower for about 3–4 minutes, until it is barely tender.

5 Stir the lentils and cauliflower into the tomato mixture, taste and adjust seasoning if necessary. The mixture may be placed in a covered container and stored overnight in the refrigerator, or frozen.

6 Heat the oven to 190°C/375°F/Gas 5. Cut a thin slice from the top of each pepper and remove the cores and seeds. Spoon the vegetable mixture into the peppers and replace the caps. Pour the oil into a baking dish and brush over the peppers.

7 Bake in the oven, uncovered, for 40–45 minutes, until the peppers are tender but have not collapsed. Serve hot.

Serves 4

ABOVE: *Red, yellow, orange and green peppers filled with lentils and split peas and other vegetables make an extremely colourful combination.*

BELOW: *Straight from the oven, the dish benefits visually from the contrast of colours and textures and has an irresistible, spicy aroma.*

CHESTNUT AND MUSHROOM LOAF

You can freeze the unbaked dish. Allow it to thaw at room temperature overnight before baking.

INGREDIENTS

3 tbsp olive oil, plus extra for
brushing
2 medium onions, chopped
2 cloves garlic, chopped
75g/3oz button mushrooms,
chopped
100ml/4fl oz/½ cup red wine
225g/8oz can unsweetened chestnut
purée
50g/2oz/1 cup fresh wholewheat
breadcrumbs
salt and freshly ground black
pepper
75g/3oz fresh cranberries, plus
extra to decorate
water
450g/1lb pastry
flour for dusting
1 small egg, beaten, to glaze

1 Heat the oven to 190°C/
375°F/Gas 5. Heat the oil
in a pan and fry the onions over a
moderate heat until they are
translucent. Add the garlic and
mushrooms and fry for a further
3 minutes. Pour on the wine, stir
well and simmer over a low heat
until it has evaporated, stirring
occasionally. Remove from the
heat, stir in the chestnut purée
and breadcrumbs and season with
salt and pepper. Cool.

2 Simmer the cranberries in a
little water for 5 minutes
then drain and cool.

3 Lightly brush a 600-ml/1-
pt loaf tin (bread pan) with
oil. Roll out the pastry to a
thickness of about 3mm/⅛in.
Cut rectangles to fit the base and
sides of the pan and press them in
place. Press the edges to seal
them. Cut a piece of pastry to fit
the top of the pan and set it aside.

4 Spoon half of the chestnut
mixture into the pan and
level the surface. Sprinkle on the
cranberries and cover with the
remaining chestnut mixture.
Cover the filling with the pastry
lid and pinch the edges to join
them to the sides. Cut holly
leaves or other shapes from the
pastry trimmings.

5 Brush the pastry top and
the decorative shapes with
the beaten egg and arrange the
shapes in a pattern on top.

6 Bake the loaf in the oven
for 35 minutes, or until the
top is golden brown. Decorate the
top with cranberries. Serve hot.

Serves 8

THE VEGETABLES

THE VEGETABLES accompanying the main dish have a very high standard to live up to and should be planned, timed and presented with equal care.

If you choose fresh vegetables, buy them as close to Christmas Day as possible, making them the last purchase on the shopping list. Buy them from an outlet which has a good reputation and a quick turn-over, and do not be afraid to scrutinize them carefully. Green vegetables such as Brussels sprouts and broccoli should be crisp and bright green. Limpness and yellowing are signs of age. Cauliflowers should be tightly closed and pure creamy-white. Dark patches or opened florets (flowerets) are tell-tale signs of lack of freshness. Root vegetables should be crisp and firm. Discoloured and limp leaves are the first signs of a fast-approaching sell-by date.

BRUSSELS SPROUTS AND CHESTNUTS

INGREDIENTS
1kg/2¼lb Brussels sprouts
about 450ml/¾pt/2 cups water or
chicken stock
salt (optional)
25g/1oz/2tbsp butter
225g-/8oz-can chestnuts, rinsed
and drained
freshly ground black pepper

1 Cut a slice from the base of each Brussels sprout, cut a cross in the base of large ones so that they cook evenly, and tear off the outer leaves.

2 Bring the water (salted, if you wish) or chicken stock to the boil in a pan, place a steamer over it, add the sprouts and cover. Steam over boiling liquid for 6–8 minutes, according to size, until the sprouts are just tender.

3 Melt the butter in a frying pan, add the sprouts and chestnuts and stir them carefully over a medium heat for 2–3 minutes. Transfer them to a warm serving dish, season with pepper, cover with foil and keep warm until ready to serve.

Serves 8

LEFT: Brussels Sprouts with Chestnuts and Caramelized Carrots and Onions make colourful vegetable dishes.

CARAMELIZED CARROTS AND BUTTON (PEARL) ONIONS

INGREDIENTS
750g/1½lb carrots, trimmed,
scraped and cut into thin rings
225g/8oz button (pearl) onions,
peeled
water to cover
salt
40g/1½oz butter
6tbsp chicken stock
1tbsp sugar
freshly ground black pepper

1 Put the carrots and onions into a pan, cover with salted water and bring to the boil over a high heat. Boil for 1 minute, then drain the vegetables.

2 Return them to the pan, add the butter, chicken stock and sugar and bring to the boil over a moderate heat, stirring occasionally. Cover the pan and simmer over a low heat for about 10 minutes until the vegetables have absorbed all the liquid and are glossy and dry.

3 Season with salt and pepper and transfer to a warm serving dish. Cover with foil and keep warm until ready to serve.

Serves 8

LEFT: Vegetable Bundles of carrot, parsnip and celery are tied with chive leaves. Cauliflower florets and snap peas are arranged in the shape of a flower and decorated with a tomato rose.

VEGETABLE BUNDLES

INGREDIENTS
450g/1lb carrots, trimmed and scrubbed
450g/1lb parsnips, trimmed and scrubbed
4 stalks celery, washed
about 450ml/3/4pt/2 cups water or chicken stock
salt (optional)
a few chive leaves
25g/1oz/2tbsp butter, melted

1 Cut the carrots, parsnips and celery into matchstick strips 7.5cm/3in long. (Reserve the trimmings to flavour soup.) Steam the vegetables over boiling, salted water or stock for 2–3 minutes, or until they are barely tender.

2 Remove the vegetables from the steamer and set them aside to cool.

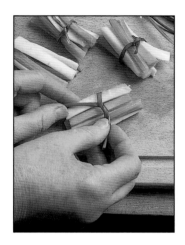

3 Separate the vegetables into groups of 2 or 3 of a kind and tie them into bundles with chive leaves. You can prepare the vegetables to this point the day before you plan to serve them. In this case, cover them with plastic wrap and store them in the refrigerator.

4 To reheat the vegetables, steam them for 1–2 minutes over boiling liquid. Or cover them with plastic wrap and heat them in a microwave at full power for 1–1 1/2 minutes. Arrange the vegetables on a heated serving dish and brush them with melted butter.

Serves 8

CAULIFLOWER AND PEA 'FLOWER'

INGREDIENTS
1 cauliflower, cut into florets (flowerets)
225g/8oz snap (edible pod) peas, trimmed or mange-tout (snow) peas
about 450ml/3/4pt/2 cups water or chicken stock
salt (optional)
1 firm tomato
15g/1/2oz/1tbsp butter, melted

1 Steam the cauliflower and peas over boiling salted water or stock for 5–7 minutes, until they are just tender.

2 Using a sharp knife or a rotary peeler, peel a long strip about 1.5cm/1/2in wide from the tomato. Coil the strip and pull up the centre to form the shape of a rose.

3 Remove the cauliflower and peas. Arrange the peas in a wheel pattern in the centre of a warmed serving dish. Arrange the cauliflower around the outside and place the tomato rose in the centre. Brush the vegetables with melted butter, cover the dish with foil and keep warm.

Serves 6–8

CHRISTMAS PUDDING AND MINCE PIES

FOR MANY people, this is the moment they have been waiting for; the moment when the lights are turned down low and the host or hostess brings in the Christmas pudding, wreathed in dramatic blue flames.

It is a matter of family custom whether the mince pies, are enjoyed at the same time as the pudding or as a second dessert course (in which case they must be kept warm or reheated, so that they will be hot enough to melt the traditional topping of rum or brandy butter).

It is also a matter of preference whether the 'hard sauce' is flavoured with one or other spirit – there will often be a no-alcohol version for the children – and whether there is custard sauce, creamy mousseline sauce or a slightly tipsy low-fat alternative.

CUMBERLAND RUM BUTTER

INGREDIENTS
225g/8oz/1 cup unsalted butter,
at room temperature
225g/8oz/1 cup soft light brown
sugar
6tbsp dark rum, or to taste

1 Beat the butter and sugar until the mixture is soft, creamy and pale in colour. Gradually add the rum almost drop by drop, beating to incorporate each addition before adding more. If you are too hasty in adding the rum, the mixture may curdle.

2 When all the rum has been added, spoon the mixture into a covered container and chill for at least 1 hour. It will keep well in the refrigerator for about 4 weeks.

Makes about 450g/1lb

RIGHT: In true Victorian tradition, a rich, dark and round Christmas pudding is decorated with a sprig of holly and flamed with brandy. A ruched ribbon around the base is a festive finishing touch.

ABOVE: Individual puddings make an attractive alternative presentation. Here they are ringed around and garnished with lightly poached cranberries.

MOUSSELINE SAUCE

INGREDIENTS
4 eggs
2 egg yolks
50g/2oz/¼ cup caster (superfine) sugar
150ml/¼pt/⅔ cup single (light) cream

1 Put all the ingredients in a double boiler or a bowl over a pan of simmering water. Do not allow the water to come into contact with the base of the bowl or upper pan.

2 Whisk until the mixture is pale and frothy. It should have a thick, creamy consistency. Serve at once.

Makes about 450ml/16floz

ORANGE BUTTER

This non-alcoholic sauce may be made for children, but it has many adult followers, too.

INGREDIENTS
100g/4oz/½ cup unsalted butter, at room temperature
100g/4oz/½ cup soft light brown sugar
grated rind of 2 oranges
juice of 1 orange

Make the sauce in a similar way to Cumberland Rum Butter, beating the orange rind with the butter and sugar and adding the orange juice gradually.

Makes about 225g/8oz

RIGHT: Mince pies decorated with holly-leaf shapes and dusted with icing (confectioners') sugar.

CUSTARD SAUCE

INGREDIENTS
4 eggs
75g/3oz/⅓ cup caster (superfine) sugar
150ml/¼pt/⅔ cup milk
300ml/½pt/⅔ cup single (light) cream
2 bay leaves

1 Beat together the eggs, sugar and milk. Beat in the cream and pour the mixture into a double boiler or a bowl over a pan of simmering water. Do not allow the water to come into contact with the base of the bowl.

2 Add the bay leaves and stir constantly with a wooden spoon for about 15 minutes, until the sauce thickens. Remove the bay leaves. Serve hot or cold.

Makes about 600ml/1pt

TIPSY YOGHURT

INGREDIENTS
4tbsp clear honey, plus extra for serving (optional)
3tbsp brandy
grated rind of 1 orange
300ml/½pt/1¼ cups Greek-style yoghurt

1 Stir the honey, brandy and orange rind until they are well blended, then gradually stir in the yoghurt.

2 Spoon the sauce into a covered container and chill in the refrigerator. If you wish, drizzle a little extra honey over the sauce an hour or so before serving. Transfer it to a serving dish before doing so.

Makes about 400ml/14floz

SPOILT FOR CHOICE

I F YOU wish to offer an alternative dessert for the Christmas meal, your guests will be spoilt for choice between refreshing Caramelized Oranges, Chocolate Meringue Yule Log, and Nesselrode Ice-cream.

CHOCOLATE MERINGUE YULE LOG

INGREDIENTS
6 eggs, separated
125g/5oz/⅔ cup caster (superfine) sugar
50g/2oz/½ cup unsweetened cocoa powder, sifted
300ml/½pt/1¼ cups double (heavy) cream, whipped

FOR THE TOPPING
2 egg whites
100g/4oz/½ cup caster (superfine) sugar
cranberries and holly leaves, to decorate (optional)

1 Heat the oven to 180°C/ 375°F/Gas 4. Line a Swiss roll tin (jelly roll pan) with non-stick baking paper.

2 Whisk the egg yolks until they are pale and creamy. Add the sugar and cocoa powder and continue whisking until the mixture thickens enough to hold its shape.

3 In a separate bowl, whisk the egg whites until they form soft peaks.

4 Spoon a little of the egg white into the cocoa mixture then carefully fold it into the remaining egg white.

5 Spread the mixture into the tin (pan). Bake in the oven for 20 minutes. Cool.

6 Sprinkle a little caster (superfine) sugar over a sheet of baking paper on a work surface. Invert the tin (pan) over the paper and shake it to release the cake. Peel off the paper from the base.

7 Spread the cream over the cake and roll it up from one long side. Cut a piece diagonally from one end. Place the main 'log' on a heat-proof dish and with the 'branch' at an angle.

8 For the topping, whisk the egg whites until they are stiff and glossy. Sprinkle on half the sugar and whisk until the meringue is stiff again. Fold in the remaining sugar.

9 Spread the meringue over the log to cover it completely. Return it to the oven for 6–7 minutes, until the meringue is pale brown. Allow the meringue to cool, then decorate it with cranberries and leaves, if you wish.

Serves 8

BELOW: Caramelized Oranges, Chocolate Meringue Yule Log and Nesselrode Ice- cream.

LEFT: *A hand-painted plate, a crisp napkin with a gold-edged bow and a shining blue star decoration – a stylish presentation for the festive meal.*

4 When the custard is cool, fold in the whipped cream and stir in the soaked fruit and wine.

5 Pour the mixture into a decorative 1.2-l/2-pt ring mould, cover and freeze for at least 4 hours.

6 Remove from the freezer and leave the ice-cream at room temperature for about 30 minutes before serving.

7 Fill the centre of the ice-cream with crystallized (candied) fruits.

Serves 8

CARAMELIZED ORANGES WITH PRALINE

INGREDIENTS
8 large oranges
175g/6oz/3/4 cup granulated sugar
100ml/4fl oz/1/2 cup water
75g/3oz/1/2 cup unblanched almonds
75g/3oz/1/3 cup caster (superfine) sugar
·oil, for brushing

1 Brush a small baking tin (pan) with oil. First make the praline. Place the almonds and caster (superfine) sugar in a small, heavy pan over a low heat. When the sugar has melted and become dark brown liquid caramel, stir with a metal spoon to toast the nuts on all sides. Turn the mixture into the oiled tin and leave to set.

2 Place the oranges in the freezer for 10 minutes.

3 Put the sugar and water into a pan, stir over a moderate heat to dissolve, then bring to the boil and boil for 5 minutes to form a syrup. Remove from the heat.

4 Using a very sharp knife, remove the peel and pith from each orange, working over a dish to retain the juice. Slice the oranges as thinly as possible – an electric carving knife is useful for this – and arrange the slices in a serving dish.

5 Pour the orange juice into the syrup. Crush the praline into small pieces, using nutcrackers or a rolling pin.

6 Pour the syrup over the oranges and, just before serving, scatter on the praline. Serve chilled.

Serves 8

NESSELRODE ICE-CREAM

INGREDIENTS
300ml/1/2pt/1 1/4 cups single (light) cream
5 egg yolks
100g/4oz/1/2 cup sugar
1/2tsp vanilla extract
75–100g/3–4oz unsweetened chestnut purée
50g/2oz/1/3 cup seedless raisins
50g/2oz/1/3 cup sultanas (golden raisins)
50g/2oz/1/3 cup crystallized (candied) cherries, chopped
50g/2oz/1/3 cup Candied orange peel, chopped
150ml/1/4pt/2/3 cup Marsala or sweet sherry
300ml/1/2pt/1 1/4 cups double (heavy) cream, whipped
Crystallized fruits, to serve

1 Pour the single (light) cream into a heavy pan and bring it to the boil. Pour it over the egg yolks in a bowl and beat well. Stir in the sugar and vanilla extract.

2 Pour the mixture into the top of a double boiler or a bowl over a pan of simmering water. Do not allow the water to touch the base of the pan or the mixture may overheat. Stir until the mixture thickens, then strain into a bowl and stir in the chestnut purée. Set aside to cool.

3 Meanwhile, place the raisins, sultanas (golden raisins), cherries and orange peel in a bowl, pour on the Marsala and leave to soak.

SWEET TREATS

Just when everyone thinks the meal is finished, you could offer guests an irresistible selection of chocolates and candies, sweetmeats and sweet treats. Call them what you will, and serve them at the table or later with coffee, guests are guaranteed to try just one – or two – of these wicked temptations.

If you plan ahead and preserve a selection of fruits and flowers by the crystallizing and sugaring processes, you can put on the style with a piled-high bowl that would inspire an artist. Select and arrange fruits and petals so that their contrasting colours and textures bring out the best visual qualities in each other.

Make quick and easy marzipan logs and give them the Midas look by dipping them first in golden granulated (light brown) sugar and then dusting them lightly with edible gold powder available from specialist shops. Dip others in melted bitter (semi-sweet) chocolate and, before it has time to set, press in a gold- or silver-coated candy.

Continue the temptation scene with a dish of chocolate truffles coated, for a contrast of flavours and appearances, with white chocolate, milk chocolate and bitter (semi-sweet) chocolate. Store them in a box in the refrigerator, but remember to bring them to room temperature before serving. They are not meant to have the texture of ice cream!

For a completely different flavour, and to tempt guests who may not care for chocolate, make a batch of sugared nuts. You can use walnuts, pecans, almonds or Brazil nuts; coat them in dark brown sugar spiced with curry powder and you will spend the rest of the holiday writing out the recipe for appreciative guests.

SUGARED NUTS

INGREDIENTS

oil, for brushing
100ml/4fl oz/½ cup water
225g/8oz/1 cup soft dark brown sugar
1 tbsp medium curry powder
large pinch of salt
450g/1lb shelled nuts such as walnuts, pecans, almonds or Brazil nuts

1 Lightly brush a baking sheet with oil.

2 Put the water, sugar, curry powder and salt into a large, heavy pan. Cover the pan and bring the mixture to the boil.

3 Remove the lid and continue boiling until the mixture reaches 120°C/248°F, the 'hard-ball' stage, when a small amount of the syrup dropped into a cup of cold water forms a ball, but still feels sticky when you mould it between your fingers.

4 Lower the heat and, holding the nuts in a pair of tongs or well-scrubbed tweezers, dip them one by one quickly into the syrup so that it coats them on all sides. Place the nuts on the greased baking sheet and leave them in a dry, warm, airy place until the coating has set.

Makes 450g/1lb

RIGHT: A pewter dish of fresh and sugared fruits decorated with pale pink roses makes a tempting offering at the end of a meal.

MARZIPAN LOGS

INGREDIENTS
225g/8oz Marzipan, at room temperature
100g/4oz/¾ cup Candied orange peel, chopped
2tbsp orange liqueur, or orange juice
1tbsp golden granulated (light brown) sugar
edible gold powder
75g/3oz bitter (semi-sweet) chocolate, melted
gold-coated sweets (candies)

1 Knead the marzipan until it is soft and pliable. Mix in the chopped peel (it is easier to do this with your fingers) and gradually mix in the liqueur or orange juice. Set aside for about 1 hour, to dry.

LEFT: A selection of truffles coated with white chocolate, milk chocolate and bitter (semi-sweet) chocolate.

ABOVE: Marzipan Logs. Some are coated in bitter (semi-sweet) chocolate, others dipped in golden granulated sugar and dusted with edible gold powder.

2 Break off small pieces of the mixture, about the size of pecan nuts, and roll them into log shapes.

3 Dip the tops of half of the marzipan logs in the sugar and brush them lightly with edible gold powder.

4 Dip the other half of the logs in the melted chocolate – it is easiest to do this if you pierce them with a wooden toothpick. Place the chocolate-dipped logs on non-stick baking paper and press a gold-coated sweet (candy) in the centre of each. When the logs are dry, store them in a box in the refrigerator. Bring them to room temperature before serving.

THE CHEESEBOARD AND THE WINES

WHETHER YOU offer guests the cheeseboard before or after the dessert is of little consequence, except for the order in which you serve the wines.

In either case, it is advisable to offer a small selection of cheeses carefully chosen for the variety of texture, flavour and appearance. If the cheese is served before the dessert, guests will be aware of the continuing feast that is to come. If you serve it afterwards, they may only have room for the smallest of tastings.

You may decide to offer a selection of, say, six cheeses in sections small enough to excite the palate without overwhelming the diner. Such a selection should include at least one or preferably two hard cheeses like Cheddar, one blue-veined type in addition to Stilton, one semi-hard variety such as Port Salut, and perhaps two creamy cheeses. If you can include at least one which is a little unusual or special, so much the better.

Think carefully about the cheeseboard itself, which does not have to be a board at all. You may use a serving dish, from your dinner set, an antique dish or large decorative plate, or even a small silver tray. If you do opt for a 'high-days and holidays' container check that it sits well with the tablecloth and tableware you plan to use.

Take the cheeses from the refrigerator an hour or two in advance of serving so that they have time to return to their full flavour potential. Cover them loosely with a cloth and keep them in a not-too-warm room. Look critically at the cheeses and decide whether they appear as appetizing as you would like. They may be visually improved by a small decorative garnish cut from peppers, olives or gherkins.

BELOW: A cheeseboard that offers variety. There is a heart-shaped goats' cheese, a wedge of creamy Cambozola and a small round Munster, a piece of mature English Cheddar, black wax Cheddar and Port Salut decorated with a gherkin fan and olive 'petal'.

LEFT: You may like to 'pass the port' at the dinner table, or offer guests this traditional fortified wine as a digestif with coffee in the living room.

THE WINES

If you have served Champagne or Champagne cocktails before the meal, you may like to serve a chilled dry Champagne with the first course. It would be a superb accompaniment to both the Gravad lax and the Melon and Cranberry Basket.

If your choice of aperitif has been chilled dry sherry or chilled white port, either of these, too, could be served with the opening course. If your preference is for a table wine, the Gravad lax would be well complemented by a dry, fairly full-bodied white wine such as Alsatian Riesling or Gerwürztraminer, and the fruit cocktail by a wine of similar dryish character such as an Alsatian Muscat or a Sancerre.

Moving on to the main course and it is a matter of personal preference whether turkey and goose are best complemented by red or white wines. If your choice is for a

white wine, then a good, full-flavoured white Burgundy should have enough 'body' to compete successfully with the stuffing and other accompaniments. Goose, especially, is favoured by a crisp and rather fine Riesling from the Mosel or Alsace regions.

If your choice is for a red wine, then it is again important to take into account the diversity of flavours to be encountered in the stuffing. Apricots and raisins, cranberries, apples, herbs and spices have more assertive flavours than the meat itself, especially chicken or turkey, and call for a full-bodied, full-flavoured wine.

As for the dessert, it takes a superb dessert wine to live up to the sense of occasion created by a gleaming, glistening, pudding. Your choice may rest on a great (and expensive) Sauternes, a lightly honeyed sweet wine from the Loire, or Hungarian Tokay.

CHRISTMAS CAKES

CHRISTMAS WOULD not be Christmas for a great many families without a traditional cake. No matter how sumptuous the Christmas dinner only the most resolute guest will refuse a small slice of rich fruit cake covered with butter-yellow almond paste and frosted with royal icing.

This round cake is covered with the smoothest of smooth snow-white icing, and decorated with piped whirls reminiscent of drifting snow. Silver dragées – an edible confection you can buy in specialist shops – highlight the edging and represent glistening baubles on the central decoration, a moulded Christmas tree design. A tartan ribbon encircling the cake is matched by a miniature bow on the tree.

You can make the cake at least a month before Christmas; the flavour and texture will be all the better for this maturing time. Close-wrap the cake in a double thickness of foil and store it in an airtight tin. You may, if you wish, 'feed' the cake with a few drops of brandy once or twice a week, to give it an even more festive flavour. Cover the cake with almond paste a week or so before Christmas, and ice it before your kitchen schedule becomes really hectic.

CHRISTMAS CAKE

The quantities given are enough to make and decorate one 17.5-cm/7-in square cake.

INGREDIENTS
450g/1lb/2²/₃ cups currants
225g/8oz/1¹/₃ cups seedless raisins
100g/4oz/²/₃ cup sultanas (golden raisins)
100g/4oz/³/₄ cup Candied orange peel, chopped
4tbsp brandy
225g/8oz/2 cups plain (all-purpose) flour
1tsp salt
1tsp ground cinnamon
¹/₄tsp grated nutmeg
225g/8oz/1 cup soft light brown sugar
225g/8oz/1 cup unsalted butter, at room temperature
4 eggs
100g/4oz/²/₃ cup blanched almonds, chopped
grated rind and juice of 1 orange

FOR THE ALMOND PASTE
175g/6oz/1¹/₂ cups icing (confectioners') sugar, plus extra for dusting
175g/6oz/³/₄ cup caster (superfine) sugar
2 eggs
1 egg yolk (reserve the egg white)
2–3 drops vanilla extract
1tbsp lemon juice
350g/12oz/3 good cups ground almonds

FOR THE ROYAL ICING
3 egg whites
about 550g/1¹/₄lb/5 cups icing (confectioners') sugar
1tsp glycerin
2–3 drops green food colouring

FOR THE DECORATION
silver dragées
2.5cm/1in-wide tartan ribbon
6mm/¹/₄in-wide tartan ribbon

RIGHT: Covered with royal icing, this traditional Christmas Cake glitters with silver dragées.

LEFT: An alternative decoration features gold dragées and designs piped in icing.

1 Line a 20-cm/8-in round cake tin (pan) with non-stick baking paper.

2 Place the currants, raisins, sultanas (golden raisins) and orange peel in a bowl, pour on the brandy and stir well. Cover and set aside for at least 4 hours, or overnight.

3 To cook the cake, heat the oven to 140°C/275°F/Gas

1. Sift the flour, salt and spices into a bowl. Beat the sugar and butter together in a large mixing bowl until the texture is pale and creamy. Beat the eggs one at a time into the butter mixture, beating well between each addition to prevent the mixture curdling. Fold in the flour and spices, using a metal spoon, stir in the soaked fruit, the almonds and the orange rind and juice.

4 Spoon the mixture into the prepared tin (pan) and level the top. Cover the top of the cake with a double thickness of non-stick baking paper and bake in the oven for 4¼–4½ hours.

5 Stand the cake tin (pan) to cool on a wire rack. When it is completely cold, remove it from the tin, wrap it in a double thickness of foil and store it in an airtight container.

6 To make the almond paste, sift all the sugar into a heatproof bowl and stir in the eggs and extra egg yolk. Place the bowl over a pan of simmering water and whisk until the mixture thickens, about 10 minutes. Remove the bowl from the heat and stir in the vanilla and lemon juice and beat until the mixture is cool. Stir in the ground almonds, form the paste into a ball and knead on a board lightly dusted with icing (confectioners') sugar until it is smooth.

7 Cut off one-third of the paste and roll it on a lightly-sugared board to a circle just larger than the top of the cake. Brush the reserved egg white on the top of the cake. Invert the cake over the paste, and with a sharp knife, trim the paste to fit the cake. Pat the trimmings onto the remaining piece of the paste and roll it out to make a strip about 33cm/13in long and 20cm/8in wide. Cut the strip in half lengthways. Brush the sides of the cake with the remaining egg white and press the almond paste strips onto it. Trim it neatly on all sides and smooth the joins with the back of a spoon.

8 Cover the cake with non-stick baking paper and set it aside for 5–7 days, until you are ready to ice it.

9 To make the royal icing, place the egg whites in a bowl and sift in the icing (confectioners') sugar a little at a time, until the mixture is thick but pliable. It should fall easily from the spoon. Whisk the icing for about 10 minutes until it holds its shape and stands in stiff peaks. Stir in the glycerine.

10 Set aside about one-fifth of the royal icing for the decoration. Spread the remainder evenly over the top and sides of the cake, using a

palette knife. Divide the remaining icing into 2. Spoon half into a piping bag fitted with 1.5-cm/½-in fluted nozzle.

11 Stand the cake on a turntable and pipe swirls of the white icing around the base and top. Press silver dragées at the base of each swirl.

12 Colour the remaining icing with green colouring and mould a tree shape. Place the decoration in the centre of the cake and press on silver dragées.

13 Leave the cake overnight, covered lightly with a cloth, so that the icing can dry out.

14 Pin ribbon around the cake and tie a bow. Tie a small bow and attach it to the tree decoration with royal icing.

Makes 1 20-cm/8-in round cake

BAKING TIPS

1 To line a round cake tin (pan) measure the circumference of the tin (pan) and cut a double strip of non-stick baking paper 2.5cm/1in longer, to allow for overlap, and 2.5cm/1in deeper, to allow for turning. Draw around the base with a pencil and cut out.

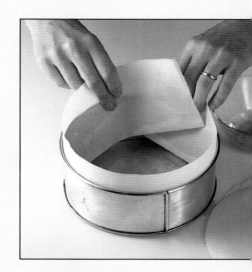

2 Brush the base and sides of the tin (pan) with vegetable oil. Place the double strip of paper inside the tin (pan), pressing against the sides. Place the cut-out base piece in the bottom of the pan.

3 Cut a double strip of brown paper long enough to wrap around the outside of the tin, 2.5cm/1in longer to allow a small overlap, and 2.5cm/1in taller than the tin (pan) tin.

4 Brush the base and side papers with vegetable oil. Place the brown paper around the outside of the tin, and tie securely with string. Line a baking (cookie) sheet with 3 or 4 layers of brown paper and stand the tin (pan) on top.

5 To test the cake is done, insert a warmed skewer into the centre of the cake. If it comes out clean it is ready. If not, return the cake to the oven and re-test at 10 minute intervals.

FRUIT CAKES WITH A DIFFERENCE

I F YOU wish to serve a cake that is even richer, more moist and even more self-indulgent than the traditional Christmas cake, try this Creole Christmas Cake recipe. However, be prepared for the shock to the budget occasioned by the inclusion of three kinds of spirit and one fortified wine!

The cake is made in celebration of Christmas and other festivals in the West Indies where it has become *the* cake for high-days and holidays among the sugar planters.

By contrast, and in a lighter vein, there is a recipe for Dundee Cake, a preferred option for those who do not care for or cannot take the richer delights of the season.

LEFT: *Oozing with the fruits of a week-long marinade, the Creole Cake is a tempting tea-time treat.*

CREOLE CHRISTMAS CAKE

This is a plan-ahead cake which is made in two stages. First the fruit and spices are soaked in the alcohol for 1 week, and the remaining ingredients are added just before baking. It is best made at least 4 weeks before Christmas.

INGREDIENTS

450g/1lb/2²/₃ cups seedless raisins
225g/8oz/1¹/₃ cups currants
100g/4oz/²/₃ cup sultanas (golden raisins)
100g/4oz/²/₃ cup pitted no-soak prunes, chopped
100g/4oz/³/₄ cup candied orange peel, chopped
100g/4oz/²/₃ cup chopped walnuts
4tbsp soft dark brown sugar
1tsp vanilla extract
1tsp ground cinnamon
¹/₄tsp grated nutmeg
¹/₄tsp ground cloves
1tsp salt
4tbsp dark rum
4tbsp brandy
4tbsp whisky
4tbsp port

FOR THE SECOND STAGE

225g/8oz/2 cups plain (all-purpose) flour
1tsp baking powder
225g/8oz/1 cup demerara (light brown) sugar
225g/8oz/1 cup unsalted butter, at room temperature, plus extra for greasing
4 eggs, beaten

FOR THE TOPPING

225g/8oz/1 cup apricot jam, sieved
2tbsp water
pecan halves, to decorate
crystallized tangerine or kumquat slices, to decorate

1 Put all the first list of ingredients into a large, heavy pan, stir and mix well and heat very gently to simmering point. On no account allow the mixture to boil, or the flavour of the alcohol will be lost. Simmer, still very gently, for 15 minutes.

2 Remove the pan from the heat and set aside to cool. Pour the mixture into a lidded jar and leave in the refrigerator for 7 days, stirring at least once every day.

3 To cook the cake, line a 22.5-cm/9-in round cake tin (pan) with a double thickness of non-stick baking paper and grease it well. Heat the oven to 140°C/275°F/Gas 1.

4 Place the flour, baking powder, sugar and butter in a large mixing bowl and beat until smooth. Beat in the eggs, a little at a time, until the mixture is smooth and well blended.

5 Gradually fold in the fruit mixture and stir until it is well blended. Lack of care at this stage could result in an uneven distribution of the fruit.

6 Spoon the mixture into the prepared tin and level the surface. Bake in the centre of the oven for 3 hours, then cover with a double thickness of non-stick baking paper or foil and continue baking for 1 hour, or until the cake feels springy when pressed in the centre.

7 Transfer the tin to a wire rack and leave it to cool. When the cake is completely cold, remove it from the tin, peel off the baking papers and wrap it closely in two thicknesses of foil. The cake will keep well for up to 1 year.

8 A day or two before serving, decorate the top of the cake. Heat the sieved apricot jam and water in a small pan and brush half of it over the top of the cake. Arrange the nuts and kumquat slices in rows or rings and brush them with the remaining apricot glaze.

Makes 1 22.5-cm/9-in cake

DUNDEE CAKE

INGREDIENTS
225g/8oz/1 cup unsalted butter, softened
225g/8oz/1 cup caster (superfine) sugar
grated rind of 1 orange
5 eggs
225g/8oz/2 cups plain (all-purpose) flour, sifted
50g/2oz/⅓ cup ground almonds
100g/4oz/⅔ cup currants
100g/4oz/⅔ cup sultanas (golden raisins)
100g/4oz/⅔ cup seedless raisins
50g/2oz/⅓ cup Candied orange peel, chopped

FOR THE TOPPING
50g/2oz/⅓ cup blanched halved almonds

1 Line a 17.5-cm/7-in round cake tin (pan) with a double thickness of non-stick baking paper . Heat the oven to 150°C/300°F/Gas 2.

2 Beat the butter, sugar and orange rind until the mixture is light and fluffy. Beat in the eggs one at a time with 1 tbsp of the flour. Gradually fold in the remaining flour with a large metal spoon. Stir in the almonds, currants, sultanas (golden raisins), raisins and chopped peel and stir until they are evenly distributed.

3 Spoon the mixture into the prepared tin (pan), level the top and arrange the almonds in a wheel pattern.

4 Bake in the centre of the oven for 2½–3 hours, until a skewer inserted into the centre of the cake comes out clean.

5 Cool the cake in the tin (pan) on a wire rack. When it is cold, remove it from the tin (pan), remove the baking papers and closely wrap it in a double thickness of foil. Store in an airtight tin. It should keep well for 6 months.

Makes 1 17.5-cm/7-in cake

ABOVE: A lighter alternative to a rich fruit cake, Dundee Cake is traditionally decorated with rings of blanched almonds.

FESTIVE FOOD AND DRINKS

Welcome and pamper your Christmas guests with drinks that sparkle and bubble, with colourful cocktails tingling with ice, and with mulls and punches heady with the aroma of fruit and spices, spirits and wine.

Throughout the holidays there may be times when only chilled Champagne or classic Champagne cocktails will match the mood of the moment. At other times it may be more appropriate to serve a heart-warming mull that makes it easy for guests to be of good cheer.

Whatever the occasion, rise to it with a selection of snacks and nibbles, most of which you can have in store before you even issue any invitations.

WELCOME, CHRISTMAS

CHAMPAGNE AND other sparkling wine cocktails have just what it takes to welcome Christmas guests and callers. Buck's fizz is a sparky accompaniment to a late breakfast or a leisurely brunch when the main meal is to be served in the evening, and bubbly cocktails have the sparkle to set the scene as the family – or at least the adult members of it – get into the swing of Christmas mid-morning.

Purists avow that nothing but the best is good enough to comprise Christmas Day cocktails – and Champagne certainly has a quality and taste that no other sparkling wine can quite match. However, when the cocktails are to be flavoured – and delightfully coloured, too – with Cassis, grenadine syrup or peach syrup – as the trio of drinks here – then who is to quibble if you use a good-quality sparkling white wine? The French Veuve du Vernay, a German sparkling hock, the New Zealand Lindauer

Brut or the Californian Domaine Chandon are all suitable candidates.

Experiment with fruit juices and flavourings such as cranberry juice, peach and apricot nectar and elderflower cordial. Add a dash of brandy, white rum or vodka to give the cocktail an extra kick and a scattering of fruit to give it style. Twists and slices of lemon, lime and orange decorating the rim of each glass create definite eye appeal, and strawberries and raspberries, grapes, sliced mangoes, kiwi fruits (Chinese gooseberries) and passion fruits add immeasurably to the appeal of 'wine cups' from a bowl.

Remember to chill white or rosé wines well in advance of serving and, for the extra tingle factor, chill the glasses too. Then dip the moist rims in caster (superfine) sugar to give them a seasonally frosty look. Have all the other ingredients ready, the flavourings, fruit and mixers such as lemonade and mineral water, and add the bubbly last of all.

POMEGRANATE PINKER

INGREDIENTS
30ml/1fl oz/2tbsp grenadine syrup
15ml/¹/₂fl oz/1tbsp brandy
(optional)
250ml/8fl oz/1 cup Champagne or other sparkling white wine, chilled
twist of thinly pared lemon peel

Put the grenadine syrup into a chilled glass, mix in the brandy if you use it and pour on the wine. Mix the drink with a swizzle stick or slender spoon and add the lemon peel. Serve at once.

Makes 1 glass

A PEACH OF A DRINK

INGREDIENTS
30ml/1fl oz/2tbsp peach syrup
15ml/¹/₂fl oz/1 tbsp vodka
(optional)
250ml/8fl oz/1 cup Champagne or other sparkling white wine, chilled
2 thin slices of lime

Put the peach syrup into a chilled glass, mix in the vodka if you use it and pour on the wine. Mix the drink with a swizzle stick or slender spoon. Cut the lime slices from the outside to the centre and balance them on the rim of the glass. Serve at once.

Makes 1 glass

SPARKLING KIR

INGREDIENTS
330ml/1fl oz/2 tbsp Cassis
250ml/8fl oz/1 cup Champagne or other sparkling white wine, chilled
1 slice of orange, halved

Put the Cassis into a chilled glass, top it up with the wine and mix well. Garnish with an orange slice. Serve at once.

Makes 1 glass

ABOVE: Three Champagne cocktails match the mood of the moment. Pomegranate Pinker decorated with a twist of lemon peel, a Peach of a Drink, with slices of lime, and Sparkling Kir with orange slices.

COCKTAIL TIME

Turn back the clock sometime over Christmas and serve thirties-style cocktails. Put cracked ice into a cocktail shaker or a glass, add a dash of this, a measure of that and a spark of ingenuity and serve the concoction with style. This may mean a twist of orange or lemon peel for its colour, its oil and its aroma, or a sprig of mint, a maraschino cherry, a cocktail onion or an olive speared on a pretty cocktail umbrella.

Serve cocktails in glasses that have been polished until they shine and, whenever possible, chilled to the same low temperature as the drink itself. Where refrigerator space is at a premium and a tray of glasses placed on the lowest shelf is not an option, if the weather is cold, the outside temperature may come to the rescue. Cover the glasses with a cloth and leave them in the garage, car port or on the balcony while you make the final preparations. The cocktails will be all the more refreshing if the glasses are chilled.

GRENADINE SLING

INGREDIENTS
3 dashes of Angostura bitters
juice of ½ lime
15ml/½fl oz/1 tbsp grenadine syrup
45ml/1½fl oz/3 tbsp gin
cracked ice
soda water
twist of orange peel

Put the bitters, lime juice, grenadine and gin into a 300-ml/ ½-pt/1¼-cup glass and add cracked ice. Fill with soda water and stir lightly. Decorate with orange peel.

Makes 1 glass

HORSE'S NECK

INGREDIENTS
1 lemon
8 ice cubes
200ml/8fl oz/1 cup gin
600ml/1pt/2½ cups ginger ale, chilled

Thinly pare the lemon so that the rind comes off in one long strip, then cut it into 4 thin, curling strips.

Put 2 ice cubes into each of 4 tumblers. Squeeze the juice of the lemon, mix it with the gin and split between the glasses. Top up with ginger ale and add a twist of peel to each.

Makes 4 tumblers

APRICOT SOUR

INGREDIENTS
8 dashes Angostura bitters
200ml/6fl oz/¾ cup apricot brandy
2tsp caster (superfine) sugar
30ml/2fl oz/¼ cup lemon juice
cracked ice
4 maraschino cherries, to decorate

Put all the ingredients except the cherries into a cocktail shaker or screw-top jar and shake vigorously. Strain into 4 chilled glasses and decorate each with a cocktail cherry.

Makes 4 glasses

LEFT: *Horse's Neck, a gin and ginger ale cocktail, is sharpened with lemon juice and twists of peel.*

ICE FANCIES

SCARLETT O'HARA COCKTAIL

This rich-ruby-red-coloured cocktail looks like Christmas all the way. For added style serve it in 'cranberry' glasses.

INGREDIENTS
350ml/12fl oz/1½ cups Southern Comfort
200ml/6fl oz/¾ cup cranberry juice
juice of 1 lime
cracked ice
maraschino cherries, to serve

Put all the ingredients except the cherries into a jug and stir well. Strain into chilled glasses and decorate each one with a cherry.

Makes 8 glasses

You can add fun and flair to cocktails and chilled fruit punches by presenting the ice in stylish ways. For coloured ice cubes, put a few drops of food colouring into a jug of water before pouring it into ice-cube trays, then harmonize the colours of the ice and cocktails, red ice with a pink-hued drink, green ice with a lime-based cocktail, blue-tinged ice with a colourless blend.

Freeze small strawberries, raspberries, blackberries or melon balls in the ice-trays. Place the fruit in each section and then fill it up with water. Ring the changes and freeze a small flower or blossom in a similar way.

You can multiply these notions for a chilled cocktail bowl, so that you can serve a fruit or flower cube with each drink. For an added dimension, freeze ice in biscuit (cookie) cutters covered in foil. Wrap the foil tightly around the base and sides of star, bell, Santa, Christmas tree and other seasonal shapes and place them on a baking sheet.

BELOW: Ice cubes look more festive if you freeze them with fruit and small edible flowers.

BUCK'S FIZZ (MIMOSA)

This delightfully refreshing drink, invented by the barman at the Buck's Club in London in 1921, has achieved star status. In France it is known as 'Champagne-orange' and in Italy and the United States as 'Mimosa'.

BELOW: It's Christmas morning, and present-opening time. A glass of ice-cold Buck's Fizz decorated with a slice of tangy lime adds to the air of excitement.

INGREDIENTS

100ml/4fl oz/¹/₂ cup fresh orange juice
1tsp grenadine syrup
200ml/6fl oz/³/₄ cup Champagne or other sparkling white wine, chilled

Put the orange juice and grenadine into a chilled glass and top up with wine. Serve at once.

Makes 1 glass

CHAMPAGNE CUP

Layers and layers of pineapple slices over cracked ice, a trio of liqueurs and the fizz of Champagne — what better way to celebrate!

ABOVE: Champagne Cup, with ice-cold layers of fruit and sparkling wine, is a perfect Christmas-morning cocktail.

INGREDIENTS

cracked ice
1 large pineapple, trimmed and thinly sliced
3 large oranges, thinly sliced
1 large cucumber, thinly sliced
45ml/1¹/₂fl oz/¹/₄ cup Maraschino liqueur
45ml/1¹/₂fl oz/¹/₄ cup green Chartreuse
45ml/1¹/₂fl oz/¹/₄ cup brandy
1 bottle dry Champagne or other sparkling white wine, chilled

Place a layer of cracked ice in a chilled punch bowl or serving bowl and arrange layers of pineapple, orange and cucumber slices over it. Repeat the layers of ice and fruit, finishing with fruit. Pour on the liqueurs and brandy and just before serving, pour on the Champagne or wine. Serve in chilled glasses with a little of the fruit in each.

Serves 6–8

ORCHARD FIZZ

Sparkling apple juice has enough of the rising-bubbles factor to qualify as a Christmas morning cocktail for the younger members of the family.

INGREDIENTS
10 sugar cubes
2 lemons, thinly sliced
200ml/6fl oz/¾ cup lime juice
1l/1¾pt/4⅓ cups sparkling apple juice
250ml/8fl oz/1 cup soda water (club soda)
2 limes, thinly sliced
2 kiwi fruits, peeled and thinly sliced
mint sprigs

Rub the sugar cubes over the lemons to remove the zest and place one in each glass. Squeeze the juice of the lemons and put the juice in a chilled jug with the lime juice, apple juice and soda water. Mix together and float the fruit slices and mint sprigs on top. Serve in chilled glasses.

Makes 10 glasses

BELOW: Orchard Fizz, a non-alcoholic cocktail, is decorated with thinly sliced limes and kiwi fruit (Chinese gooseberries).

CRANBERRY FROST

A non-alcoholic cocktail with the colour of holly berries will delight younger and older guests alike. It is the perfect 'one for the road' drink to serve at the end of a gathering.

INGREDIENTS
100g/4oz/½ cup caster (superfine) sugar
juice of 2 oranges
100ml/4fl oz/½ cup cranberry juice
1l/1¾pt/4⅓ cups sparkling mineral water (seltzer)
2–3tbsp fresh cranberries, to decorate
sprigs of mint, to decorate

ABOVE: The very essence of festive colour, non-alcoholic Cranberry Frost is chilled with fruited ice cubes and decorated with fresh berries.

Put the sugar, orange juice and water into a small pan and stir over a low heat to dissolve the sugar. Bring to the boil and boil for 3 minutes. Set aside to cool. The syrup can be made in advance and stored in a covered container in the refrigerator. Pour the syrup into a chilled bowl, pour on the cranberry juice and mix well. To serve, pour on the mineral water and decorate with cranberries and mint leaves.

Serves 10

APPETIZERS

BALANCE IS the key word when you are planning the dips and dunks, pastries and nibbles to serve with drinks. Whether the snacks are to be enjoyed as appetizers before a meal or represent the food element of a drinks party, make your selections as varied as possible.

If you use cream cheese as the already-thickened, dairy-rich basis of some of your dips, include at least one such as Chick-pea Dip or Taramasalata that has no cheese, and at least one which is suitable for vegetarians.

Even if pastry-making and shaping is your strong point,

vary your selection of tartlet cases – cut down on preparation time too – by making some from crisply-baked sliced bread and pitta bread rounds, and include some hot finger foods such as Mini Meatballs and Devils on Horseback.

If the snacks are to be served before a meal, allow two or three for each guest. If they are to be served at an informal gathering, allow three or four per guest at lunchtime, four or five in the evening, and be sure to have a supply of nuts, olives and crackers for variety. Provides a stack of small plates or waxed paper plates and napkins to avoid spills.

MINI MEATBALLS

INGREDIENTS
350g/12oz/1½ cups lean minced (ground) beef
100g/4oz/ bacon, rind removed, minced
1tsp dried thyme
grated nutmeg
salt and black pepper
flour, for dusting
vegetable oil, for frying

BARBECUE SAUCE
3tbsp olive oil
1 large onion, finely chopped
1 clove garlic, finely chopped
2tsp tomato purée
2tbsp demerara (light brown) sugar
2tbsp red wine vinegar
2tbsp Worcestershire sauce
150ml/¼pt/⅔ cup chicken stock or water

1 Mix the beef and bacon together with a wooden spoon until it forms a smooth paste. Stir in the thyme and season with nutmeg, salt and pepper. Cover and chill for at least 1 hour.

2 Dust your hands with flour. Scoop the mixture with a teaspoon and shape it into balls slightly larger than a walnut.

3 Heat some oil in a heavy frying pan (skillet) and fry the meatballs over a moderate heat for about 7 minutes, turning them until they are cooked and evenly brown on all sides. Serve warm, with Barbecue sauce.

4 To make the sauce, heat the oil in a pan and fry the onion and garlic over a moderate heat until the onion is translucent. Stir in the tomato purée and then the remaining ingredients and simmer for 10 minutes. Serve hot.

Makes about 24 meatballs

RIGHT: For eye-catching garnishes press out vegetable shapes using biscuit (cookie) cutters.

CHEESE AND OLIVE BITES

Serve these delicious bite-sized morsels chilled and speared with toothpicks, as an appetizer at a cheese and wine party or a drinks party.

INGREDIENTS
225g/8oz/1 cup soft cream cheese
about 16 stuffed green olives
50g/2oz/⅓ cup chopped walnuts

1 Beat the cheese until it is soft. Take heaped teaspoonfuls of the cheese and shape them around each olive. Roll them between your palms to form neat spherical shapes. Put the chopped walnuts in a saucer and roll the cheese bites in them to cover them evenly. Chill.

2 You can, if you wish, cut the bites in half to show the olives and make the savouries more colourful.

Makes about 16 bites

SCRAMBLED EGGS AND MUSHROOM TARTLETS

INGREDIENTS

*Shortcrust pastry made with 225g/
8oz/2 cups plain (all-purpose)
flour
beaten egg, for glazing
25g/1oz/2tbsp butter, plus extra
for greasing
4 eggs
3tbsp single (light) cream
salt and freshly ground black
pepper
100g/4oz/½ cup oyster or button
mushrooms, chopped
black olive 'petals', to garnish*

1 Heat the oven to 190°C/
375°F/Gas 5. Make the
pastry and leave it to rest for
15–20 minutes.

2 Roll out the pastry and use
it to line 24 greased tartlet
tins (small baking pans). Brush
the rims with beaten egg and
prick the bases with a fork. Line
each pastry case with a circle of
non-stick baking paper and fill it
with baking beans. Bake the
pastry cases 'blind' for 10
minutes, then remove the beans
and paper and bake for a further
5–7 minutes to dry the pastry.
Remove the tins and stand on a
wire rack.

3 Melt the butter in a small
pan over a moderate heat.
Beat the eggs and cream together
and season with salt and pepper.
Pour the mixture into the pan
and stir until it is beginning to
set. Stir in the chopped
mushrooms and stir until the
mixture is just set but
still creamy.

4 Spoon the filling into the
warm pastry cases and
decorate some with olive 'petals'.
Serve warm.

Makes 24 tartlets

BACON CRISPIES

INGREDIENTS

*150g/6oz bacon, rind removed,
finely chopped
150g/6oz/¾ cup butter, softened
175g/6oz/1½ cups plain (all-
purpose) flour
salt and pepper
100g/4oz/½ cup grated Cheddar*

1 Fry the bacon in a non-stick
pan over a moderate heat,
stirring frequently, until it is
crisp and dry. Transfer it to a
plate covered with paper towels
and set aside to cool.

ABOVE: *Individual tartlet
cases are filled with scrambled
egg and oyster mushrooms and
garnished with black olive
'petals'.*

2 Heat the oven to 170°C/
325°F/Gas 3. Beat
together the butter, flour, salt
and pepper until smooth. Stir ⅔
of the bacon and the grated cheese
into the mixture and mix well.

3 Place teaspoonfuls of the
mixture well apart on a
greased baking sheet and sprinkle
with the remaining bacon.

4 Bake in the oven for 30
minutes, until lightly
brown. Cool on a wire rack, and
store in an airtight tin.

Makes 28–30 snacks

ABOVE: On the blue plate, Talmouse, shortcrust pastry tricorns filled with a creamy tuna sauce, and on the red plate, mini choux buns filled with cream cheese and chopped prawns (shrimp).

TALMOUSE

These bite-sized pastry tricorns can have a variety of fillings. In place of the canned tuna in this recipe you could use 225g/8oz/1 cup cooked smoked haddock fillet, skinned and flaked or, for a vegetarian alternative, a 225-g/8-oz can artichoke hearts, drained and chopped.

INGREDIENTS

375g/13oz packet frozen puff pastry, thawed
1 small egg, beaten

FOR THE FILLING

150g/6oz can tuna, flaked
15g/¹/₂oz/1tbsp butter
15g/¹/₂oz/²/₃ cup plain (all-purpose) flour
150ml/¹/₄pt/²/₃ cup single (light) cream
2tbsp milk
salt and black pepper
large pinch cayenne

1 First make the filling. Melt the butter in a small pan over a moderate heat. Remove from the heat and stir in the flour. Return to the heat and stir until the mixture forms a roux. Stir in the cream and milk and season with salt, pepper and cayenne. Bring the sauce to the boil and boil for 3 minutes, stirring. Remove from the heat. Stir in the tuna and leave to cool.

2 Heat the oven to 200°C/ 400°F/Gas 6. Roll out the pastry on a floured board to a thickness of about 4mm/¹/₆in. Using a 7.5-cm/3-in fluted cutter, cut into rounds. Re-roll the trimmings and cut out more rounds. Brush the rim of each round with beaten egg.

3 Spoon a little of the fish filling in the centre of each round and shape the pastry into a tricorn. Brush with beaten egg.

4 Place on a baking sheet and bake in the oven for 18–20 minutes, until golden brown. Serve hot.

Makes about 24 snacks

OPPOSITE: Cream Cheese Dip garnished with red pepper hearts, Avocado Dip with green pepper hearts, Chick-pea Dip and Mexican Dip garnished with carrot shapes.

CHICK-PEA DIP

INGREDIENTS
225g/8oz can chick-peas, rinsed
and drained
2 garlic cloves, crushed
4tbsp olive oil
225g/8oz/1 cup cottage cheese
large pinch ground cumin
salt and freshly ground black
pepper

1 Put the chick-peas in a
blender or food processor
with the garlic, olive oil and
cottage cheese and process to a
purée.

2 Season with cumin, salt
and pepper and beat in a
little more olive oil if the mixture
is too stiff (this will depend on
the consistency of the cheese).

3 Transfer to a serving dish.
Serve chilled.

Serves 12

MEXICAN DIP

INGREDIENTS
350g/12oz/1½ cups soft cream
cheese
150g/5oz/½ cup Greek-style or
plain yoghurt
1tsp Worcestershire sauce
1tsp hot pepper sauce
2 tomatoes, skinned, seeded and
chopped
1 clove garlic, crushed
salt
carrot or other vegetable shapes, to
garnish

1 Beat the cheese until soft,
then beat in the yoghurt,
sauces, tomato and garlic. Season
to taste with salt.

2 Transfer to a serving dish,
garnish with carrot shapes
or other vegetable garnishes cut
with biscuit (cookie) cutters, or
cut into small petals and cover.
Serve chilled.

Serves 12

AVOCADO DIP

INGREDIENTS
225g/8oz/1 cup soft cream cheese
1 large, ripe avocado
2tbsp lemon juice
salt and freshly ground black
pepper
2 drops green food colouring
(optional)
pinch of cayenne
green pepper hearts, to garnish

1 Beat the cream cheese until
it is soft. Halve the
avocado, remove the stone and,
using a teaspoon, scoop the flesh
into the cheese.

2 Add the lemon juice and
beat until the mixture is
smooth. Season with salt and
pepper and a pinch of cayenne.

3 Transfer to a serving dish,
garnish with green pepper
hearts and cover. Serve chilled.

Serves 12

CREAM CHEESE DIP

INGREDIENTS
350g/12oz/1½ cups soft cream
cheese
150ml/5oz carton soured cream
salt and freshly ground black
pepper
red pepper hearts, to garnish

VARIATIONS
100g/4oz/⅔ cup chopped walnuts
100g/4oz/⅔ cup chopped cooked
shrimps
100g/4oz/⅔ cup chopped bacon,
crisply fried
10cm/4in cucumber, peeled and
chopped
1 red pepper, cored, seeded and
chopped

1 Put the cream cheese into a
bowl and beat until it is
smooth. Beat in the soured
cream, which will lighten the
mixture. If you wish to serve the
dip plain, season it with salt and
pepper. Otherwise, add one of
the suggested variations – the
addition of chopped cucumber,
for example, makes the popular
Greek dip, Tzatziki. Season to
taste with salt and pepper.

2 Transfer to a serving dish,
garnish with red pepper
hearts and cover. Serve chilled.

Serves 12

BE OF GOOD CHEER!

THERE CAN be few things more warmly welcoming at Christmas than a glass or two of steaming, spicy, aromatic mulled wine. It is the perfect – indeed the traditional – drink to offer visiting carol singers, and the one to come home to after you yourself have been in good voice. Mulled wine is a sure way to break the ice at a party and, as long as the mixture is not too potent, to serve as a nightcap before guests leave. What could be more enjoyable than a glass of mulled wine, ale or cider served piping hot, perhaps with mince pies, on an evening at home, when the family is relaxing round the fire?

The following recipes for punches and mulls may serve as a springboard to your own unique blends. You can include any combination of fruits and sweet spices in the proportions you enjoy, to make the drinks piquant or mild; add honey or granulated sugar, which leave the liquid clear, or soft light brown sugar, which makes it slightly cloudy.

It is principally for this reason – the clarity of the mull – that whole and not ground spices are usually added: whole cloves stuck into oranges, apples, tangerines and kumquats, whole halved cinnamon sticks, and blades of mace, coriander seeds, juniper berries, allspice seeds and others tied into a small piece of muslin (cheesecloth) that can be retrieved and discarded, once the spices have been infused. Small whole spices floating in the drink may look decorative, but would be a problem if they were inadvertently swallowed by guests.

If you wish to use ground spices such as cinnamon, ginger, allspice and (sparingly) cloves, it is best to mix them with any sugar you may be including well in advance of making the mull. That way the sugars will absorb the flavour of the spices and you will avoid the somewhat 'raw' taste that powdered spices can have.

You may wish to serve mulled wine laced with a little brandy or rum as a welcoming drink and then, as the party progresses, to lower the alcohol level by adding orange juice, pineapple juice, cider or even water. The sugar, fruit and spice elements should amply compensate for any loss of 'body' in the blend.

LEFT: Travellers used to take their spices with them in silver carriers to ensure that their mulls had plenty of flavour. From top left, clockwise, silver punch ladle, mace holder in the shape of a mace, long-handled spoon, used as a swizzle stick, nutmeg holder with grater in the base, another holder with no grater and a lidded spice box; most of the items are Georgian.

OPPOSITE: Some of the flavourings that may be used to add zest and spice to mulled wine, ale and cider. From top left, clockwise, orange peel, fresh ginger, juniper berries, cinnamon sticks, star anise, vanilla pods, allspice berries, coriander seeds, cloves, orange slices and nutmegs.

RIGHT: Fruits have always been used to add depth of flavour to mulls and punches. Limes and lemons, tangerines, clementines and their variants, oranges, kumquats and apples can all be used whole, studded with cloves, or spiced. Raisins are delicious when soaked in the hot liquor.

INFORMAL DRINKS PARTY

When the music's playing, the candles are flickering and your guests are in the mood to enjoy themselves, a party planned on informal lines or on the spur of the moment can perfectly capture the festive spirit. The drinks can be relatively cheap, with a selection of beer, lager, cider and mineral water and a sparkling cider and fruit cup. And the food can be an appetizing example of self-assembly.

At a 'roll-filling' party, people can help themselves to what they want. You provide a choice of crisp and crunchy, soft and seed-topped white and wholewheat rolls and pitta bread, a platter of cold meats, kebabs and salads for your guests to fill them with – and a warm, relaxed welcome.

SANDWICH FILLINGS

Cold sandwich fillings could include the following:

Meat Slice roast beef, spiced beef, baked ham, roast turkey or salami, garlic sausage and other prepared meats.

Fish This could include smoked salmon, Gravad lax, smoked trout, or smoked mackerel.

Pâté These could be meat- or fish-based, including pheasant and pork pâté or smoked trout pâté.

Eggs Serve scrambled eggs embellished with smoked salmon or oyster mushrooms.

Cheeses Offer a choice of soft and hard cheeses. This might be cream cheese with chopped dates, Mozzarella or Mascarpone cheese. Hard cheeses could include Cheddar, Cheshire or Gloucester. These should be thinly sliced or grated. For ease of serving, they could be mixed with a little cream cheese or lightly whipped double (heavy) cream. Stilton, Gorgonzola or other blue-veined cheese should be thinly sliced.

Hot fillings These could include crisply-fried bacon, frankfurters, pork sausages, herbed sausages, venison sausages and any other favourites; Lamb kebabs; or Stir-fried prawns (shrimp) in tomato sauce.

CIDER CUP

INGREDIENTS

2l/3¹/2pt/8³/4 cups dry cider, chilled
1l/1³/4pt/4¹/3 cups sparkling apple juice, chilled
300ml/¹/2pt/1¹/4 cups sweet sherry
600ml/1pt/2¹/2 cups soda water, chilled
225g/8oz/1 cup frozen blackberries, thawed
2 dessert apples, cored and thinly sliced
2tbsp lemon juice

1 Mix the cider, apple juice and sherry in a large punch bowl and, just before serving, pour on the soda water.

2 Add the blackberries and the apple slices tossed in lemon juice.

Serves 20–24

LEFT: Cider Cup, decorated with apple slices and blackberries.

OPPOSITE: Herb-flavoured Lamb Kebabs and warm pitta bread served with Barbecue Sauce.

LAMB KEBABS

These are particularly appropriate to serve in warm pitta bread, with shredded lettuce and onion rings.

INGREDIENTS
1kg/2¼lb lean lamb, trimmed and cut into 1.5-cm/½-in cubes
juice of 1 lemon

FOR THE MARINADE
3tbsp olive oil
1tsp dried oregano
½tsp dried thyme
2tbsp red wine vinegar
freshly ground black pepper

1 Mix the marinade ingredients together and pour the mixture into a large shallow dish.

2 Thread the lamb onto small wooden skewers and place them in the marinade. Spoon the liquid over the meat, cover and set aside for about 1 hour. Heat the grill (broiler) to medium.

3 Remove the skewers from the marinade and grill (broil) them for 6–7 minutes, turning them frequently and basting them with the marinade.

4 Transfer the kebabs to a warmed serving dish, sprinkle them with lemon juice and a few grindings of pepper.

STIR-FRIED PRAWNS (SHRIMP)

INGREDIENTS
5tbsp vegetable oil
4 cloves garlic, finely chopped
4 spring onions
1kg/2¼lb frozen prawns (shrimps), thawed
450g/1lb tomatoes, skinned and chopped
2tbsp soy sauce
1tsp sugar
1tsp cornflour (cornstarch)
1tbsp water

1 Heat the oil in a wok or frying pan until it is just beginning to smoke. Add the garlic and the onions and stir-fry over a high heat for 1 minute.

2 Add the prawns (shrimp) and stir-fry for 2–3 minutes, until they become firm. Remove the onions and prawns with a draining spoon and add the tomatoes, soy sauce and sugar.

3 Stir the cornflour (cornstarch) into the water, pour into the pan and cook over a moderate heat for 5–7 minutes, until the mixture forms a thick paste.

4 Return the onion and prawn (shrimp) mixture and just heat through. Serve hot.

Fills about 20 rolls

BARBECUE SAUCE

INGREDIENTS
3tbsp olive oil
1 large onion, finely chopped
1 red pepper, cored, seeded and chopped
2 cloves garlic, finely chopped
2tbsp tomato purée
225g/8oz can chopped tomatoes
2 bay leaves
1tsp dried oregano
salt and black pepper

1 Heat the oil in a pan and fry the onion, pepper and garlic over a moderate heat for about 3 minutes, until the onion is translucent.

2 Add the tomatoes, bay leaves and oregano and season with salt and pepper.

3 Bring to the boil and simmer for 10–15 minutes, until the mixture forms a paste.

4 Discard the bay leaves, and season.

Makes about 450ml/¾pt/2 cups

MULLED CLARET

A blend of claret, cider and orange juice, this mull can be varied to suit the occasion by increasing or decreasing the proportion of fruit juice or, to give the mull more pep, by adding up to 150ml/¼pt/⅔ cup brandy.

INGREDIENTS

1½l/2½pt/6¼ cups inexpensive
claret
600ml/1pt/2½ cups medium cider
300ml/½pt/1¼ cups orange juice
1 orange
5tbsp clear honey
2tbsp seedless raisins
2 clementines
a few cloves
4tbsp demerara (light brown)
sugar
grated nutmeg
2 cinnamon sticks

1 With a sharp knife or a rotary peeler, pare off a long strip of orange peel.

2 Place the peel, honey and raisins in a large pan. Stud the clementines with cloves and add them.

3 Grate a little nutmeg into the sugar and add to the pan with the cinnamon sticks. Pour on the wine and heat over a low heat, stirring until the sugar has dissolved and the honey melted.

RIGHT: Mulled Claret makes a welcoming drink to break the ice.

4 Pour in the cider and the orange juice and continue to heat the mull gently. Do not allow it to boil.

5 Warm a punch bowl or other serving bowl. Remove the clementines and cinnamon sticks and strain the mull into the bowl to remove the raisins. Add the clementines studded with cloves, and serve hot in warmed glasses or in glasses containing a silver spoon (to prevent the glass breaking). Grate a little nutmeg over each serving, if you wish.

Makes 16 150ml/¼pt glasses

JAMAICA SUNSET

This frothy blend of eggs, milk and spirits definitely comes into the just-before-bedtime category of drink.

INGREDIENTS
4 eggs, separated
2tbsp caster (superfine) sugar
4tbsp dark rum
4tbsp brandy
300ml/½pt/1¼ cups milk, hot
(or according to the volume of the glasses)
nutmeg

2 Pour on the rum and brandy, 1tbsp of each in each glass.

1 Beat the egg yolks with the sugar. Beat the whites to soft peaks. Mix together and pour into 4 heatproof glasses.

3 Top up with hot milk. Grate nutmeg on top.

Serves 4

MULLED CIDER

Another way to impart the tangy flavour of orange or other citrus fruit zest — without using the whole fruit or a twist of peel — is to rub sugar lumps over the rind. The rough surface of the sugar acts as a grater and removes the essential oils from just below the surface.

INGREDIENTS
20 sugar lumps
2 oranges, well washed
1 lemon
1 apple, thickly sliced
a few cloves
1 cinnamon stick
1l/1¾pt/4⅓ cups medium cider
4tbsp brandy
a few fresh strawberries, sliced, to decorate

1 Rub the sugar lumps over the zest of the oranges and put the sugar into a pan. Squeeze the juice from the oranges and add to the pan. Squeeze the juice from the lemon and brush some over the apple slices to prevent them from discolouring. Add the remaining lemon juice to the pan. Stud the apple slices with cloves and add together with cinnamon, cider and brandy.

2 Heat over a low heat, stirring to dissolve the sugar.

3 Pour the mull into a warmed punch bowl or serving dish and float a few strawberries on to decorate. Serve in heated glasses.

Makes about 18 glasses

HOW MUCH FOR HOW MANY

ESTIMATING HOW much food and drink to provide for your party guests over the festive season can never be an exact science. Use the tables on these pages as a general guide, but build in your own variable factors. Just how much to provide for how many guests will depend on the duration of the party, the time of the day and, to an extent, the age of the gathering. A group of hungry teenagers may consume more than an older age group.

ESTIMATING DRINKS

These are the numbers you can expect to serve, giving a standard measure, from a standard bottle:

Drink	Glasses per bottle or carton
Sherry, 75cl	12–16
Port, 75cl	12–16
Table wine, 70–75cl	6–8
Champagne and other sparkling wines, 75cl	6–7
Gin, whisky, vodka and other spirits served as cocktails, or with 'mixers', 70–75cl	30
Tonic water, ginger ale or dry ginger, soda water and other 'mixers', 500ml/18floz	4–5
Vermouth, 70cl	12–14
Liqueurs, 70cl	30
Tomato juice, 1l/1¾pt	10–12
Orange, pineapple and other fruit juices, 1l/1¾pt	8–10
Fruit cordials (add 3.5l/6pt water to each bottle)	16–18

The number of glasses you may expect to serve with mulled wine or punch will depend to an extent on the potency or otherwise of the drink. Guests are likely to treat a potent mixture such as one laced with port and brandy with more restraint, at least after the first glass, than a less heady concoction which contains a high proportion of fruit juice or water. The approximate number of servings is given with each recipe in this section, though this also depends on what size of glasses you wish to use.

LEFT: Quantities for parties can never be exact, and will depend to a large extent on the type of party, time of day and nature of the guests.

ESTIMATING FOOD

Hors d'œuvres

When you are making cocktail savouries other than those featured in our recipes, calculate the ingredients you will need as follows:

Item	Notes	Ingredients	Quantity
Sausage rolls	Pastry calculated at 675g/1½lb/3 cups plain (all-purpose) flour, 350–450g/12oz–1lb/1½–2 cups fat	675g/1½lb/3 cups shortcrust or flaky pastry, 900g/2lb sausagemeat	30 medium-sized rolls, 50 small ones
Vol-au-vents	Fillings, such as chopped chicken, turkey, ham, salmon, tuna, prawns or mushrooms with white sauce	900g/2lb/4 cups puff pastry, 300g/10oz savoury filling, 600ml/1pt white sauce	25 vol-au-vents 7.5cm/3in diameter, or 40 5cm/2in diameter
Bouchées (pastry boats)	Fillings as above, or soft cream cheese mixed with yoghurt and one of the savoury ingredients	675g/1½lb/3 cups shortcrust pastry, 300g/10oz savoury filling, 600ml/1pt/2½ cups white sauce	50 bouchées 7.5cm/3in in length

You may expect to serve the following quantities of food and drink to guests at gatherings of various kinds.

Cocktail party – Lunchtime

3–4 savouries such as tartlets, mini choux buns and Palmiers

1–1½tbsp savoury dip

5–6 crudités

3–4 drinks, including soft drinks

Cocktail party – Evening

4–5 savouries such as Mini meatballs, Talmouse and cocktail scones

1½–2tbsp savoury dip

6–8 crudités

4–5 drinks, including soft drinks

Informal drinks party (extended duration)

2–3 filled rolls

1–2 other, small savouries

5–6 drinks, including soft drinks

1–2 cups of coffee

Teenage party

5–6 savouries

2–3 sweet items, such as mince pies or brownies

4–5 drinks, including soft drinks

CHRISTMAS BAKING

❧❦❧

This chapter enables you to build on your own repertoire of Christmas specials, from a rich and fragrant pudding to spirit-soaked mincemeat, from fancy gingerbread men to moist gingerbread cake, both among the oldest of festival offerings and as popular now as they ever were. Through sweet pastry cases and gooey chocolate cakes, the section moves on to cocktail snacks and hors d'œuvres, and then, in a sweeter vein, to chocolates and candies for children to make; from chocolate truffles and other sweetmeats to delectable sugared fruits, flowers and petals to serve with pride at the end of a perfect meal.

CHRISTMAS PUDDING

THE LUXURIOUS pudding with which Christmas is celebrated today, rich with dried fruits, sugar and spices and usually enlivened with a dash of alcohol, has derived over several centuries from frumenty, a thick porridge that was eaten on Christmas Eve. Over the years a variety of fruits and other ingredients were added to the basic mixture – first prunes, which gave rise to the name 'plum pudding', and then meat and suet, the fat that gives the pudding its richness.

You can serve one large pudding or make it in individual moulds. When making the pudding mixture, it is customary to ask everyone in the family, and anyone who happens to be visiting, to stir the pudding and make a secret wish.

TRADITIONAL CHRISTMAS PUDDING

INGREDIENTS

225g/8oz/2 cups plain (all-purpose) flour
1tsp ground cinnamon
1/2tsp grated nutmeg
1/2tsp ground allspice
1tbsp salt
100g/4oz/1 cup fresh breadcrumbs
550g/1 1/4lb/2 3/4 cups seedless raisins
350g/12oz/2 cups sultanas (golden raisins)
350g/12oz/2 cups currants
150g/6oz/1 cup candied peel, sugar coating removed, chopped
50g/2oz/1/3 cup blanched almonds, chopped
225g/8oz/2 cups soft dark brown sugar
225g/8oz/1 cup shredded suet or soft margarine
4 eggs
200ml/6fl oz/1 cup milk
100ml/4fl oz/1/2 cup brandy or substitute more milk
melted butter, for greasing

1 Sift the flour, spices and
salt into a large mixing
bowl. Stir in the breadcrumbs,
dried fruits, peel, almonds and
sugar. Add the suet or margarine
and stir well until all the
ingredients are well mixed. Beat
together the eggs, milk and
brandy if you use it and stir the
mixture into the dry ingredients.

2 If you intend to cook the
pudding in moulds or
pudding basins, brush them
lightly with melted butter. Cut
circles of non-stick baking paper
large enough to cover the top of
each mould, allowing for a pleat
from side to side which will
unfold as the mixture expands.
Cut pieces of cloth to similar
sizes; unbleached calico or muslin
(cheesecloth) is traditional, but
you can also use foil. Brush the
baking paper with butter.

**OPPOSITE: Pottery moulds
were often used in Victorian
times to give variety to the
shape of the pudding. Silver
coins and charms were
sometimes pressed into the
mixture and cooked with the
pudding as lucky tokens.**

3 Spoon the mixture into the
moulds to come level with
the rims. Cover with the greased
and pleated non-stick baking
paper and then with a cloth or
foil and tie securely with string.

4 To make a round pudding
without using a mould, first
brush a piece of non-stick baking
paper with butter. Place this as a
lining on clean, unbleached calico
(cheesecloth). Shape the mixture
into a round between your hands
and bring the paper and the cloth
over it. Tie two of the four
corners of the cloth into a knot
and then, crosswise, tie the other
two.

5 Place a trivet of a piece of
folded cloth in a large
saucepan, add water to come
half-way up the mould or the
pudding cloth and bring it to the
boil. Add the puddings, cover the
pan and boil for 5 hours;
individual puddings for 2 hours.
Top up with more boiling water
as needed.

6 Take out the puddings and
allow them to cool. Replace
the non-stick baking paper and
cloths with fresh ones. Store in a
cool, dry, airy place. The
puddings should keep well for 1
year.

Makes 5 450g/1lb puddings

SERVING CHRISTMAS PUDDINGS

To reheat the puddings on a conventional cooker, boil for a
further 3 hours; individual ones for 1 hour. You can do
this in a slow cooker (electric crock pot) to relieve pressure
on hob (stove top) space.

You can save a considerable amount of time by cooking
Christmas puddings in a microwave. Cover the top of a
mould with plastic wrap. Place the pudding on the
turntable and cook at Medium for 5 minutes. Leave the
pudding for 5 minutes, then cook on medium heat for a
further 3 minutes. Allow to cool, then cover with a second
layer of plastic wrap. Be sure to use microwave-safe moulds
and basins, and not metal ones. To reheat the pudding,
cook on medium heat for 2 minutes.

To release a pudding from a mould, run a knife around
the inside of the mould. Place a warmed plate over the
mould, hold it and the mould firmly together and invert to
release the pudding. If it does not easily slide out of the
mould, shake it up and down.

MINCEMEAT AND MINCE PIES

MINCE PIES are an essential part of the British culinary tradition, enjoyed with great enthusiasm and in great quantity throughout the Christmas holiday, and then rarely, if ever, offered again until the following year.

Originally mincemeat was, as its name implies, made from minced (ground) meat, as a way of preserving the last scraps of meat culled in the autumn so that it would last throughout the winter. The mixture, which also included fresh and dried fruits, spices and sugar, was simmered for several days and then stored in sealed jars in the cellar or in an outhouse. A seventeenth-century writer described the contemporary mince pie, a huge dish called 'Christmas pie',

as 'a most learned mixture of Neats-tongues [ox tongues], chicken, eggs, sugar, raisins, lemon and orange peel, various kinds of Spicery, etc'.

Today's mincemeat no longer contains meat or poultry, except in the form of suet. Those who do not wish to eat animal fats may substitute vegetarian suet, which is a saturated vegetable fat, or use polyunsaturated margarine.

The mixture may be used to fill tray bakes (bars) such as Mincemeat Slice and open lattice flans (pies); spooned into partly baked individual tart shells topped with fancy cut-out pastry shapes, or, when baked and cooled, drizzled with glacé icing.

LEFT: Mincemeat should be made at least 4 weeks before Christmas and left in a cool, dry, dark place to mature.

TRADITIONAL MINCEMEAT

INGREDIENTS

225g/8oz/1⅓ cups currants
225g/8oz/1⅓ cups sultanas (golden raisins)
450g/1lb/2⅔ cups seedless raisins
450g/1lb cooking apples, peeled, cored and chopped
225g/8oz/1½ cups Candied citrus peel, chopped
100g/4oz/⅔ cup blanched almonds, chopped
225g/8oz/1 cup shredded suet, or vegetarian suet
225g/8oz/1 cup soft dark brown sugar
1tsp ground cinnamon
1tsp ground allspice
1tsp ground ginger
½tsp grated nutmeg
grated rind and juice of 2 oranges
grated rind and juice of 2 lemons
about 150ml/¼pt/⅔ cup brandy or port

1 *Place all the ingredients except the brandy or port in a large mixing bowl. Stir well, cover the bowl with a cloth and set aside in a cool place overnight.*

2 *The following day, stir in enough brandy or port to make a mixture moist enough to drop from a spoon.*

3 *Spoon the mixture into sterilized jars and cover and store in a cool, dry place.*

ABOVE RIGHT: Three ways of decorating mince pies: dusted with icing (confectioners') sugar, decorated with holly-leaf shape cut-outs and, open top, drizzled with glacé icing.

DOUBLE-CRUST MINCE PIES

INGREDIENTS

Shortcrust pastry made with 350g/
12oz/3 cups flour
flour for dusting
450g/1lb/2 cups mincemeat
butter, for greasing
milk, for brushing
icing (confectioners') sugar or caster
(superfine) sugar, for dusting

1 Heat the oven to 200°C/
400°F/Gas 6. Roll out the
pastry as thinly as possible on a
lightly floured board. Using a
7.5-cm/3-in plain round cutter,
cut out 24 circles. With a 5-cm/
2-in plain round cutter, cut out
another 24 circles.

2 Grease 24 patty tins
(muffin pans), dust them
with flour and line them with the
larger circles. Fill each one with
mincemeat, then brush the edges
with milk. Press the smaller
rounds on top and seal the edges.
Brush the tops with milk.

3 Bake for 25–30 minutes
until the pastry is light
golden brown. Cool in the tins
(pans), then transfer the pies to a
wire rack to become cold. Store
them in an airtight tin. Just
before serving, dust the tops with
sugar. Serve warm.

Makes 24 pies

MINCEMEAT LATTICE FLAN

Mincemeat Lattice Flan is
traditionally served warm
with brandy butter or rum
butter spooned on top.

1 Line a 20-cm/8-in flan case
with shortcrust pastry made
with 225g/8oz/2 cups flour.

2 Spoon in 225g/8oz/1 cup
mincemeat and cut the
remaining pastry in strips 6mm/
1/4in wide.

3 Dampen the edges of the
flan case and arrange the
strips to criss-cross each other to
form a lattice effect. Brush the
strips with milk before baking.
Serve warm.

MINCEMEAT SLICE

1 Make Mincemeat Slice in a
similar way to Double-
crust Mince Pies. Use just over
half the rolled pastry to line the
base and sides of a greased tin or
loaf pan 25 × 17.5 cm/10
× 7 in.

2 Brush the side edges with
milk, spoon on the
mincemeat and level the surface
with a knife.

3 Cover with the remaining
pastry, press it firmly on
the edges and trim it neatly all
round. Brush the top with milk
before baking.

4 Just before serving, dust the
top with icing
(confectioners') sugar or caster
(superfine) sugar. Serve warm.

GINGERBREAD

I_{N ALL} its forms, gingerbread has been part of the Christmas tradition for generations. Nowhere was ginger more prized than in Germany, and it is from that country that many present-day traditions originate. By the seventeenth century, every northern-European country had its regional variations of the spiced bread. There were Flemish, Dutch and Swiss specialities, all recognizably closely related to the German ones, and in England gingerbread sold at country fairs, as 'fairings', was often gilded with edible gold leaf. In the United States, gingerbread has been popular since the early colonial days, when Salem, Massachusetts, was an important spice-trading centre.

DARK GINGERBREAD

An alternative and somewhat richer recipe than is traditional, this mixture can be used to shape the gingerbread tree ornaments and biscuits (cookies) shown throughout this book; the hearts that comprise the table-centre ring on these pages; and family traditions of your own.

INGREDIENTS

350g/12oz/3 cups plain (all-purpose) flour, plus extra for dusting
2tsp ground ginger
1tsp ground allspice
1tsp ground cinnamon
pinch of salt
1/2tsp bicarbonate of soda (baking soda)
175g/6oz/3/4 cup unsalted butter, at room temperature, plus extra for greasing
4tbsp soft light or dark brown sugar
8tbsp molasses
6tbsp milk

TO DECORATE

100g/4oz/1 cup icing (confectioners') sugar
4–5tsp water or lemon juice
colouring, optional

ABOVE: These gingerbread shapes have been 'gilded' with gold-coloured powder. This is available in both edible and inedible forms.

LEFT: An old Dutch gingerbread mould, shown with fresh, dry and ground ginger, is an example of the intricate shapes that were baked in the eighteenth century.

1 Sift the flour, ginger, allspice, cinnamon, salt and bicarbonate of soda (baking soda) into a bowl.

2 Beat the butter until it is soft, then beat in the sugar and molasses until the mixture is light and fluffy. Gradually stir in the flour and milk alternately, continuing to stir until it is well blended.

3 Knead the dough on a lightly floured board until it is smooth. Place it in a polythene bag and chill in the refrigerator for at least 2 hours or overnight.

4 Heat the oven to 190°C/ 375°F/Gas 5. Lightly grease 2 baking sheets. Roll out the dough to a thickness of 4mm/ ⅛in and cut it to the required shapes. Gather up the trimmings, re-roll the dough and cut out more shapes. If the shapes are to be hung on the tree, push a hole near the top of each one with a skewer.

5 Transfer the shapes to the baking sheets and bake for 10–12 minutes, until the gingerbread is golden brown and beginning to darken at the edges. Leave it to cool slightly on the baking sheets, then transfer to a wire rack to cool.

6 To decorate the shapes, sift the icing (confectioners') sugar into a bowl, mix it to a stiff paste with the water or lemon juice and add colouring of your choice. Spoon the glacé icing into a piping bag and pipe lines, stars, names and other designs.

MOIST GINGERBREAD CAKE

INGREDIENTS

225g/8oz/2 cups plain (all-
purpose) flour
2tsp ground ginger
1tsp ground cinnamon
1/4tsp grated nutmeg
pinch of salt
50g/2oz/1/3 cup pitted dates,
chopped
50g/2oz/1/3 cup crystallized
(candied) ginger, chopped
125g/5oz/1/2 cup black treacle
(molasses)
50g/2oz/1/4 cup butter
1 egg
75g/3oz/1/2 cup dark brown sugar
4tbsp milk
1/2tsp bicarbonate of soda (baking
soda)

1 Heat the oven to 180°C/
350°F/Gas 4. Sift the
flour, ginger, cinnamon, nutmeg
and salt and stir in the chopped
dates and ginger.

2 Melt the treacle (molasses)
and butter in a small pan.
Beat the egg and beat in the
sugar. Add the two mixtures
alternately to the dry ingredients,
beating all the time. Stir the
bicarbonate of soda (baking soda)
into the milk, and stir into the
mixture.

3 Pour the mixture into a
20cm-/8in square baking
tin (pan) lined with non-stick
baking paper. Level the top and
bake for 45–50 minutes·

**BELOW: Use the illustration
as a guide for the stencil.**

4 Stand the tin on a wire
rack to cool. Remove the
cake from the tin (pan), strip off
the baking paper and wrap the
cake in foil. Store it in an
airtight tin. It will keep fresh for
up to 8 weeks.

5 Use stiff card (posterboard)
for the stencil, so that it can
be lifted off without bending. Sift
the icing (confectioners') sugar
evenly over the top of the cake.

6 Lift off the stencil
carefully, holding it at each
side.

GINGERBREAD HEART RING

This table centre-piece is inspired by traditional Polish Christmas decorations. You could make one with other cut-out shapes such as gingerbread men and women, teddy bears or stars.

EQUIPMENT

* 7 heart-shaped gingerbread biscuits, baked and decorated
* stiff cardboard ring, outer diameter 25cm/10in, inner measurement 15cm/6in
* glacé icing made with 100g/4oz/1 cup sifted icing (confectioners') sugar and, if you wish, coloured red
* 5cm/2in-wide ribbon
* Victorian-style paper scraps (optional)

1 Cover the cardboard ring with glacé icing and quickly – before it sets – press on the heart-shaped gingerbread to cover it.

RIGHT: *Victorian scraps or other paper decorations can be fixed to the centre of each biscuit with a dab of glacé icing.*

2 Tie the ribbon into a bow, trim the ends and fix it to the ring with a generous dab of glacé icing to ensure it stays securely in place throughout the season. To preserve the ring as a decoration throughout the Christmas holidays, it may be as well to make extra heart-shaped biscuits (cookies) for young gingerbread enthusiasts to eat!

PASTRY AND CAKES

Astock of shortcrust or *pâte brisée* pastry cases (pie crust shells) ready-baked and stored in the refrigerator is an invaluable stand-by at Christmastime. You can fill the cases with fruits, with preserves, light chiffon mixtures, lemon meringue, mincemeat, or whatever you choose.

It is advisable to have at least one chocolate cake in store, ready to decorate as soon as friends ring up to say they are dropping in for coffee or tea. Chocolate Pecan Cake, made with ground nuts in place of flour, keeps especially well and can be decorated in a variety of ways.

CHOCOLATE PECAN CAKE

INGREDIENTS
250g/9oz/1½ cups plain (semi-sweet) chocolate, broken into pieces
125g/5oz/⅔ cup butter, cut into pieces
4 eggs
75g/3oz/⅓ cup caster (superfine) sugar
1 tsp vanilla extract
100g/4oz/1 cup pecans, ground
about 28 pecan halves
6.5cm/2½in-wide ribbon (optional)
leaves and berries, to decorate (optional)

FOR THE FROSTING
100g/4oz/¾ cup plain (semi-sweet) chocolate, broken into pieces
50g/2oz/⅔ cup butter, cut into pieces
2 tbsp clear honey

1 Heat the oven to 180°C/350°F/Gas 4. Line a 20-cm/8-in baking tin (pan) with non-stick baking paper.

2 Place the chocolate and butter in a small pan over low heat, stir until it has melted and remove from the heat.

LEFT: Rich, glossy Chocolate Pecan Cake is decorated with a sprig of holly and a wide tartan bow.

3 Beat the eggs, sugar and vanilla extract until light and pale coloured. Stir in the chocolate mixture and ground pecans and mix well.

4 Pour the mixture into the prepared tin and level up the top.

5 Bake the cake in the oven for 25–30 minutes, until the centre feels springy when touched. Stand the cake on a wire rack to cool.

6 To make the frosting, melt the chocolate, butter and honey in a small pan over a low heat. Remove the pan from the heat and dip the pecan halves into the frosting so that it coats them half-way. Spread them on non-stick baking paper to dry.

7 Remove the cake from the tin (pan), peel off the baking paper and invert the cake onto the wire rack, so that it is upside-down. Put a plate under the rack to catch the drips.

8 Spread the frosting over the cake and arrange the nuts in a pattern around the edge and in the centre. Transfer the cake to a serving plate and, when the frosting is set, tie a ribbon around it and decorate it with a bow, leaves, and berries, if you wish.

Serves 8

PÂTE BRISÉE CASES (PIE CRUST SHELLS)

INGREDIENTS

225g/8oz/2 cups plain (all-purpose) flour
1tsp icing (confectioners') sugar
½tsp salt
150g/5oz/⅔ cup butter, cut into cubes
1 egg yolk
1tsp lemon juice
about 2tbsp iced water
milk, for brushing

1 Sift together the flour, icing (confectioners') sugar and salt and rub in the butter, using 2 knives or a pastry blender, until the mixture is like fine breadcrumbs. Mix together the egg yolk, lemon juice and water, sprinkle the liquid over the dry ingredients and mix with a fork. When the liquid is well blended, form the mixture into a dough, wrap it in non-stick baking paper or foil and chill for 1 hour.

2 Remove the dough from the refrigerator and leave it at room temperature for 15–20 minutes.

3 Heat the oven to 200°C/400°F/Gas 6. Roll out the pastry on a lightly floured board to a thickness of 6mm/¼in. Roll the pastry over a rolling pin and lower it into a 22.5-cm/9-in tart tin (pan). Press the pastry evenly all around the base and trim off the excess around the rim by rolling the rolling pin over it.

4 Brush the rim with milk. Cut decorative shapes such as holly leaves, flowers and stars from the trimmings, using confectionery cutters. Arrange them around the rim and brush them with milk. Prick the base of the pastry with a fork.

5 Line the pastry case with non-stick baking paper and fill it with dried beans, known in this context as baking beans. Bake the lined case in the oven for 10 minutes. Remove the case from the oven and lower the heat to 180°C/350°F/Gas 4. Remove the beans (store them for future use in this way) and return the pastry to the oven for 8–10 minutes if it is to be recooked with a filling, or for 12–15 minutes if it is to be fully cooked at this stage.

Makes 1 22.5-cm/9-in pastry case (pie crust shell)

HORS D'OEUVRES AND CANAPÉS

PASTRY PLAYS a leading role at Christmastime, whether for delicious appetizers before an extended meal, or a tray of hors d'œuvres to serve at a drinks party. These recipes will help you to plan and prepare your menus with ease.

CHEESE STRAWS

Make cheese straws in a similar way to Festive Nibbles. Replace the seed topping with 25g/1oz/½ cup grated cheese.

1 Cut the cheese pastry into fingers about 10cm/4in long and 6mm/¼in wide.

2 With the trimmings, cut rounds using 2 pastry cutters of different sizes, a 6cm/2½in one to cut out the circle and a 5cm/2in diameter one to stamp out the centre.

3 To serve the Cheese Straws push 6 or 8 straws through each ring.

Makes about 50 straws and 8 rings

FESTIVE NIBBLES

The more the merrier — stars, crescent moons, triangles, squares, hearts, fingers and rounds. Shape these spicy cheese snacks in any way you wish, serve them with drinks from ice-cold cocktails to hot and spicy mulls.

INGREDIENTS

100g/4oz/1 cup plain (all-purpose) flour, plus extra for dusting
1tsp mustard powder
salt
100g/4oz/½ cup butter, plus extra for greasing
75g/3oz Cheddar cheese, grated
pinch of cayenne
2tbsp water
1 egg, beaten
poppy seeds, sunflower seeds or sesame seeds, to decorate

1 Heat the oven to 200°C/400°F/Gas 6. Sift the flour, mustard powder and salt into a bowl and rub in the butter until the mixture resembles fine breadcrumbs. Stir in the cheese and cayenne and sprinkle on the water. Add half the beaten egg, mix to a firm dough and knead lightly until smooth.

2 Roll out the dough onto a lightly floured board and cut out a variety of shapes. Re-roll the trimmings and cut more shapes.

3 Place the shapes on a greased baking sheet and brush the tops with the remaining egg. Sprinkle on the seeds to decorate.

LEFT: *Festive fare includes Buttermilk Scones and Palmiers.*

OPPOSITE: *Cheese Straws and Festive Nibbles make an appetizing display.*

YOUNG COOKS

CHILDREN OF all ages love to help in the kitchen – rolling out pastry, licking out the cake bowl, and sometimes even helping to wash the dishes. But most of all, young cooks like to have a project of their own, a recipe they can follow from start to finish and serve or give away to friends with pride.

FRUIT AND NUT CLUSTERS

INGREDIENTS

225g/8oz white chocolate, broken into pieces

50g/2oz/⅓ cup sunflower seeds

50g/2oz/⅓ cup almond slivers

50g/2oz/⅓ cup sesame seeds

50g/2oz/⅓ cup seedless raisins

1 tsp ground cinnamon

EQUIPMENT

* weighing scales
* mixing bowl
* spoon
* wooden spoon
* heatproof bowl
* pan of simmering water
* 2 teaspoons
* about 24 paper sweet cases (candy cups)

BELOW: The chocolate mounds in paper cases are displayed on a bright fan, an attractive way to present them at a youngsters' party.

ABOVE: Nuts and seeds, raisins and white chocolate have all the makings of delicious Fruit and Nut Clusters.

1 Put the chocolate into a heatproof bowl over a pan of simmering water. Do not allow the water to touch the base of the bowl, or the chocolate may become too hot. Or you can put the chocolate in a microwave-proof container and heat it on Medium for 3 minutes. Stir the melted chocolate until it is smooth and glossy.

2 Mix all the other ingredients together, pour on the chocolate and mix well.

3 Using 2 teaspoons, spoon the mixture into paper cases and leave to set. Store in an airtight tin.

Makes about 24 clusters

CHOCOLATE MAGICS

Children will love to see the magic transformation of these biscuits (cookies) after baking.

INGREDIENTS

250g/9oz plain (semi-sweet) chocolate, broken into pieces
100g/4oz/½ cup unsalted butter, cut into pieces
75g/3oz/⅓ cup caster (superfine) sugar
3 eggs
1tsp vanilla extract
150g/6oz/1½ cups plain (all-purpose) flour
½tsp baking powder
3tbsp unsweetened cocoa powder
large pinch of salt
about 75g/3oz/1 cup icing (confectioners') sugar, for coating

EQUIPMENT

* weighing scales
* medium saucepan
* knife
* wooden spoon
* saucer
* medium-sized bowl
* tablespoon
* sieve
* plastic wrap
* 2 baking sheets
* non-stick baking paper
* small bowl
* 2 teaspoons
* 2 wire cooling racks
* spatula

1 Put the chocolate and butter into the saucepan and melt it over a low heat, stirring it with the wooden spoon several times. Remove the pan from the heat and stir in the sugar. Break each egg into a saucer and add them one at a time to the chocolate mixture. Stir in the vanilla extract.

2 Sift the flour, baking powder, cocoa and salt into the bowl. Gradually add the melted chocolate mixture, stirring all the time. When the mixture is smooth and well blended, cover the bowl with plastic wrap and place it in the refrigerator for at least 2 hours.

3 To cook the biscuits (cookies), heat the oven to 170°C/325°F/Gas 3. Cover the baking sheet with a piece of non-stick baking paper.

4 Sift the icing (confectioners') sugar into the small bowl. Using a teaspoon, scoop out the chocolate mixture and push it off the spoon and into your hand with the other teaspoon. Roll the mixture between your palms to make a ball – your hands have to be very clean to do this – and drop it into the bowl of icing (confectioners') sugar. Roll it until it is well covered in sugar then place it on the baking sheet. Continue until all the mixture is used up, placing the chocolate rounds at least 7.5cm/3in apart.

5 Bake the biscuits (cookies) for 10–12 minutes, until they feel soft and springy when touched. Place the baking sheets on the wire cooling racks for a few minutes. Lift off the biscuits (cookies) with a spatula and arrange them on the racks. When they are cold, store them in an airtight tin.

Makes about 24 biscuits (cookies)

BELOW: *The refrigerated Chocolate Magic paste is shaped into small balls and dipped in sifted icing (confectioners') sugar. At this stage they look like chocolate truffles.*

BOTTOM: *Who would guess that the chocolate rounds would have a crazy-paving, sugar topping like this? No wonder they are called Chocolate Magics!*

MAKING CANDIES

Candies and sweets of all kinds have a multiplicity of roles at Christmastime. Making them at home in a cosy kitchen is fun and children love to help. They may be able to spoon out the honey, shell the nuts, roll truffles in coloured hundreds and thousands (coloured sprinkles), or pack the finished items in a box as a special present – home-made candies and chocolate are among the most welcome of gifts. A glance at the price of the candies in specialist shops leaves no doubt that these are firmly in the luxury class. Packed in a different way, wrapped in check gingham fabric and tied with pretty ribbons, sliced candy makes delightful Christmas tree decorations which guests will just love to take home.

HONEY AND NUT CLUSTER

This is a popular candy in Italy, where it is known as 'Torrone'. To serve, cut it in squares or fingers and keep it in the refrigerator. It is delightfully sticky!

INGREDIENTS
100g/4oz/²⁄₃ cup blanched almonds
100g/4oz/1 cup shelled hazelnuts (filberts)
whites of 2 eggs
100g/4oz/½ cup clear honey
100g/4oz/½ cup caster (superfine) sugar

1 Line a 20-cm/8-in square tin (pan) with non-stick baking paper.

2 Spread the almonds and hazelnuts (filberts) on separate baking sheets and toast them in the oven at the lowest temperature for about 30 minutes. Tip onto a cloth and rub off the skins. Roughly chop both types of nut.

3 Whisk the egg whites until they are stiff and stir in the chopped nuts.

4 Put the honey and sugar into a small, heavy pan and bring to the boil. Stir in the nut mixture and continue cooking over a moderate heeat for 10 minutes.

5 Turn the mixture into the prepared tin (pan) and level the top. Cover with another piece of non-stick paper, put weights (such as food cans) on top and leave in the refrigerator for at least 2 days.

6 To present the Torrone as a tree decoration, wrap slices in non-stick baking paper and then in gift-wrap or cotton fabric, or in foil.

LEFT: Slices of the Honey and Nut Cluster, wrapped in non-stick baking paper and pink check gingham, make pretty take- home gifts.

CHOCOLATE TRUFFLES

These rich and irresistible sweet meats are always popular. Even after the most sumptuous of meals, you will not find a guest who will refuse one. You can coat the truffle mixture in a variety of ways – with melted milk or white chocolate; rolled in unsweetened cocoa powder; or covered in hundreds and thousands (coloured sprinkles).

INGREDIENTS
150ml/¼pt/⅔ cup double (heavy) cream
250g/9oz bitter or plain (semi-sweet) chocolate, broken into pieces
2tbsp brandy or rum
about 3tbsp cocoa powder, for dusting

1 Pour the cream into a heavy pan and bring to the boil. Remove from the heat and add the chocolate. Stir until melted and well blended. Stir in the brandy or rum and strain into a bowl. Set aside to cool, then chill for at least 1 hour.

2 Using a melon baller with a 2-cm/¾-in scoop, or 2 small teaspoons, form the mixture into balls and place them on a baking sheet lined with non-stick baking paper. Chill for 1 hour.

3 Sift about 3tbsp cocoa into a small bowl. Roll the truffles in the cocoa to coat them on all sides – turning them over and over with a wooden cocktail stick or toothpick keeps the coating intact. Place them in small paper cases and store them in a box in the refrigerator. Remove them about 30 minutes before serving.

RIGHT: Fancy truffles are ready to be placed in paper cases and stored in the refrigerator.

BELOW: Cocoa-coated truffles piled into an engraved glass dish are shown to advantage with a single gilded leaf. It is not customary to make these truffles perfectly round.

SUGARED FLOWERS AND FRUITS

SPARKLING UNDER a light dusting of caster (superfine) sugar like summer fruits and flowers unseasonally tinged with frost or snow, sugared sweetmeats are a delicacy especially suited to the magic of Christmas. You can prepare them several days in advance of the festivities and, once they are thoroughly dry, store them in an airtight tin.

Make your selection of flowers and fruits, petals and leaves as appetizing and visually appealing as you can. Christmas is a time for giving way to culinary temptation and visual flights of fancy.

It may be a case of gathering the last of the season's roses or using petals from a rose in a bouquet. Enjoy the flowers in an arrangement for a day or two and then, while they are still in their prime, and certainly before they begin to discolour, pluck off the petals for sugaring.

Not all flowers are edible, though many are. Check with the list on this page before gathering others for your sugar collection. Marigolds, nasturtiums and pansies were all favourites in Victorian times, and offer an attractive variety of colour and shapes.

Sugared fruits add substantially to a sweetmeat selection. You can process small fruits such as cherries, cranberries, strawberries and raspberries whole. Larger ones such as oranges and tangerines should be peeled and segmented, figs halved or quartered, according to their size, and plums and apricots halved and pitted.

Sugared leaves are a pretty contrast to both fruit and flowers. The sugared leaves can be used with fruit and flowers to add a notion of realism, or composed into dainty herbal sprays, a neat decoration for a dessert or cheesecake.

ABOVE: After dipping in egg white, a rose petal is lightly dusted with caster (superfine) sugar to cover the whole surface.

LEFT: Sugared rose petals and cranberries are arranged in the shape of a flower with variegated mint leaves. This decoration can be used on a cake or dessert.

GUIDE TO EDIBLE FLOWERS

Crystallizing (candying) flowers and petals is such a delightful task that it is easy to get carried away and preserve every flower in sight. It is important to remember that not all flowers or plants are edible, and some may be harmful. If you are in doubt about the safety or suitability of any plant, consult a reliable source, or confine your decorative activities to those on the list below.

almond blossom (*Prunus dulcis*)

apple blossom (*Malus sylvestris*)

borage (*Borago officianalis*)

carnation (*Dianthus caryophyllus*)

clover (*Trifolium sp.*)

cowslip (*Primula veris*)

daisy (*Bellis perennis*)

dandelion (*Taraxacum officinale*)

elderflower (*Sambucus nigra*)

forget-me-not (*Myosotis alpestris*)

freesia (*Freesia x kewenis*)

honeysuckle (*Lonicera periclymenum*)

hydrangea (*Hydrangea macrophylla*)

jasmine (*Jasminium officinale*)

lavender (*Lavandula vera*)

magnolia (*Magnolia grandiflora*)

may blossom (*Crataegus monogyna*)

mimosa (*Acacia dealbata*)

nasturtium (*Tropaeolum majus*)

orange blossom (*Citrus sinensis*)

pansy (*Viola tricolor*)

primrose (*Primula vulgaris*)

rose (*Rosa gallica*)

scented-leaf geranium (*Pelargonium graveolens*)

sweet william (*Dianthus barabatus*)

violet (*Viola odorata*)

yarrow (*Achillea millefolium*)

ABOVE RIGHT: An orange segment held on a skewer is dipped into a bowl of lightly beaten egg white.

RIGHT: Flowers, petals and fruits dipped in egg white and dusted with sugar are left to dry on a wire rack covered with non-stick baking paper.

BREADS, SCONES AND TEABREADS

WITH so many rich, traditional foods featured on the Christmas menus, it can be a welcome change to be offered a slice of delicious home-made bread with butter or cheese, or a light-as-a-feather scone with a choice of preserves. And with the coming and going of expected and unexpected guests, it is a good idea to have a stand-by recipe for a bread suitable for all occasions.

These three recipes offer just such versatility. The Irish Soda Bread takes only moments to make and as it uses soda as the raising agent, is not left to rise between making and baking.

The Cheese Scone recipe makes a welcome change from the rich foods of the season, and may be served at a light brunch or lunch. Vary the flavour with herbs or seeds.

Lastly Stollen, a yeast bread speckled with fruit and sprinkled with icing (confectioners') sugar, is an Austrian speciality which may be eaten plain – it is slightly sweet – or with butter or preserves, and is delicious toasted.

ABOVE AND BELOW: Soda Bread with its soft, crumbly texture is a good choice for an informal snack, and contrasts well with other breads for a cheese and wine party.

IRISH SODA BREAD

INGREDIENTS
450g/1lb/4 cups plain (all-purpose) flour
2tsp bicarbonate of soda (baking soda)
1tsp salt
300ml/½pt/1¼ cups milk

1 Heat the oven to 220°C/ 425°F/Gas 7. Sift the flour, soda and salt into a bowl. Pour on the milk and mix to a soft dough.

2 Turn the dough onto a lightly floured board and knead it lightly until smooth. Shape it into a round and stand it on a greased and floured baking sheet. Cut a cross in the top and brush with milk.

3 Bake in the oven for 35–40 minutes, until the loaf is well risen and golden brown. Cool on a wire rack.

Makes 1 loaf

CHEESE SCONES

INGREDIENTS

225g/8oz/2 cups plain (all-purpose) flour
1tsp cream of tartar
1tsp bicarbonate of soda (baking soda)
1tsp dry mustard powder
pinch salt and pepper
1–2tsp chopped fresh herbs (optional)
50g/2oz/1/2 cup butter
75g/3oz/1/3 cup grated cheese
150ml/1/4pt/2/3 cup milk or buttermilk

1 Sift the flour, cream of tartar, soda, mustard and salt and pepper into a bowl. Add the fresh herbs, if using. Rub in the fat until the mixture is like dry breadcrumbs, and gradually stir in enough milk to make a light, springy dough. Stir in the grated cheese.

2 Turn the dough onto a lightly floured board and knead until smooth. Roll it to a thickness of 2.5cm/1in. Cut into rounds with a 5-cm/2-in cutter (or a 4-cm/1½-in cutter for cocktail savouries). Place the scones on a floured baking sheet and brush the tops with milk. Bake in the oven for 7–10 minutes, until the scones are well risen and golden brown.

Makes about 16 scones

STOLLEN

INGREDIENTS

150ml/1/4pt/2/3 cup lukewarm milk
40g/1½oz/3tbsp caster (superfine) sugar
2tsp dried yeast
350g/12oz/5 cups plain (all-purpose) flour, plus extra for dusting
1/4tsp salt
100g/4oz/1/2 cup butter, softened
1 egg, beaten
50g/2oz/1/3 cup seedless raisins
25g/1oz/1/6 cup sultanas (golden raisins)
40g/1½oz/1/3 cup candied orange peel, chopped
25g/1oz/1/2 cup blanched almonds, chopped
1tbsp rum
40g/1½oz/3tbsp butter, melted
about 50g/2oz/1/2 cup icing (confectioners') sugar

1 Mix together the warm milk, sugar and yeast and leave it in a warm place until it is frothy.

2 Sift together the flour and salt, make a well in the centre, pour on the yeast mixture. Add the softened butter and egg and mix to form a soft dough. Mix in the raisins, sultanas (golden raisins), peel and almonds and sprinkle on the rum. Knead the dough on a lightly floured board until it is pliable.

3 Place the dough in a greased bowl, cover it with non-stick baking paper and set it aside in a warm place for about 2 hours, until it has doubled in size.

4 Turn the dough out onto a floured board and knead it lightly until it is smooth and elastic again. Shape the dough to a rectangle about 25 × 20cm/10 × 8in. Fold the dough over along one of the long sides and press the 2 layers together. Cover the loaf and leave it to stand for 20 minutes.

ABOVE: Stollen, a fruity yeast bread traditionally served in Austria at Christmastime, may be served at breakfast, coffee or teatime.

5 Heat the oven to 200°C/400°F/Gas 6. Bake the loaf in the oven for 25–30 minutes, until it is well risen. Allow it to cool slightly on the baking sheet, then brush it with melted butter. Sift the sugar over the top and transfer the loaf to a wire rack to cool.

Makes 1 loaf

COUNTDOWN TO CHRISTMAS

Working out the timetable for your Christmas cooking schedule is the key to the whole operation. With each task allocated its slot in the diary, and then duly completed, you can move on smoothly and confidently to the next.

As Christmas Day approaches and the cook moves into top gear, the timetable here will be invaluable as an at-a-glance reminder of when to ice (frost) the cake, prepare the stuffings and vegetables, make the sauces, put the poultry or meat into the oven, reheat the pudding and cook the vegetables to perfection. It's easy when you know how!

Countdown to Christmas

This at-a-glance timetable will help you plan ahead for the principal Christmas cooking, and suggest when to make gifts and decorations.

MIDSUMMER ONWARDS

Make Rose petal jelly, Mint jelly
Begin making soft-fruit Rumtopf from fresh fruits. You can add to it throughout the season
Make Lavender jelly, Pickled walnuts, Scented geranium leaf jelly, Rowanberry liqueur, Bullace liqueur

LATE AUTUMN

Make Sloe gin, Yellow pepper relish, Quince paste (Membrillo), Pickled vegetables in oil, Black olives in oil
Collect fallen leaves, horse chestnuts, twigs and other natural materials for decorations

NOVEMBER

FIRST WEEK
Make Christmas puddings
Make Mincemeat
Make Dundee cake
Soak fruit for Creole Christmas cake

SECOND WEEK
Make Creole Christmas cake
Make Traditional Christmas cake
Make Moist gingerbread cake

THIRD WEEK
Feed Creole Christmas cake and Traditional Christmas cake with brandy at intervals (optional)
Begin making Christmas crackers
Buy coloured tissue papers and other wrappings

FOURTH WEEK
Continue to feed Creole Christmas cake and Traditional Christmas cake with brandy at intervals (optional)
Decide on Christmas dinner menu
Order turkey, goose, beef or ham, and salmon
Make Dried-fruit Rumtopf

DECEMBER

FIRST WEEK
Make pâte brisée pastry cases to freeze
Make Cranberry conserve
Make Fondant icing for Christmas star cake
Make Fondant holly leaf sweets
Make Turkish delight
Begin making crystallized (candied) fruits
Make Praline, to decorate desserts
Continue to feed Creole Christmas cake and Traditional Christmas cake with brandy (optional)

Make Almond Paste and use it to cover Traditional Christmas cake. Make fruit shapes as *petits fours* with any left-over paste
Compile complete shopping list for main Christmas meals under headings for different stores, or for the various counters at the supermarket.
Add to the list as other items occur to you

SECOND WEEK
Shop for dry stores such as rice, dried fruits, flour
Make chocolate-covered dried fruits such as apricots, dates, figs
Make Cranberry sauce
Order special bread requirements
Order milk, cream and other dairy produce
Make Brandy, rum or orange butter
Cover Traditional Christmas cake with royal icing.
Leave one day, then cover and store

THIRD WEEK
Make Sugared fruits, flowers, and petals. Be sure to store in a dry place
Make Coconut triangles for gift basket
Make Nesselrode ice cream as alternative dessert, and store in freezer
Make Chocolate truffles, Marzipan logs, Spiced nuts
Make and decorate Gingerbread shapes for tree trims, and Gingerbread heart ring. Store in an airtight container
Make pastry-type cocktail savouries and freeze, or store in airtight tins
Make fruit bread such as Stollen and wrap it in foil. Freeze if wished
Continue feeding Creole Christmas cake with brandy (optional)
Make evergreen garland, welcome wreath and other long-lasting foliage decorations

FOURTH WEEK
Shop for chilled ingredients such as butter, cheese, yoghurt, cream
Buy wines and other drinks

DECEMBER 21

Check thawing time of frozen turkey, goose and beef. Large (11.5-kg/25-lb) turkey needs 86 hours (3½ days) to thaw in the refrigerator, 40 hours at room temperature. Make a note to take poultry or beef from the freezer at appropriate time
Make Christmas star cake
Decorate Creole Christmas cake with crystallized (candied) fruits and nuts
Prepare Gravad lax

DECEMBER 22

Make Mustard sauce to serve with Gravad lax

DECEMBER 23

Shop for fresh vegetables (or on December 24 if possible)

Make filling for Four-vegetable peppers, for vegetarian meal. Store in refrigerator to cook on Christmas Day.

Make Cumberland sauce to serve with Honey-glazed ham.

Make Horseradish cream, to serve with Roast beef.

Make Prune sauce and Apple sauce, to serve with Roast goose

Make Cranberry mould, to serve with Roast Turkey

Make chocolate Yule log, as alternative dessert

Decorate Christmas star cake

Arrange any fresh flowers

DECEMBER 24

Shop for fresh vegetables if possible (otherwise buy them on December 23)

Prepare chocolate-dip strawberries and other soft fruits

Make Chestnut and mushroom loaf, for vegetarian meal. Store in refrigerator, to cook Christmas day

Make stuffing for Roast turkey: Cranberry and rice or Apricot and raisin; Sausagemeat or Chestnut. Store in covered containers in the refrigerator

Make stuffing for Roast goose: Sage and onion and Raisin and pecan

Cook turkey or goose giblets to make gravy. Cool, strain and store in the refrigerator

Make Mince pies

Make Melon basket for first course. Prepare melon balls and cranberries for filling and store in the refrigerator

Make Custard sauce and Tipsy yoghurt, to serve with the Christmas pudding

Prepare caramelized oranges, as alternative dessert

Chill Champagne and other white wines.

Bring red wines to room temperature. Decant port and keep at room temperature

If practicable, set dining table, and set tray with coffee cups

Prepare vegetables, if you wish

Make decorative vegetable shapes to garnish cheeseboard, and tomato rose to garnish Cauliflower flower. Cover and store in the refrigerator

Prepare bacon rolls to serve with turkey by threading them onto wooden cocktail sticks (toothpicks)

If serving Christmas dinner at mid-day, remove turkey, goose, beef or ham from refrigerator and allow to come to room temperature overnight

CHRISTMAS DAY

The timetable is planned for Christmas Dinner to be served at 2.00 pm. If you wish to serve it at a different time, please adjust the times accordingly

If serving dinner in the evening, remove turkey, goose, beef or ham from refrigerator and allow to come to room temperature before cooking

9.35 am	Reduce heat to 180°C/350°F/Gas 4
	Pour off fat from roasting tin
	Turn the goose and baste it now
	and at intervals
11.05 am	Pour off fat from roasting tin (pan)
	Turn the goose and baste it now
	and at intervals
12.15 pm	Put dish of Red cabbage into oven
1.25 pm	Arrange whole apples around the
	goose, or in a separate dish
1.35 pm	Steam small new potatoes
1.45 pm	Turn off oven
	Remove the goose, potatoes and
	apples from the oven, arrange on a
	warmed serving dish, cover with
	foil and keep warm
	Fry any forcemeat balls
	Fry apple slices
	Heat Apple sauce and Prune sauce

To cook a 2.5-kg/5-lb forerib of beef

11.00 am	Set the oven to 230°C/450°F/Gas 8
(for well-done)	
or	
11.15 am	
(for medium)	
or	
11.30 am	
(for rare)	
11.20 am	Put beef in oven
or	
11.35 am	
or	
11.50 am	
11.30 am	Reduce heat to 180°C/350°F/Gas 4
or	
11.45 am	
or	
12 noon	
12.15 pm	Put potatoes around meat
1.45 pm	Remove beef and potatoes from
	oven, put it on a warm serving
	dish, cover with foil and
	keep warm
	Increase heat to 220°C/425°F/Gas 7
Early morning	Stuff turkey or goose. Make forcemeat balls with any left-over stuffing, or spoon it into greased ovenproof dishes
	Set table, if not already done
Mid Morning	Slice Gravad lax and return to refrigerator
	Assemble and decorate Melon basket and return to refrigerator
	Put steamer or large saucepan on
10.45 am	cooker and bring water to the boil
	Put Christmas pudding on to
11.00 am	steam. Remember to top up boiling water as necessary

To cook a 4.5kg/10lb turkey

9.05 am	Set oven to 220°C/425°F/Gas 7
9.25 am	Put turkey in oven
9.45 am	Reduce heat to 180°C/350°F/Gas 4. Baste turkey now and at frequent intervals
12.15 pm	Put potatoes around meat
1.15 pm	Remove foil from turkey. Baste again. Turn the potatoes Increase heat to 200°C/400°F/Gas 6 Put any dishes of stuffing in oven
1.45 pm	Remove turkey and potatoes from oven, put on heated serving dish, cover with foil and keep warm Make gravy Grill bacon rolls

To cook a 5-kg/12-lb goose

8.55 am	Set oven to 230°C/450°F/Gas 8
9.15 am	Put goose in oven
2.00 pm	Put individual Yorkshire puddings in the oven

To cook a 2-kg/4½-lb ham joint

early morning	Bring to boil, discard water Put in pan with fresh water, boil for 1 hour 35 minutes Glaze Bake for 15 minutes while oven is set at 180°C/350°F/Gas 4 Reheat Cumberland sauce

To cook vegetarian meal

12.55 pm	Set oven to 190°C/375°F/Gas 5 Pack vegetable filling into peppers
1.15 pm	Put dish of peppers in oven
1.20 pm	Put chestnuts and mushroom loaf in oven
2.00 pm	Remove both dishes from oven

The remaining courses

11.00 am	Take cheese from refrigerator and arrange on board. Cover with cloth and leave at room temperature Arrange dish of sugared fruits Arrange truffles and other sweetmeats Open red wines and leave to breathe at room temperature
1.30 pm	Grind coffee Take ice cream from freezer
1.45 pm	Cook vegetables Cover chocolate Yule log with meringue ready to cook Garnish cheeseboard with chilled fruits Scatter praline on Caramelized oranges Heat mince pies
2.00 pm	Serve first course

Index

254

ACKNOWLEDGEMENTS

THE AUTHOR and publishers would like to thank the following organizations and companies for their help and co-operation in the preparation of this book:

Appalacia, The Folk Art Shop, 14a George Street, St Albans, Herts, AL3 4ER, tel 0727 836796, for American folk art items including hand-carved wooden figures, tinware and quilted decorations

Bostik Ltd, Ulverscroft Road, Leicester, LE4 6BW, tel 0533 510015 for the hot glue gun and various adhesives used to create many of the designs

California Raisins for the raisins used in the puddings, mincemeat, etc.

Danish Bacon Council for gammon bacon joints

Evans Kitchen Shop, 19 High Street, Halstead, Essex CO9 2AS, tel 0787 473967, for the loan of china, glass and other accessories

C.M. Offrey & Son Ltd, Fir Tree Place, Church Road, Ashford, Middx, TW15 2PH, tel 0784 247281, for the wide selection of ribbons shown on the jacket and throughout the book

Paperchase, 213 Tottenham Court Road, London W1P 9AF, tel 071 581 8496, for the tree baubles shown on the jacket and many of the decorative items shown in other photographs

Prices Patent Candle Co Ltd, 1258 London Road, London SW16 4EE, tel 081 764 0640, for so many of the candles in the photographs

The author would also like to thank the following people for their help in so many ways:
Suzanne Ardley, Nelson Hargreaves, Margaret Jack, David Suckling, Anthony Thomas, Douglas Westland.